Keith Snell Piano Course
for the Adult Beginner

BOOK 2

CONTENTS

Unit 1: D Major, A Major, E Major

D Major Scale and Key Signature.......... 4
Primary Triads and Chord Progression 4
Reading in D Major 5
Believe Me............................... 6
A Major Scale and Key Signature.......... 8
Primary Triads and Chord Progression 8
Reading in A Major 9
Vive la Compagnie 10
Daydream 11
E Major Scale and Key Signature.......... 12
Primary Triads and Chord Progression 12
Reading in E Major 13
Evening on the Lake.................... 14
Theory 16
Technic 19

Unit 2: Accompaniment Patterns

Split Chord, Waltz Bass, Arpeggio,
  and Alberti Bass 20
Red River Valley 21
Ballroom Romance....................... 22
On Top of Old Smoky.................... 23
Classic Sonatina....................... 24
Music Box Waltz 26
Alberti Etude, Op. 599, No. 14 (Czerny) 27
Theory 28
Technic 30

Unit 3: A Minor, D Minor, E Minor

Relative Minor Scales and Key Signatures ... 32
Forms of Minor/A Minor Scale 33
Primary Chords in A Minor 34
Bold and Brave 34
D Minor Scales and Chords 36
Lament................................. 37
E Minor Scales and Chords 38
Tarantella 39
Theory 40
Technic 43

Unit 4: Triads and Inversions; Triplet

C Major Triad and Inversions............ 44
Triadic Fanfare 45
Royal Arrival.......................... 46
2nd Inversion Boogie 47
Triplet 48
Tarantella 48
Minuet (Telemann)...................... 49
Theory 50
Technic 52

Unit 5: Legato Pedal; Chromatic Scale

Pedal Exercises......................... 54
The Shepherd's Flute (Salutrinskaya) 55
Solemn Occasion 56
Sakura................................. 57
Chromatic Scale......................... 58
Dashing Through the Day............... 59
Theory 60
Technic 63

Unit 6: B♭ Major, G Minor

B♭ Major Scale and Key Signature 64
Primary Triads and Chord Progression 64
Reading in B♭ Major..................... 65
Amazing Grace 66
Hunting Song, Op. 82, No. 42 (Gurlitt)...... 67
G Minor Scales and Chords 68
Song without Words (Spindler) 69
Theory 70
Technic 72

Unit 7: 2/2; Dim. and Aug. Triads

Time Signature 2/2 74
Musette (Le Couppey)................... 74
Diminished Triads 76
Puck, ¢ 76
Augmented Triads 78
Expanding Horizons.................... 78
On an Escapade 79
Theory 80
Technic 82

(Contiued on next page)

Unit 8: 16th Notes; Time Signature 3/8

Sixteenth Notes 84
Four to One 84
Two to One 84
Arabesque 85
Etude in A minor, Op. 82, No. 52 (Gurlitt) . . . 86
Time Signature 3/8 87
German Dance (Haydn) 87
Dotted Eighth Note 88
Strolling 88
Singing 88
Russian Folk Song, Op. 107, No. 3 (Beethoven) 89
Theory 90
Technic 92

Unit 9: E♭ Major, A♭ Major, D♭ Major

E♭ Major Scale and Key Signature 94
Primary Triads and Chord Progression 94
Reading in E♭ Major 95
Largo (Dvořák) 96
Écossaise, WoO 86 (Beethoven) 97
A♭ Major Scale and Key Signature 98
Primary Triads and Chord Progression 98
Reading in A♭ Major 99

Sonata Theme, from K. 311 (Mozart) 100
Waltz, Op. 39, No. 15 (Brahms) 101
D♭ Major Scale and Key Signature 102
Primary Triads and Chord Progression 102
Reading in D♭ Major 103
Swanee River (Foster) 104
Barcarolle 105
Theory 106
Technic 112

Unit 10: G♭ Major, B Major

G♭ Major Scale and Key Signature 114
Primary Triads and Chord Progression 114
Reading in G♭ Major 115
America (My Country 'Tis of Thee) 116
Monument Valley 116
B Major Scale and Key Signature 118
Primary Triads and Chord Progression 118
Reading in B Major 119
La donna e mobile (Verdi) 120
Habanera 121
Theory 122
Technic 126

Music Dictionary 128

ISBN-10: 0-8497-6427-0
ISBN-13: 978-0-8497-6427-1

kjos Neil A. Kjos Music Company

© 2024 Kjos Music Press, 4382 Jutland Drive, San Diego, California 92117.
International copyright secured. All rights reserved. Printed in U.S.A.
Warning! The contents of this publication are protected by copyright law.
To copy or reproduce them by any method is an infringement of the copyright law.
Anyone who reproduces copyrighted matter is subject to substantial penalties and assessments for each infringement.

PREFACE

The Keith Snell Piano Course for the Adult Beginner, Book 2, continues from *Book 1* with the introduction of new scales and key signatures. The final units of *Book 1* present the keys of C, G, and F Major. *Book 2* begins with the introduction of D, A, and E Major. This is subsequently followed in Unit 3 with the presentation of A, D, and E minor. With these three minor keys, students learn the relative minors to C, F, and G Major, as well as the parallel minors to D, A, and E Major. The overarching goal of *Book 2* is to have students read and play in as many keys as possible, while simultaneously learning about other important aspects of keyboard technic, theory, and musicianship through a variety of music styles. After completing *Book 2*, students will have read, played, and completed theory and technic exercises in:

- Major Sharp Keys: C, G, D, A, E, and B
- Major Flat Keys: F, B♭, E♭, A♭, D♭, and G♭
- Minor Keys: A, E, D, and G

Students will become familiar with the primary triads and primary chord progression for each key and how these building blocks of harmony are used in music. These chords will be used for various accompaniment patterns such as the Waltz Bass, Alberti Bass, and arpeggio figures, in the typical ways found in different musical styles. By using these primary chords in a variety of patterns, students will gain the ability to recognize the harmonic structure of music in a more linear or horizontal fashion, rather than only seeing chords in a vertical or blocked way. The playing of varied accompaniment patterns also aids in the development of left hand coordination, balance, and technic.

Among the most important and challenging new concepts presented in *Book 2*, from both a theoretical and technical standpoint, is the introduction and use of triad inversions. Although inversions are played within the primary chord progression for each key, playing a single triad and its inversions requires a new type of intellectual and physical manipulation. While the proper hand shape and fingering solutions were established in *Book 1,* Unit 5, with opening the hand to the interval of a 6th, learning to move that shape into the first and second inversion triads requires specific practice and attention paid to correct fingering. The principal points to observe here are the placement of fingers 2–3–4–5 over consecutive keys, while maintaining the interval of a 3rd between fingers 1 and 2.

Explorations in meter and rhythm in *Book 2* include time signatures 2/2 and 3/8, as well as 16th notes and dotted eighth note rhythms. The 2/2 time signature is used in Unit 7 as a preparation for the introduction of 16th notes in Unit 8 by playing four eighth notes in one beat in 2/2. This paves the way for playing four sixteenths in one beat in 2/4. Dotted eighths rhythms are prepared first by introducing an eighth tied to a 16th note, then removing the tied note and replacing it with the dot.

The technic of legato pedaling is featured in Unit 5 and utilized throughout the rest of the book. The first step in mastering legato pedaling is coordinating the timing for using the pedal. This is initially done by playing pedal changes rhythmically. Pedal markings throughout the book are very detailed, but the most successful pedaling occurs when a student learns to listen carefully to their pedaling. We pedal with our ears, not our eyes.

The scaffolding of technical skills, rhythmic concepts, reading fluency, and musicianship is scrupulously organized in the curriculum of this course. The order of units presented in *Book 2* represents what the author believes to be most successful based on his teaching experience. That said, some flexibility and an open mind must always be present when working with the individual needs, preferences, and goals of different students. To this end, some discretion may be used in determining the introduction of a concept outside of the prescribed order if it is relevant to the student.

It is the author's sincere desire that this course will equip students with a foundation in the basic skills and knowledge necessary to continue playing the piano for many years to come with feelings of satisfaction and accomplishment.

Keith Snell

UNIT 1
D MAJOR, A MAJOR, E MAJOR

W = whole step, H = half step

D Major Scale and Key Signature

The key signature for D Major has two sharps: F♯ and C♯.

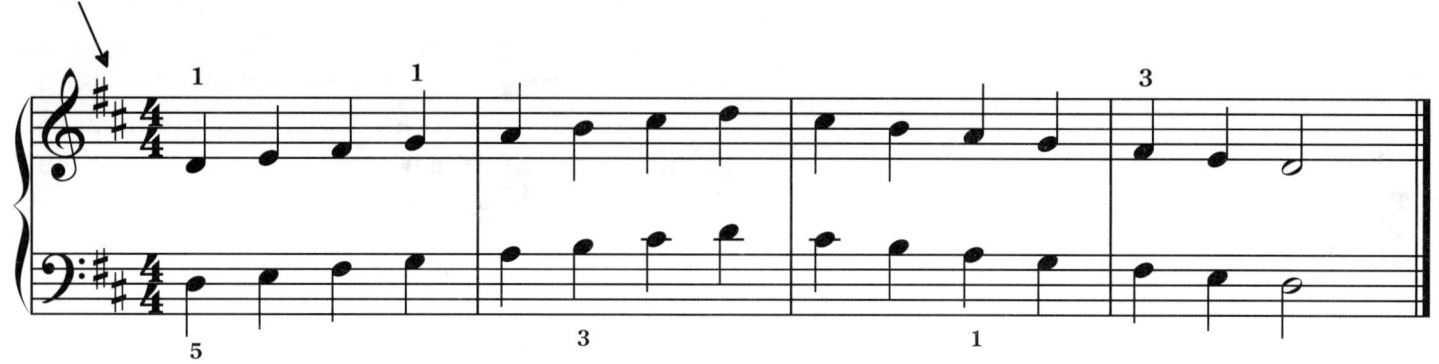

Primary Triads in D Major

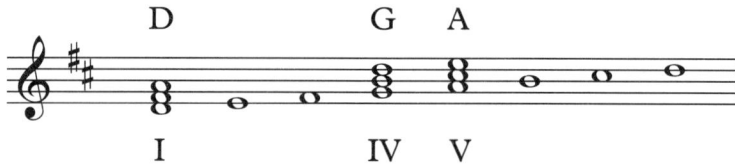

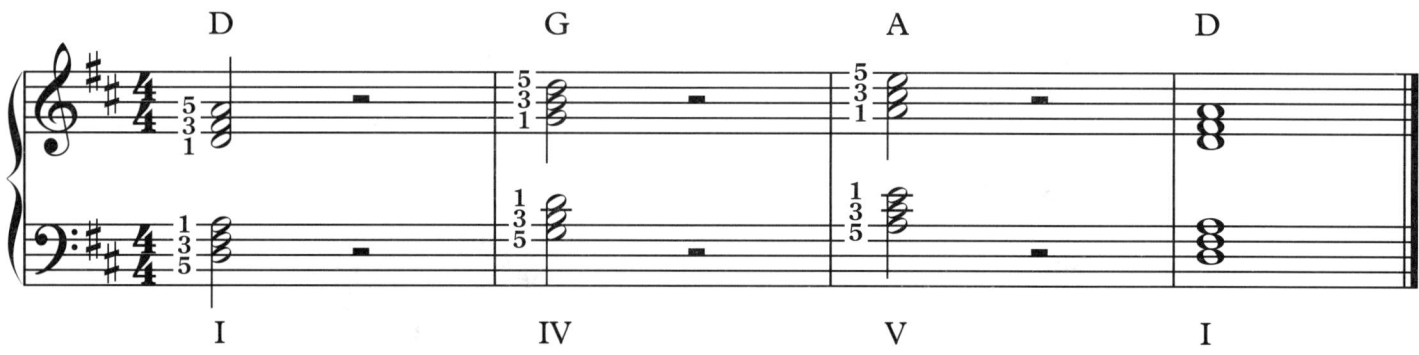

Primary Chord Progression

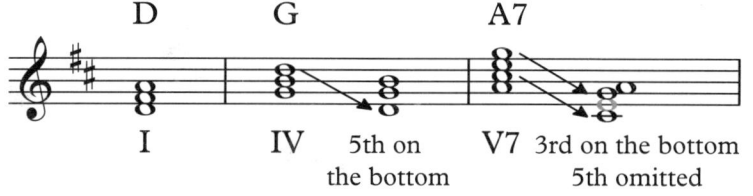

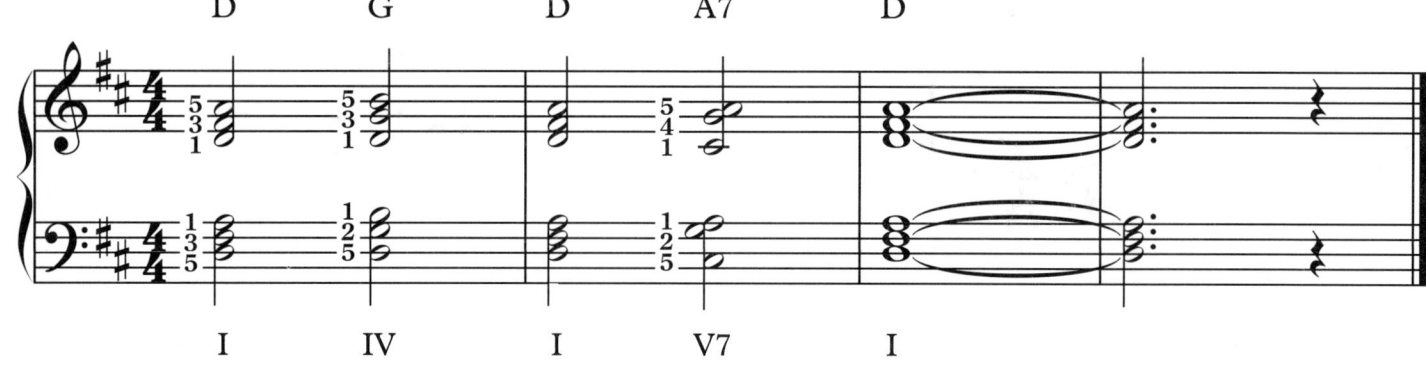

GP692

D Major, A Major, E Major 5

Reading in D Major

I.

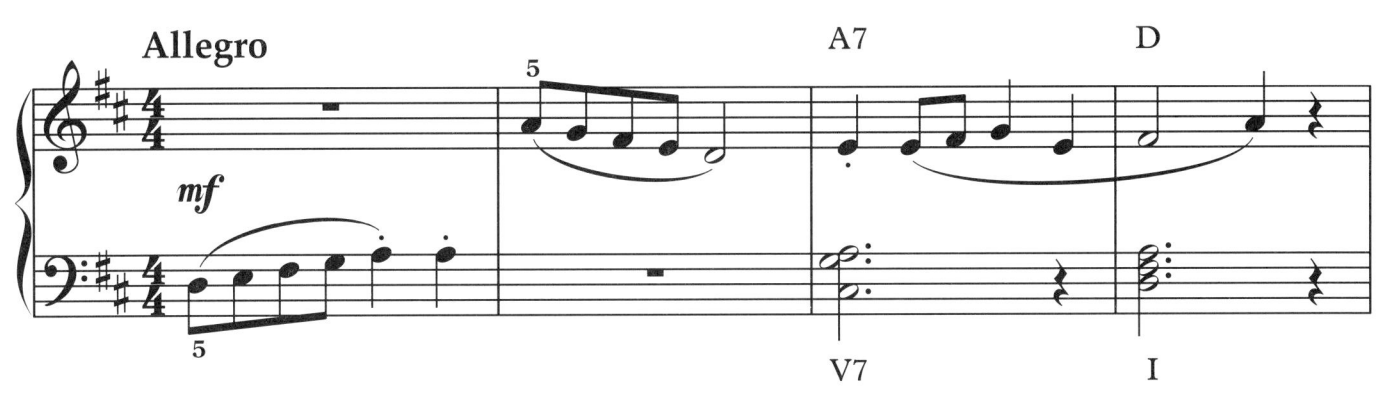

II.

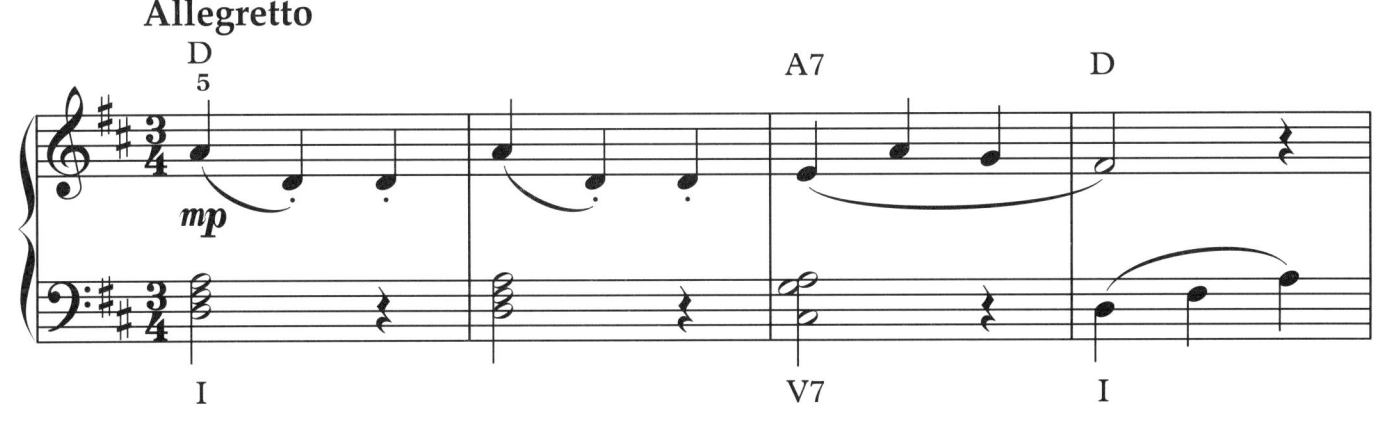

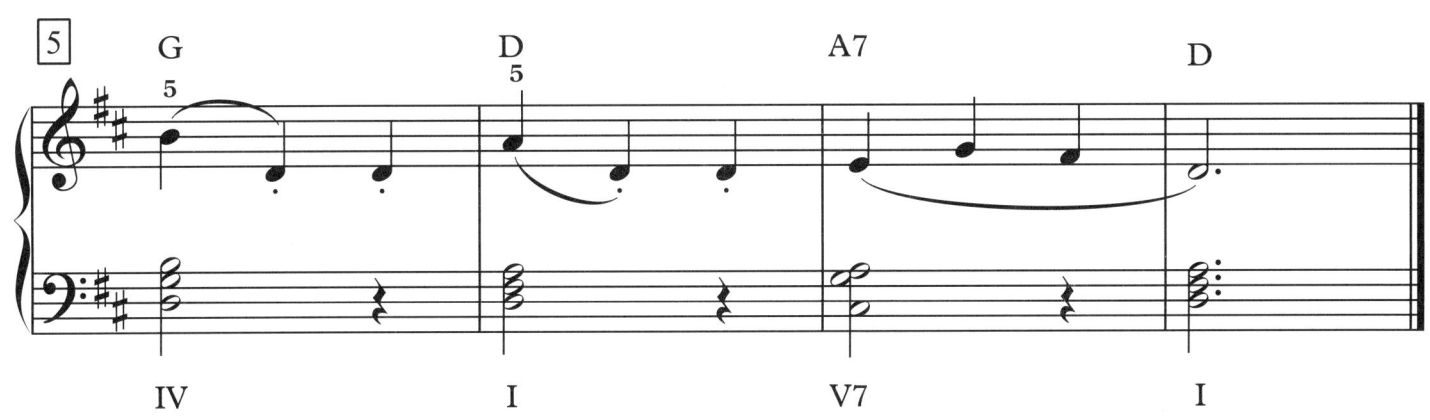

GP692

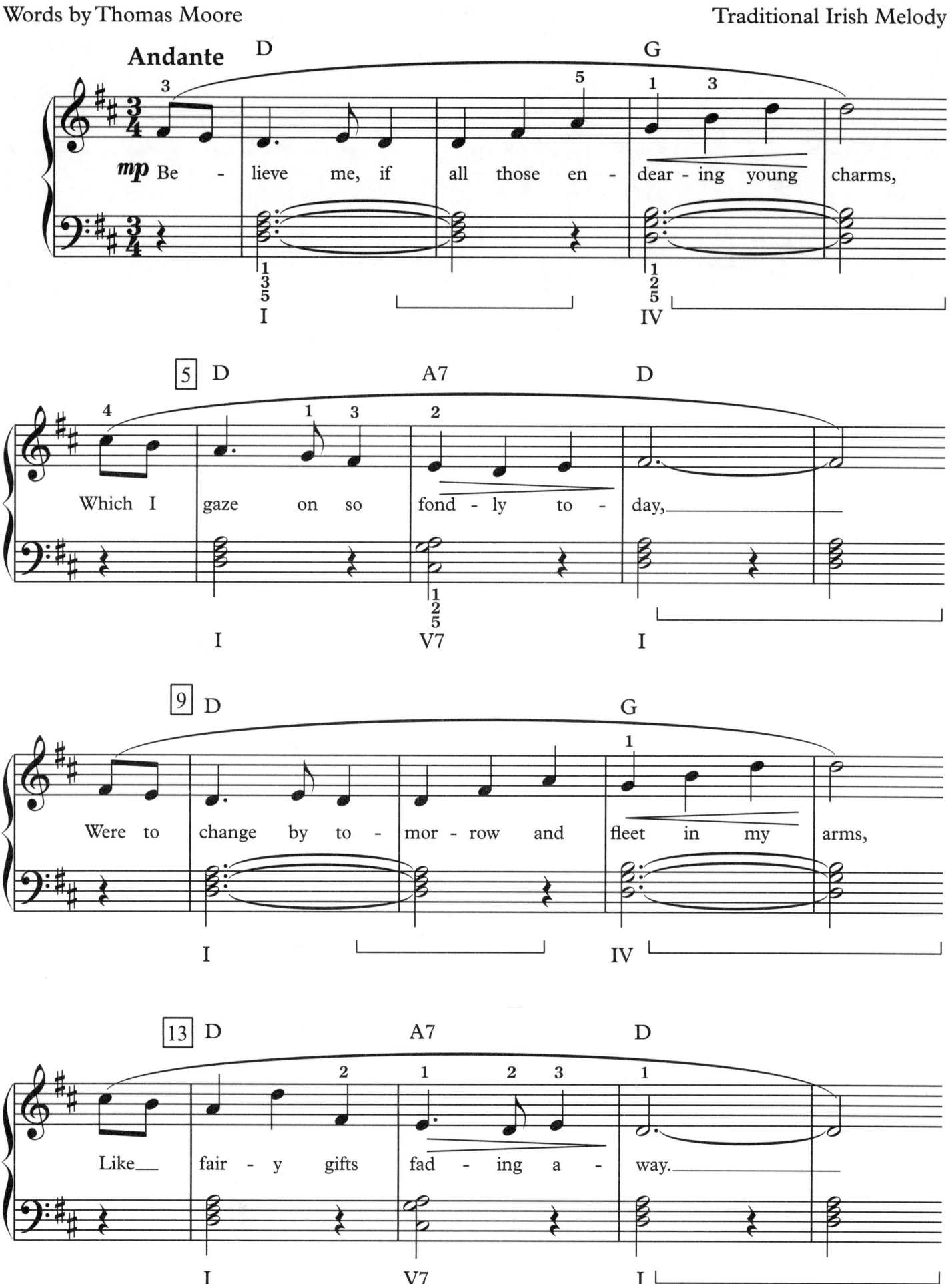

D Major, A Major, E Major 7

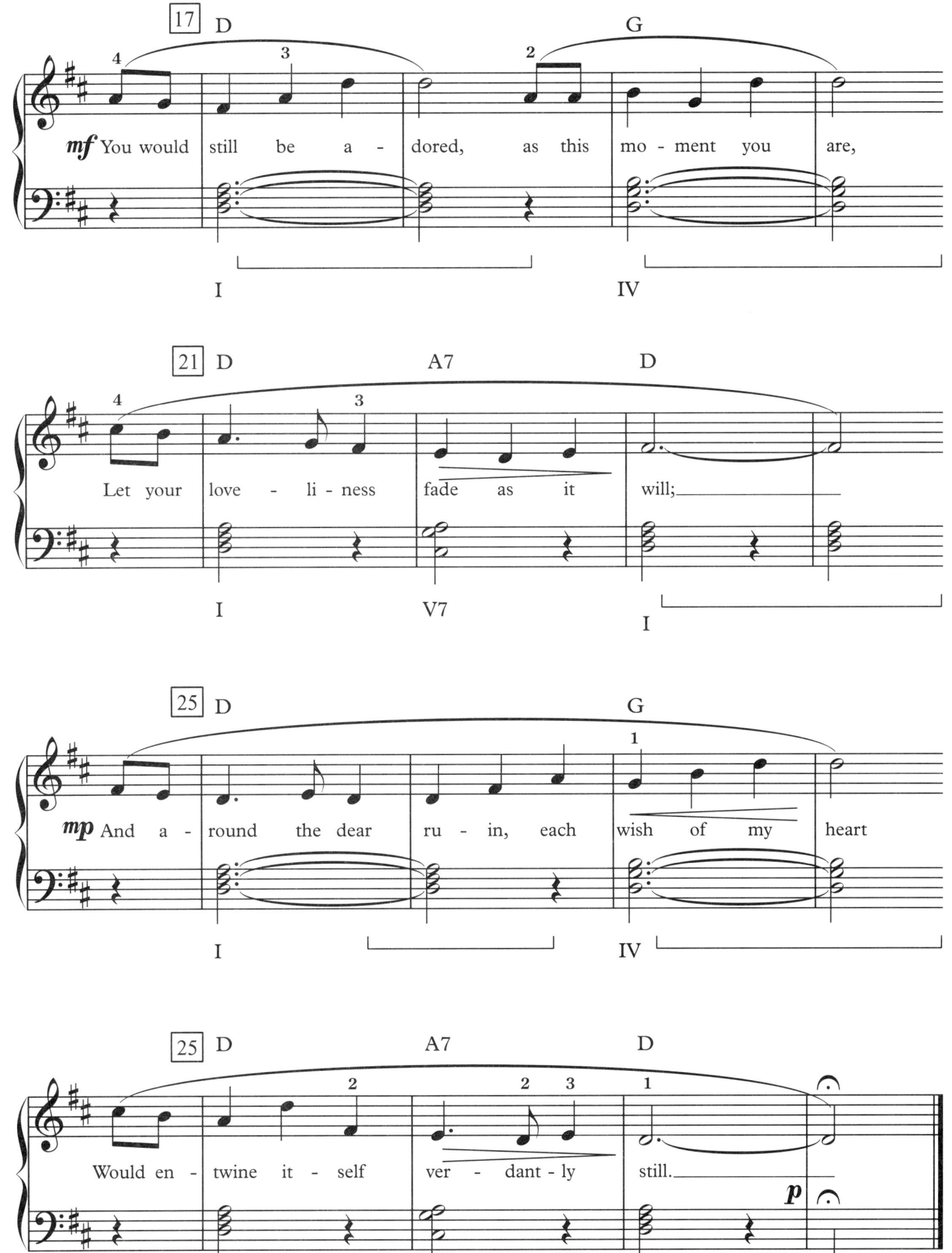

A Major Scale and Key Signature

The key signature for A Major has three sharps: F#, C#, and G#.

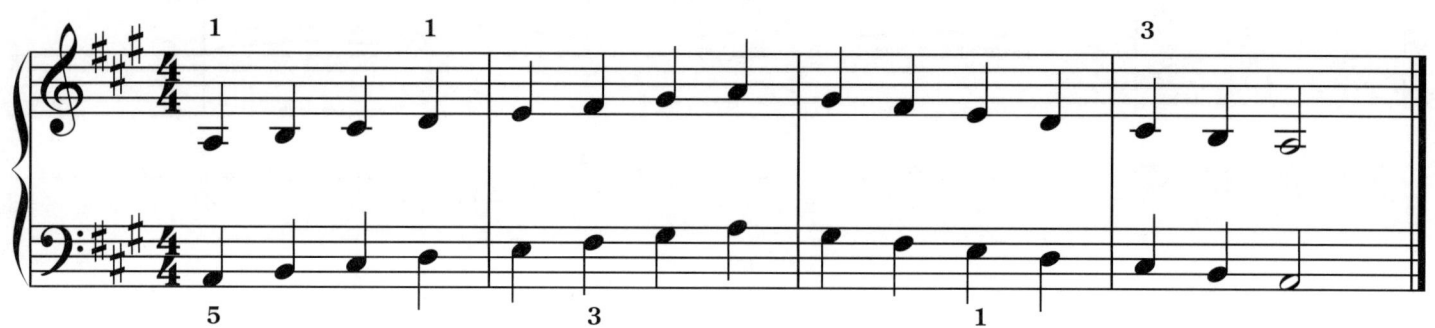

Primary Triads in A Major

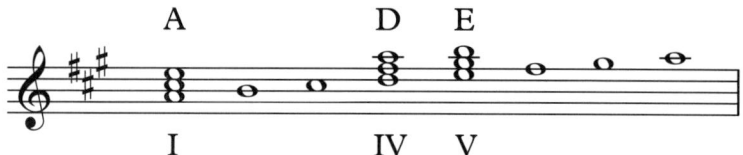

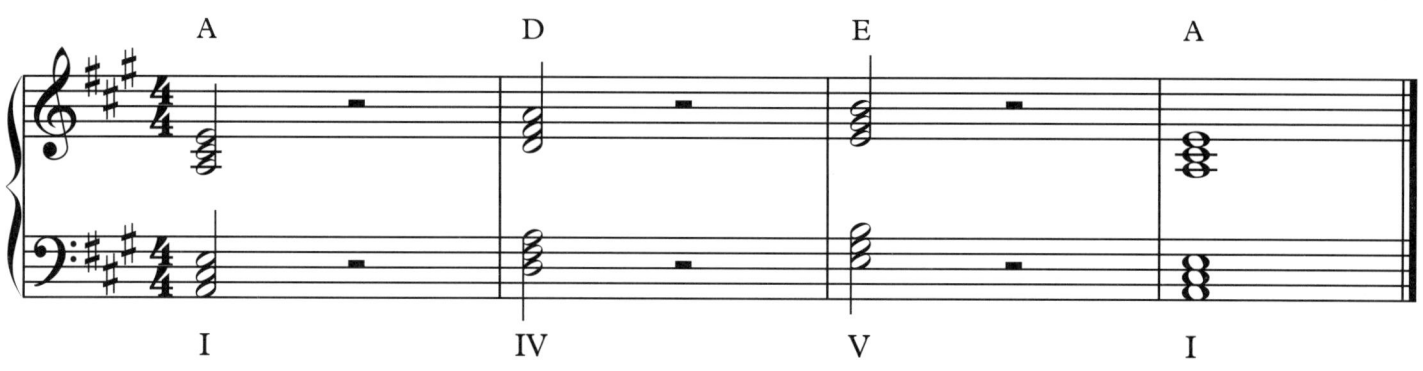

Primary Chord Progression

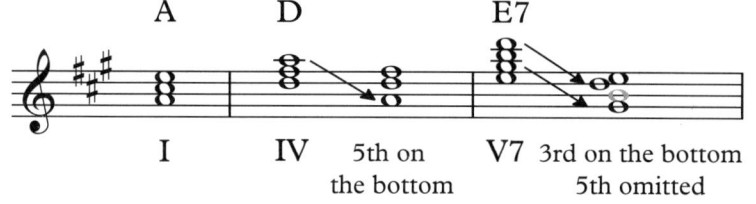

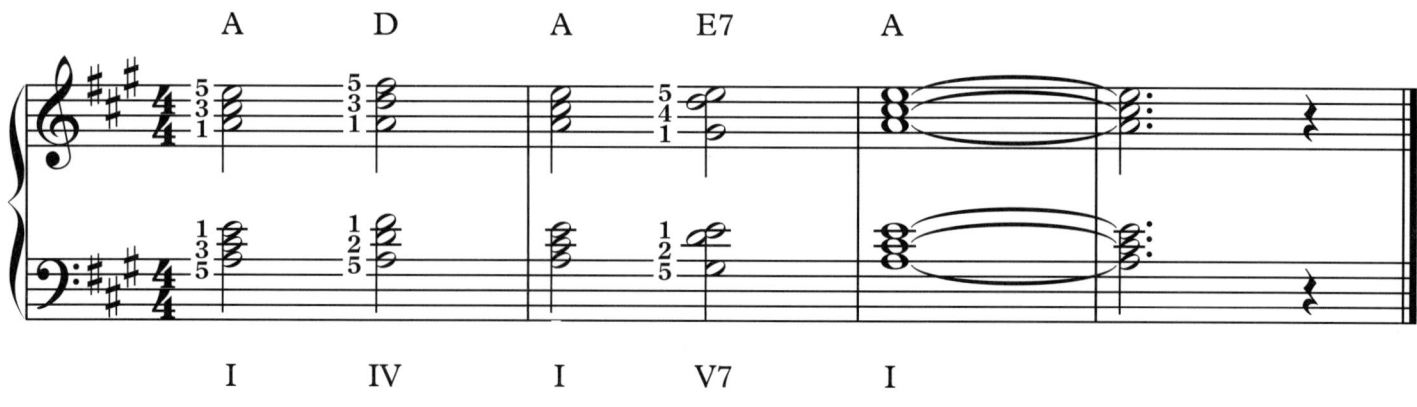

GP692

D Major, A Major, E Major — 9

Reading in A Major

I.

Moderato

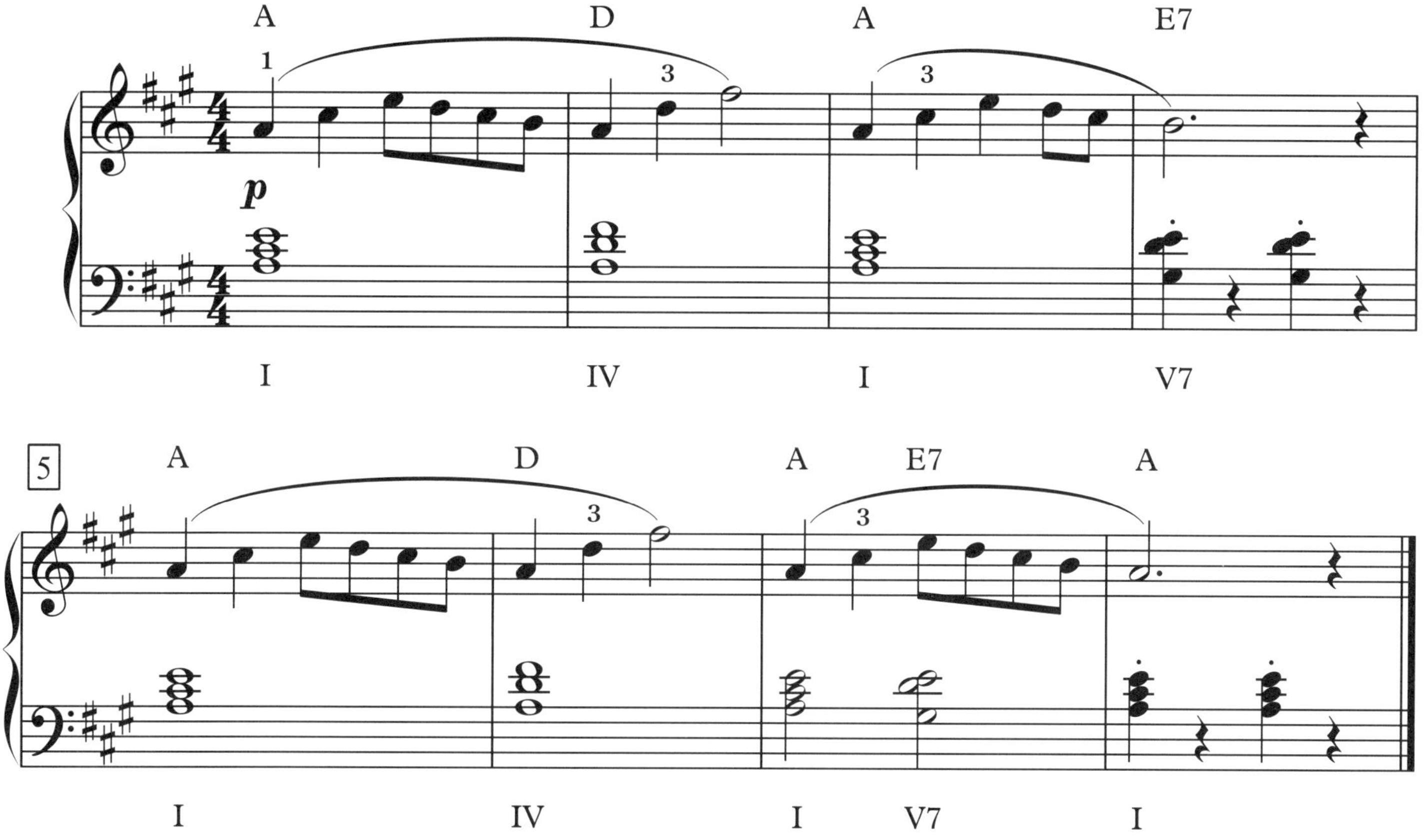

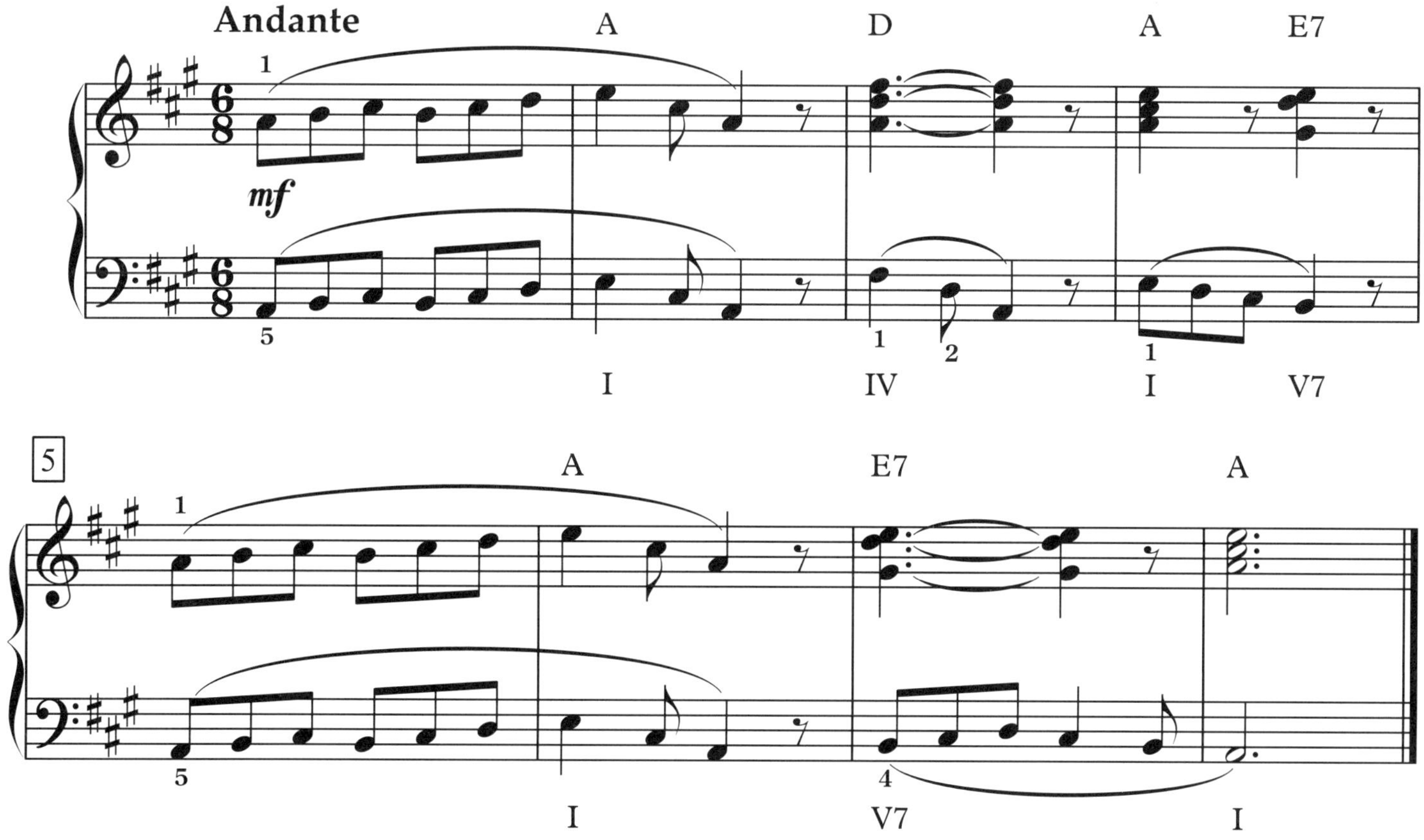

Vive la Compagnie

Traditional English Ballad

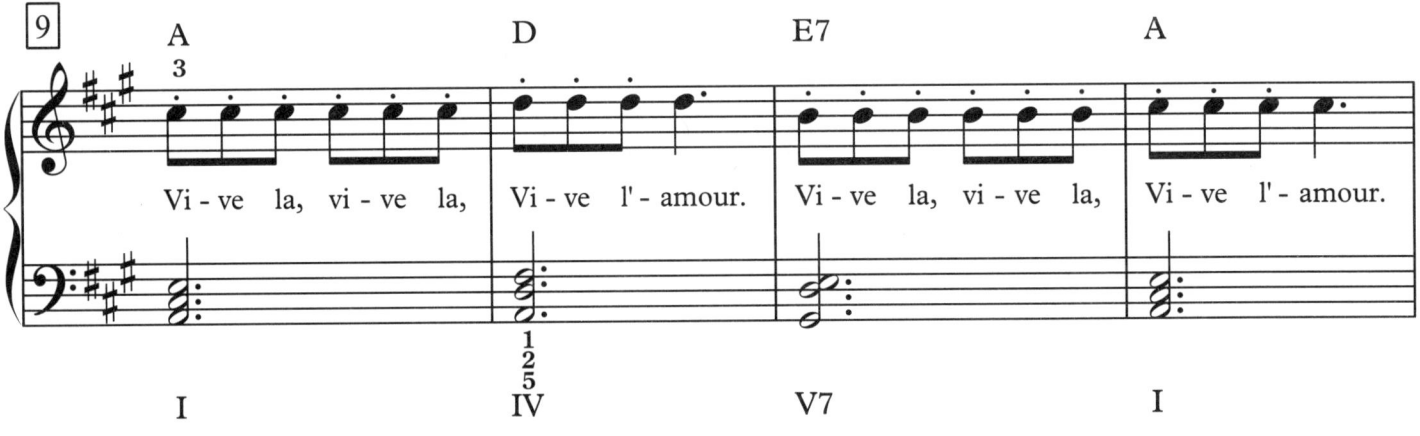
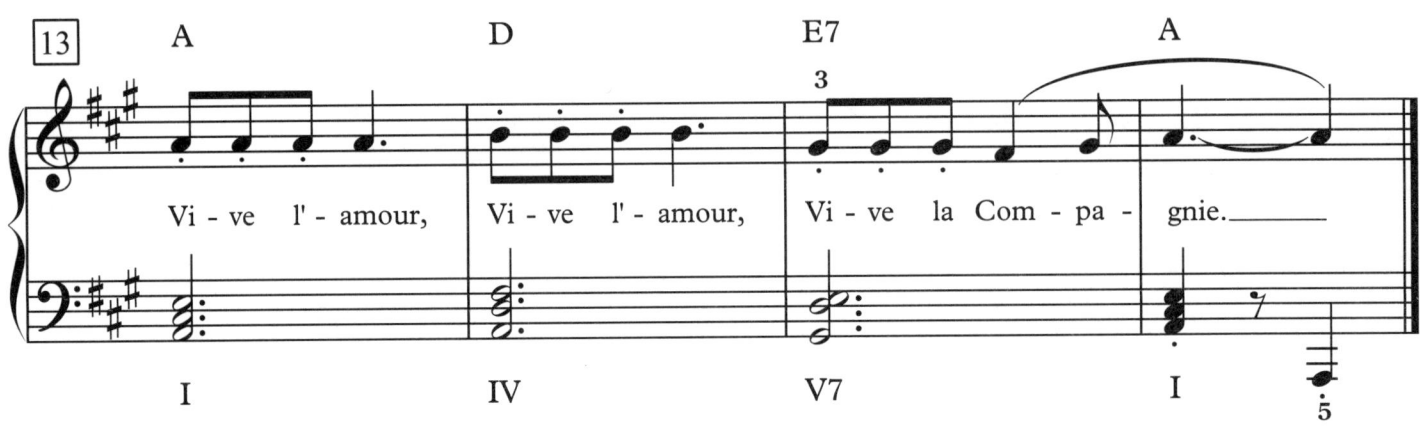

GP692

Daydream

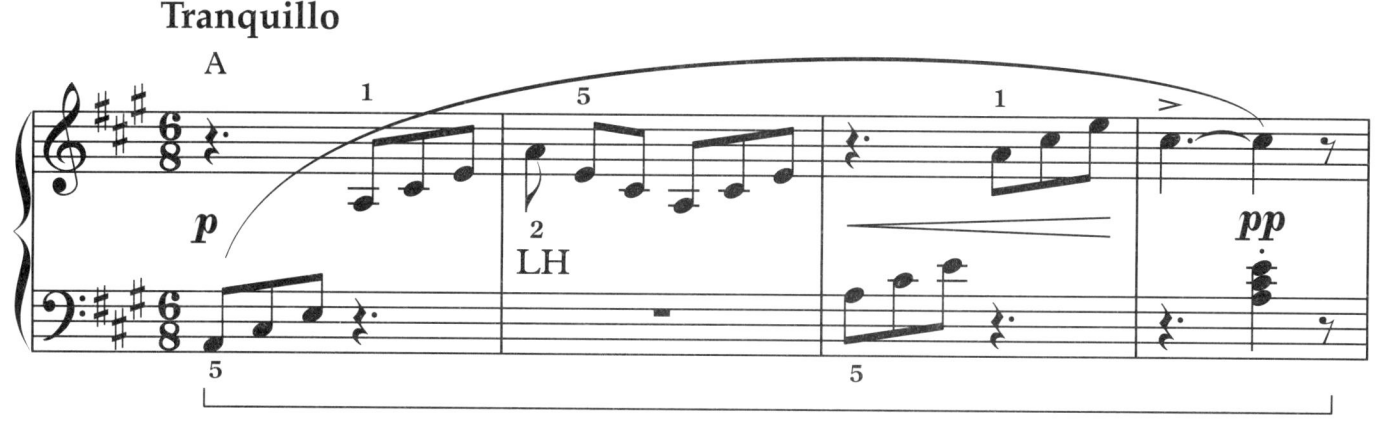

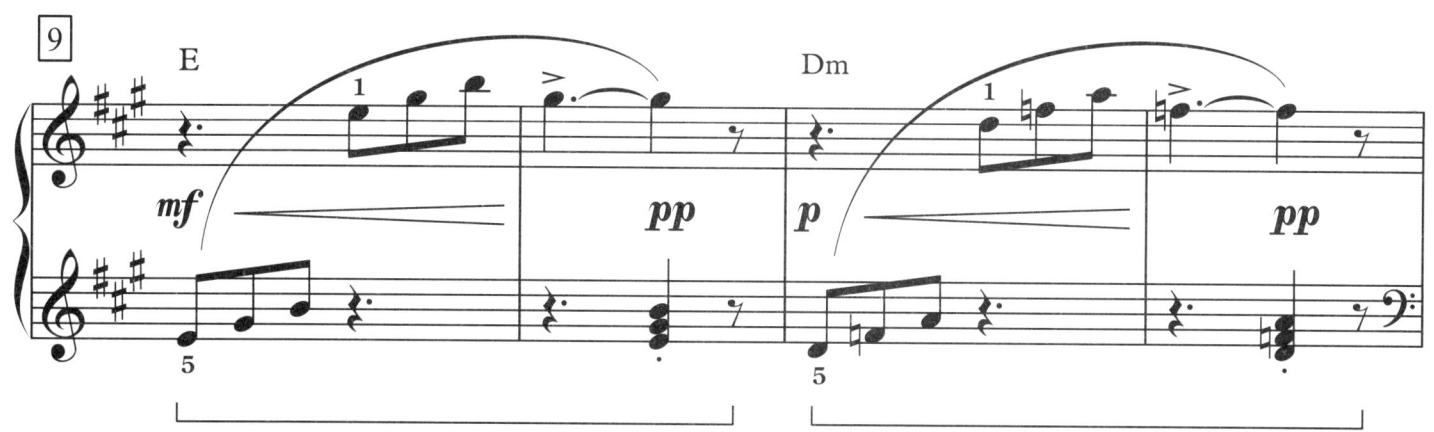
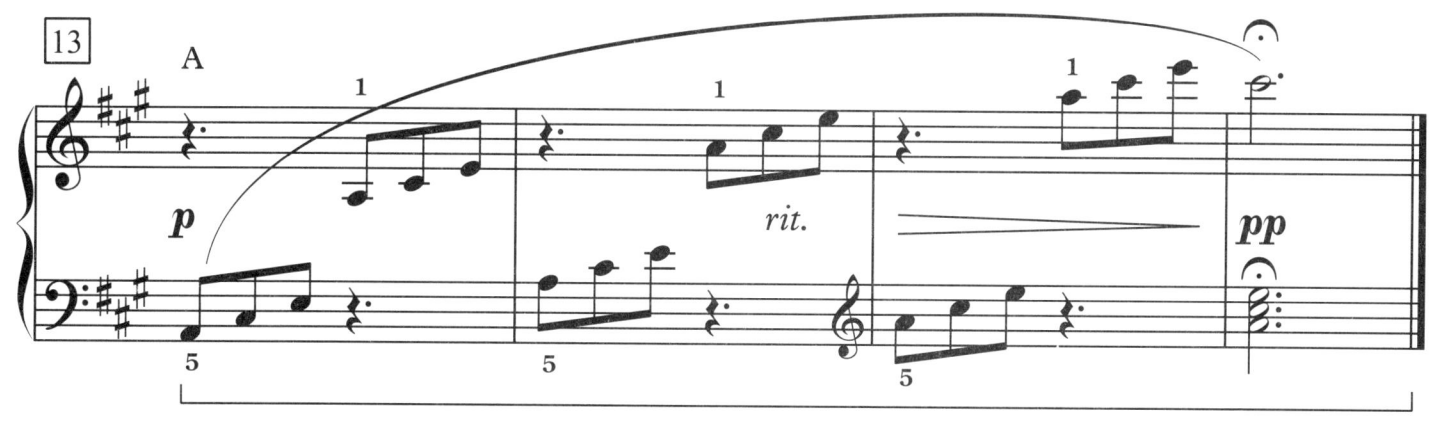

E Major Scale and Key Signature

The key signature for E Major has four sharps: F♯, C♯, G♯, and D♯.

Primary Triads in E Major

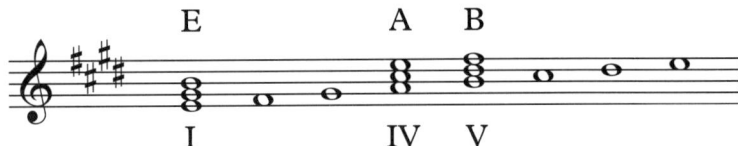

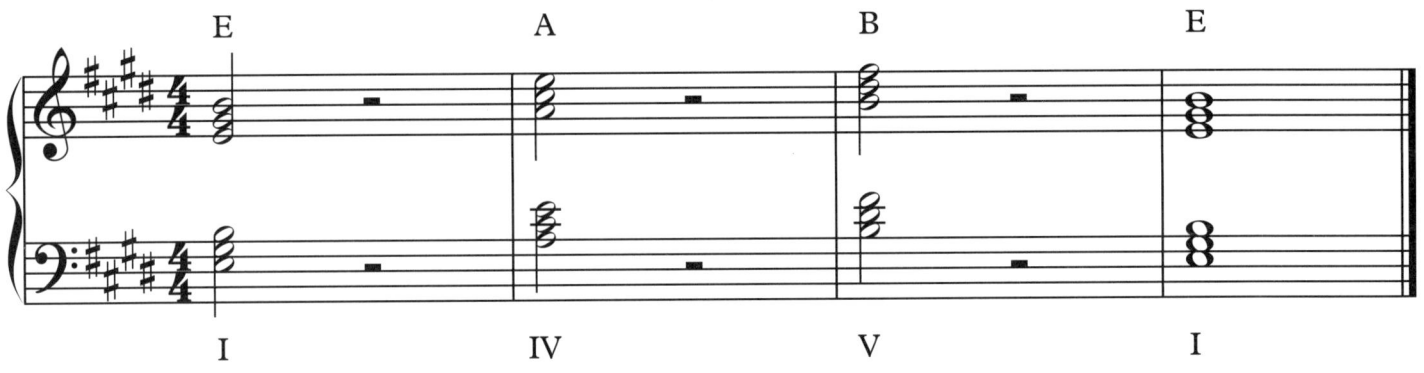

Primary Chord Progression

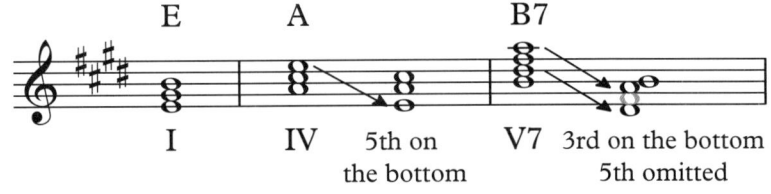

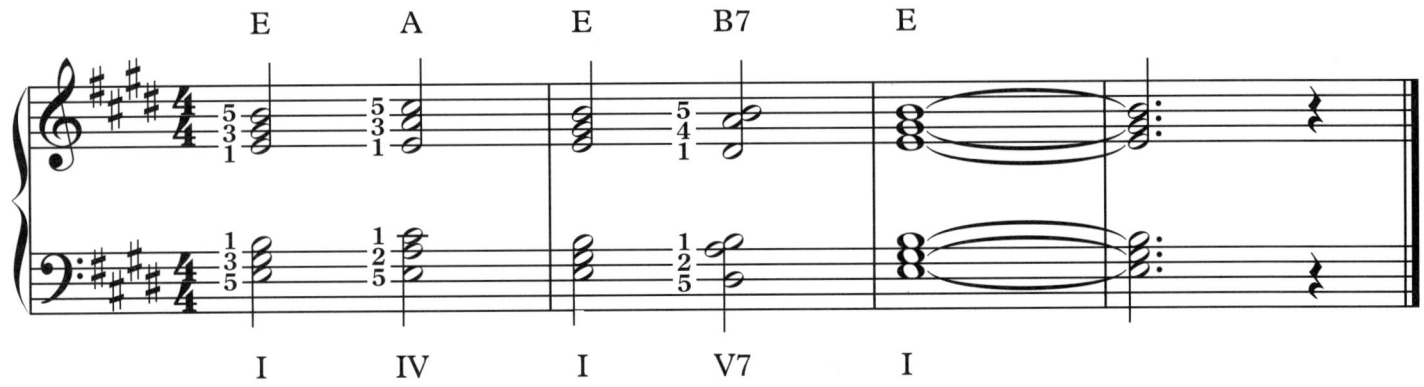

Reading in E Major

I.
Allegro

II.
Moderato

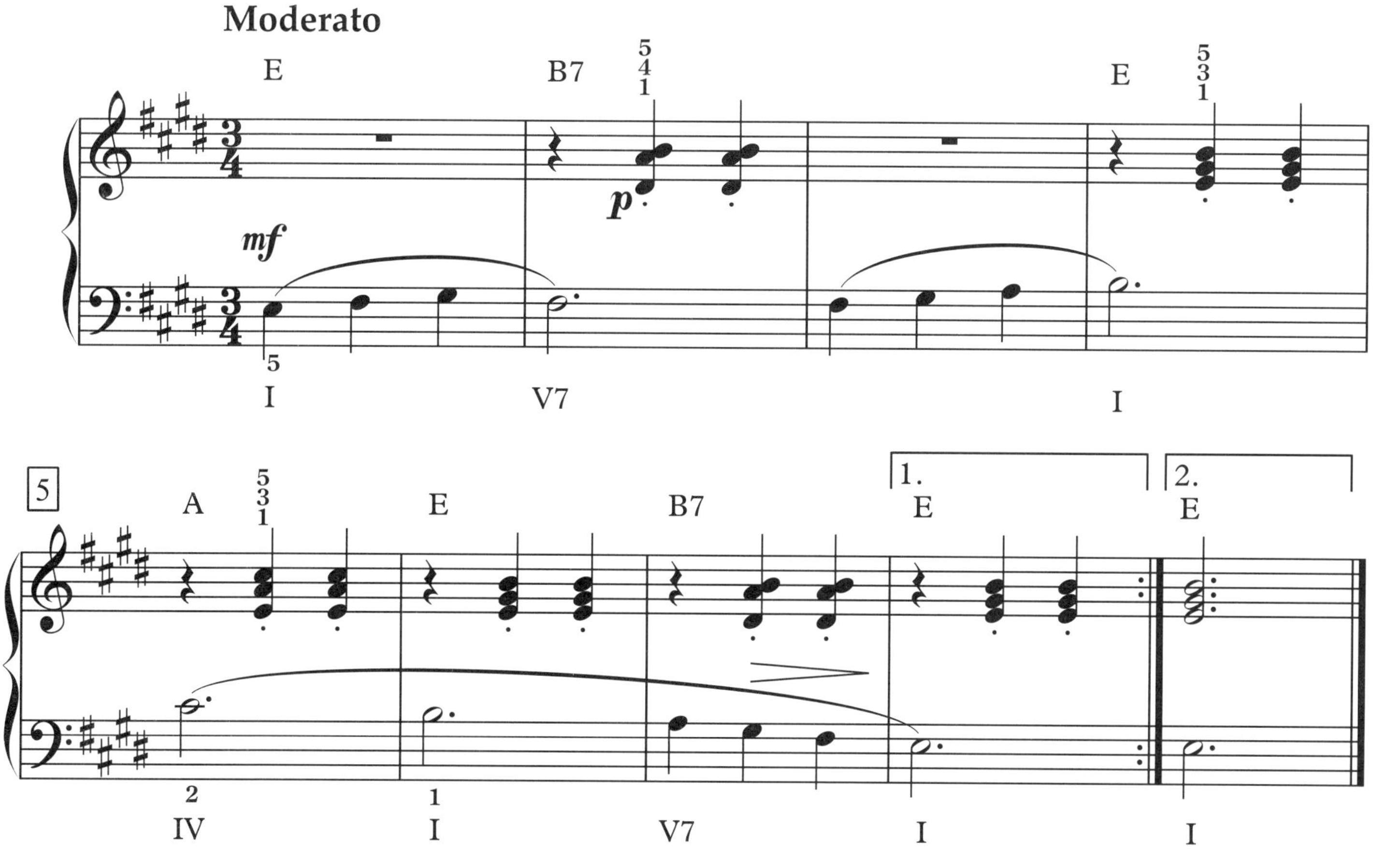

Evening on the Lake

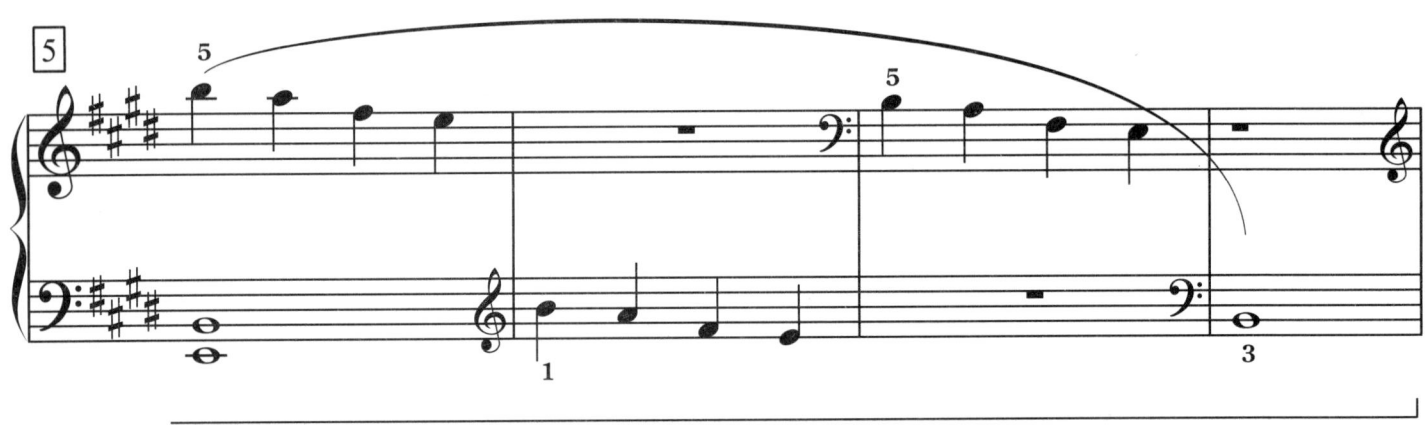
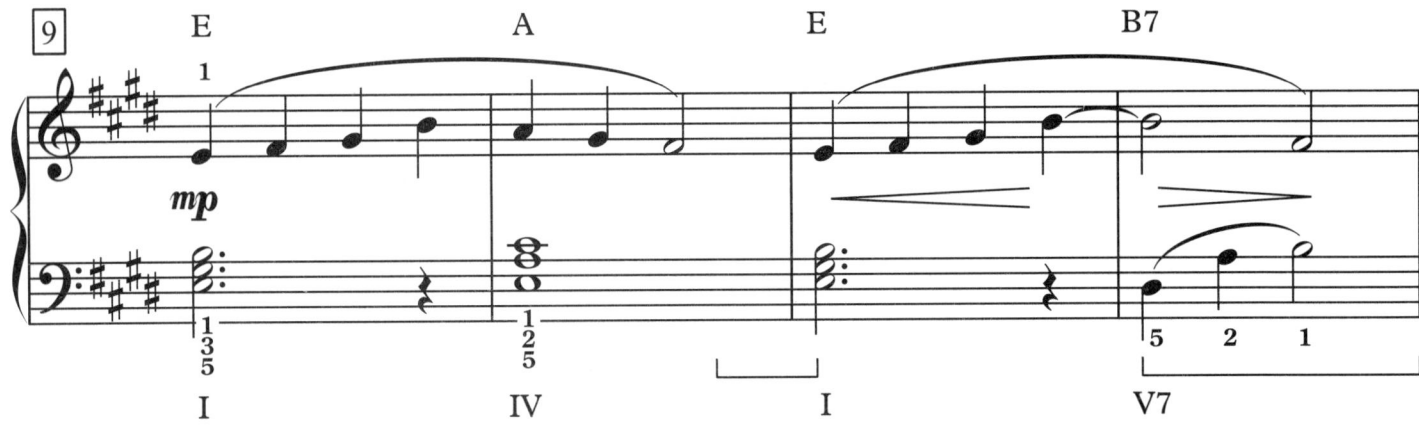
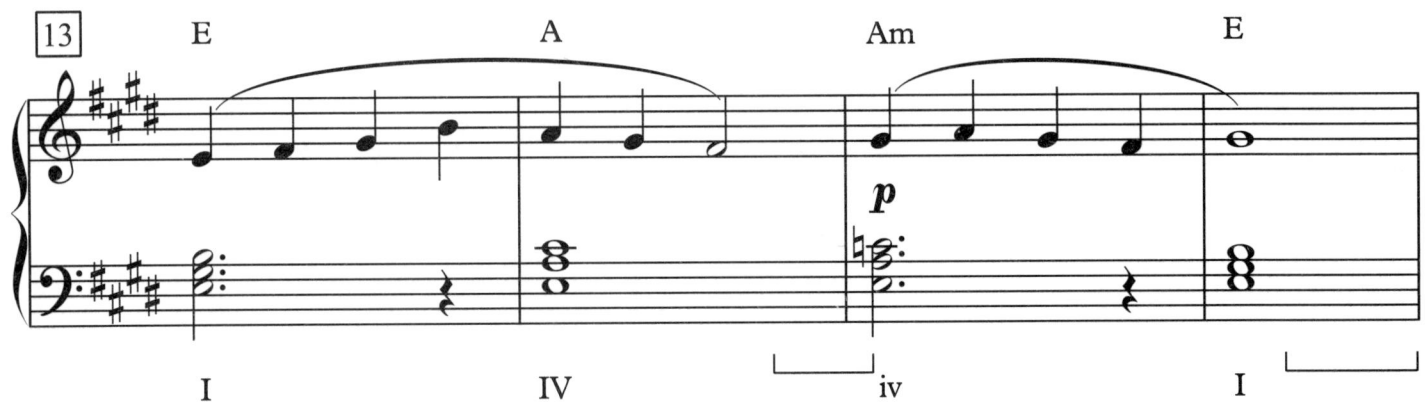

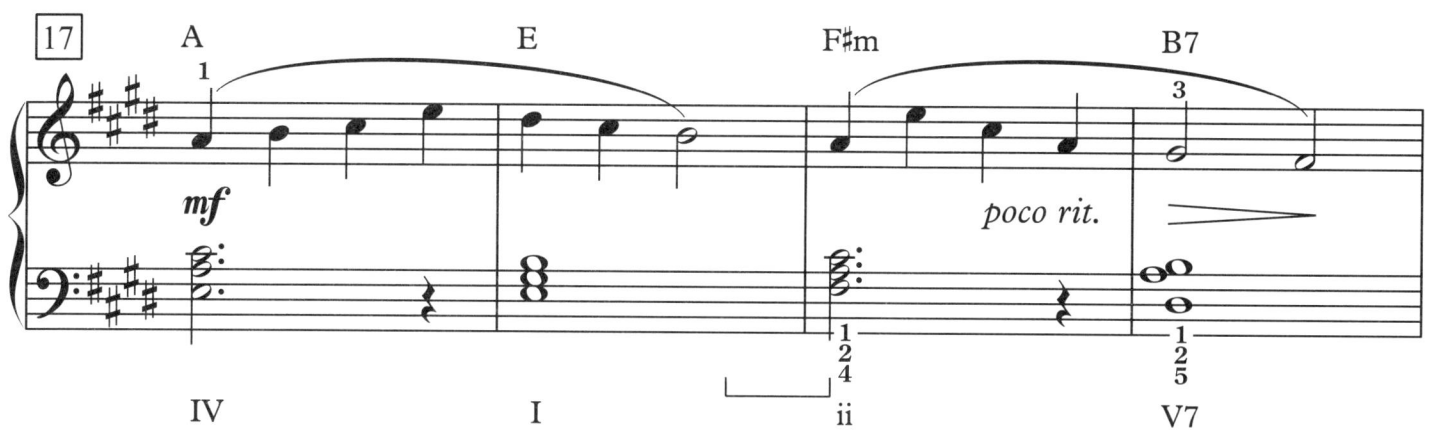
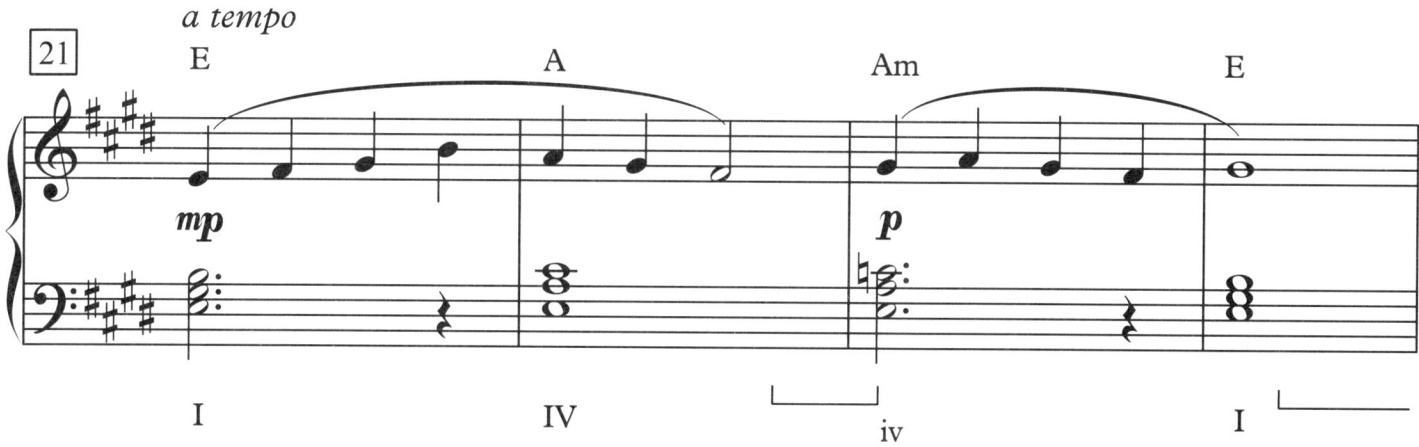

THEORY

D Major Key Signature

The key signature for D Major has two sharps: F♯ and C♯.

1. Trace the first key signature, then draw two more.

Primary Chords in D Major

Primary Chord Progression

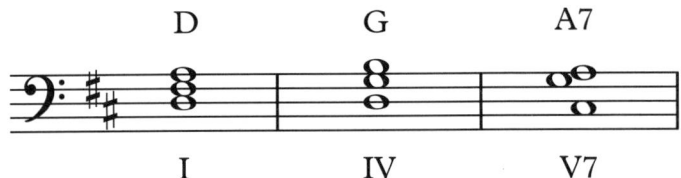

2. Draw this primary chord progression. Use whole notes.

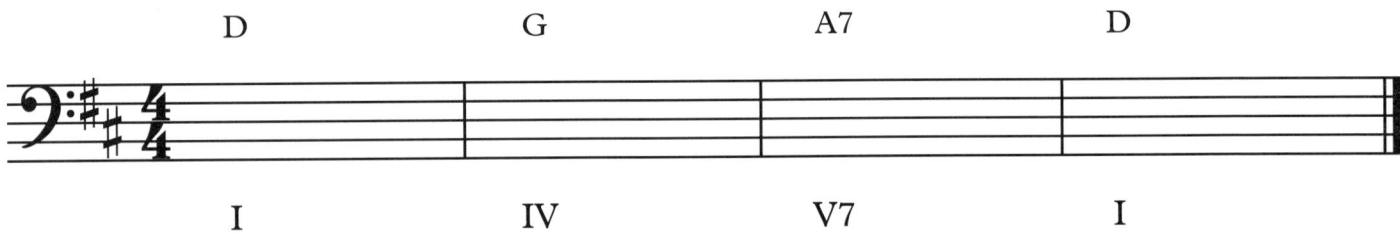

3. Harmonize each measure of this melody with I, IV, or V7. Use whole notes.
   Write Roman numerals below the staff, and chord names above the staff.
   Play what you have written.

D Major, A Major, E Major   17

A Major Key Signature

The key signature for A Major has three sharps: F♯, C♯ and G♯.

4. Trace the first key signature, then draw two more.

Primary Chords in A Major

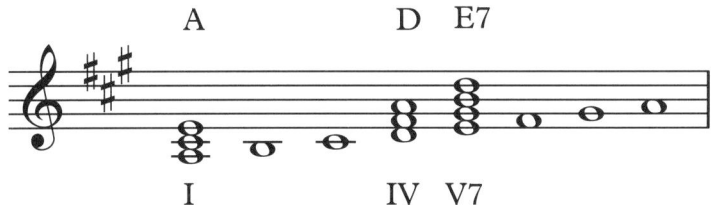

Primary Chord Progression

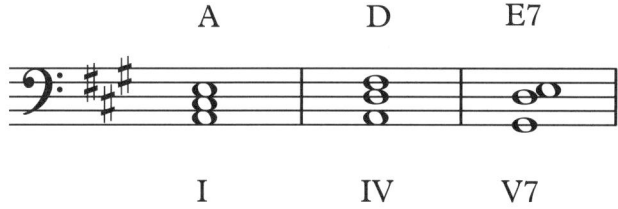

5. Draw this primary chord progression. Use whole notes.

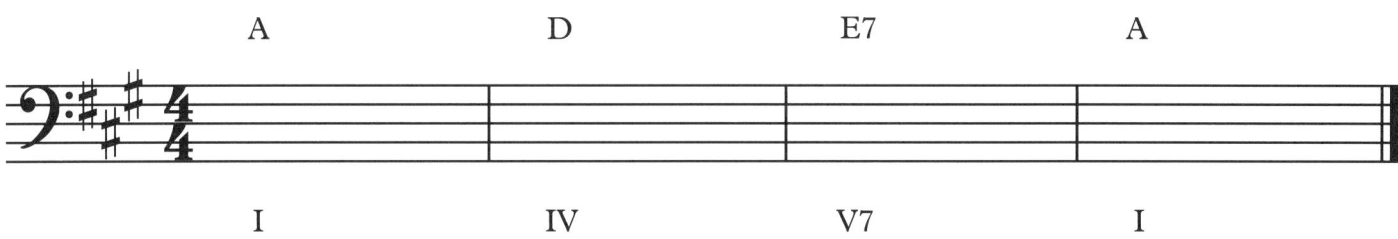

6. Harmonize each measure of this melody with I, IV, or V7. Use dotted half notes.
   Write Roman numerals below the staff, and chord names above the staff.
   Play what you have written.

GP692

E Major Key Signature

The key signature for E Major has four sharps: F♯, C♯, G♯, and D♯.

7. Trace the first key signature, then draw two more.

Primary Chords in E Major

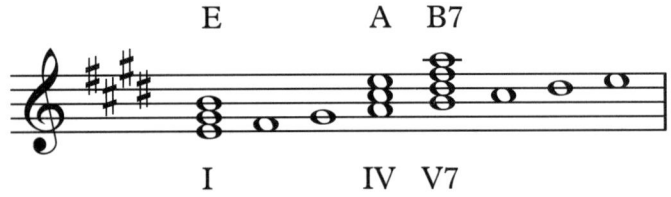

Primary Chord Progression

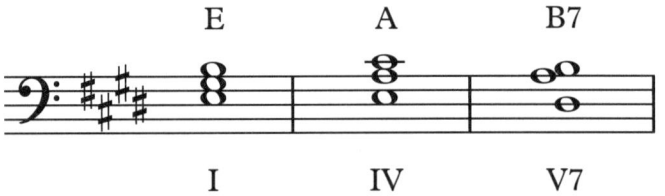

8. Draw this primary chord progression. Use whole notes.

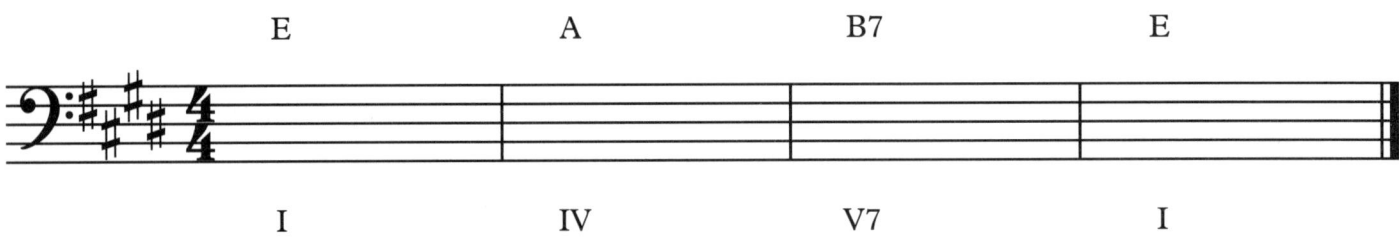

9. Harmonize each measure of this melody with I, IV, or V7. Use half notes.
   Write Roman numerals below the staff, and chord names above the staff.
   Play what you have written.

TECHNIC

D Major, A Major, E Major ■ 19

1. Etude for five-finger evenness.

Etude
Op. 82, No. 16

Cornelius Gurlitt
(1820-1901)

Transpose to A Major and E Major.

2. Primary triads in D Major.

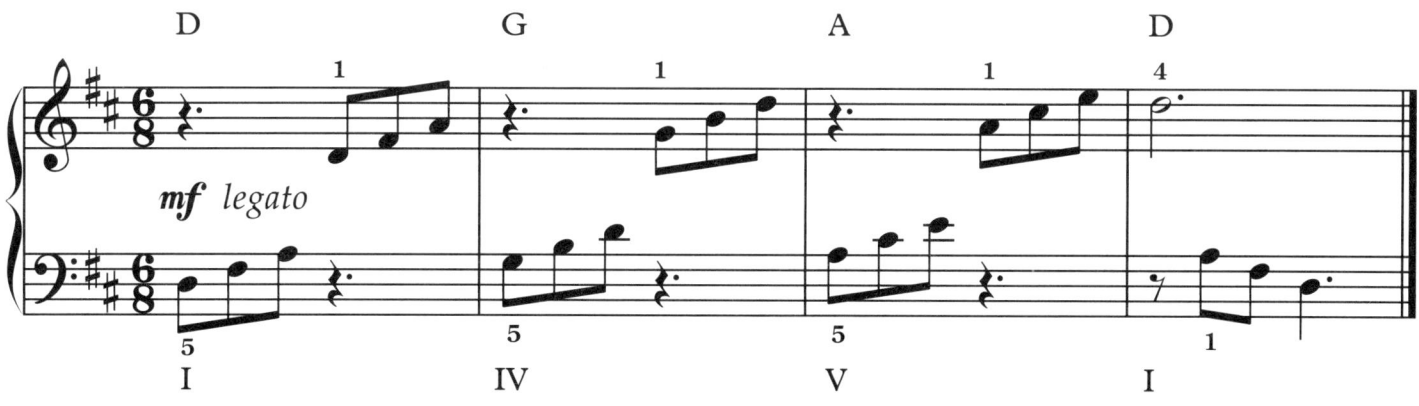

Transpose to A Major and E Major.

UNIT 2
ACCOMPANIMENT PATTERNS

Primary chords are frequently used to accompany melodies.
Play this primary chord progession with your left hand, then transpose it to G, D, A, E, and F Major.

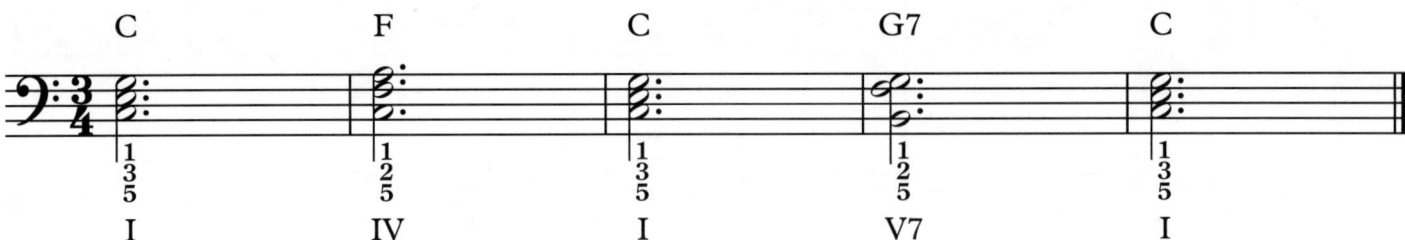

Primary chords may be used for accompaniments in a variety of broken-chord patterns as shown below.
Play each pattern with your left hand, then transpose it to the key indicated.

1. **Split Chord** (See page 21.)

Transpose to F Major.

2. **Waltz Bass** (See pages 22 and 26.)

Transpose to A Major.

3. **Arpeggio** (See page 23.)

Transpose to D Major.

4. **Alberti Bass** (See pages 24 and 27.)

Transpose to G Major.

Ballroom Romance
A Slow Waltz*

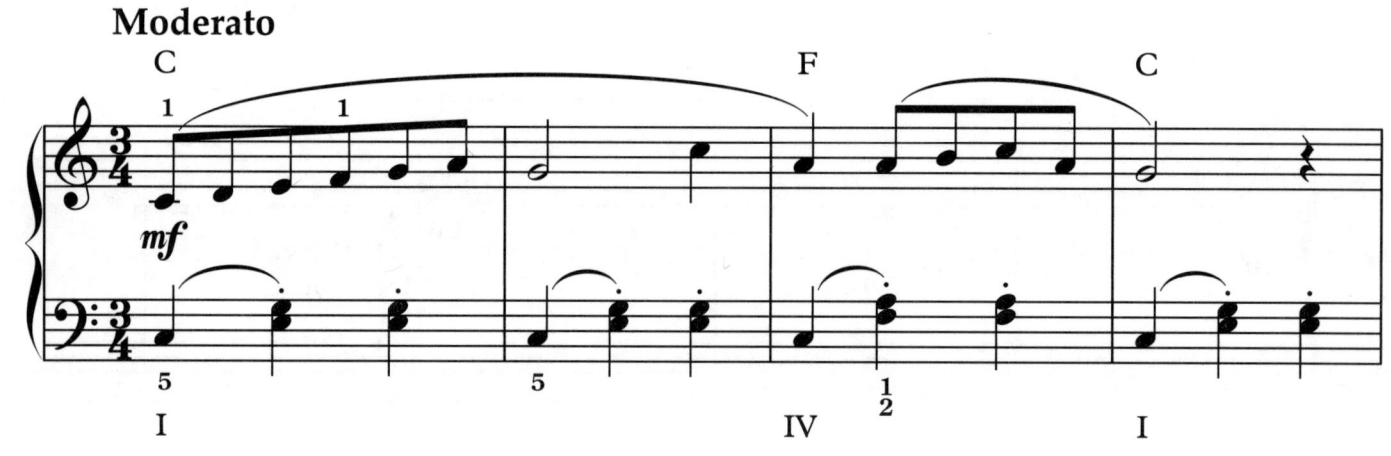

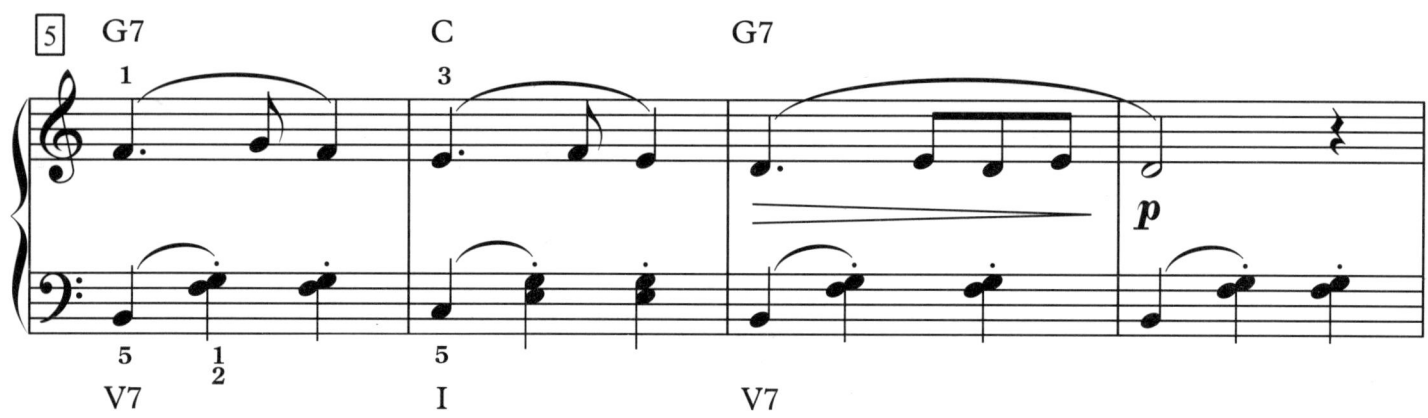

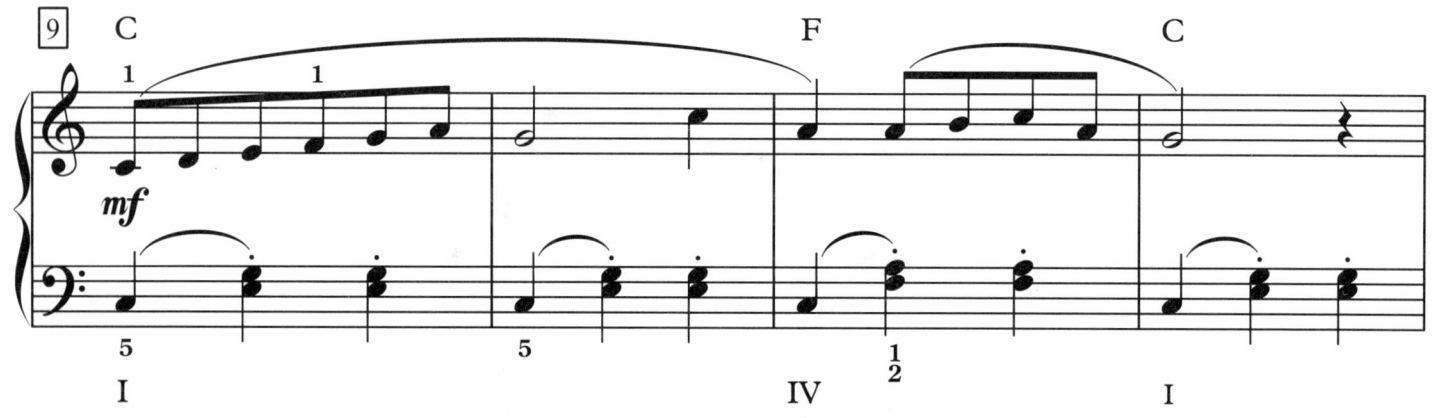

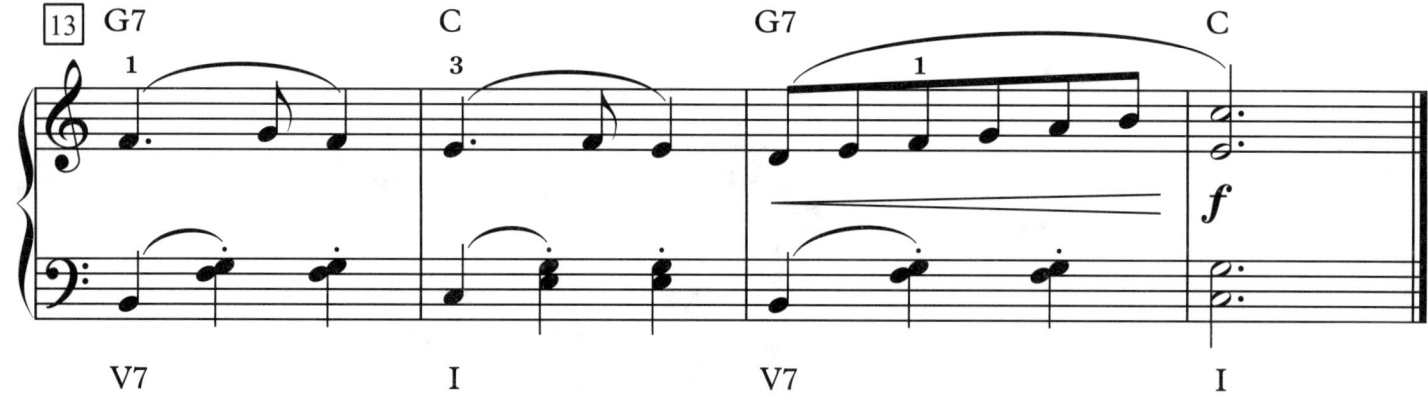

*In contemporary ballroom dance, fast waltzes are called Viennese, in contrast to the Slow Waltz.

A **sonatina** is a short sonata, and may have one, two, or three movements. *Classic Sonatina* is a one movement sonatina in traditional first movement, or **sonata allegro** form. Themes and sections of the form are indicated in the music. The **Alberti bass** was used frequently during the Classical period of music (c.1750-1825) by many composers, including Haydn, Mozart, and Beethoven.

Classic Sonatina

EXPOSITION

First Theme: C Major

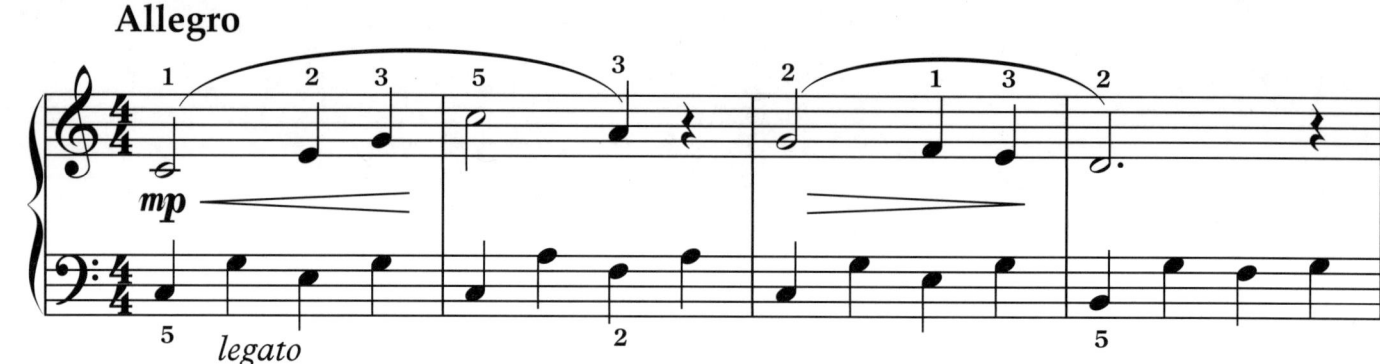

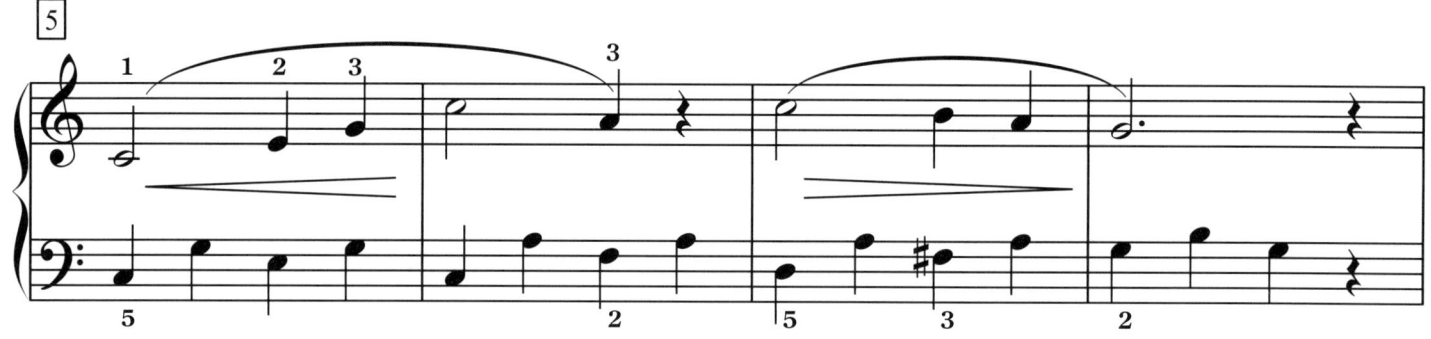

Second Theme: G Major

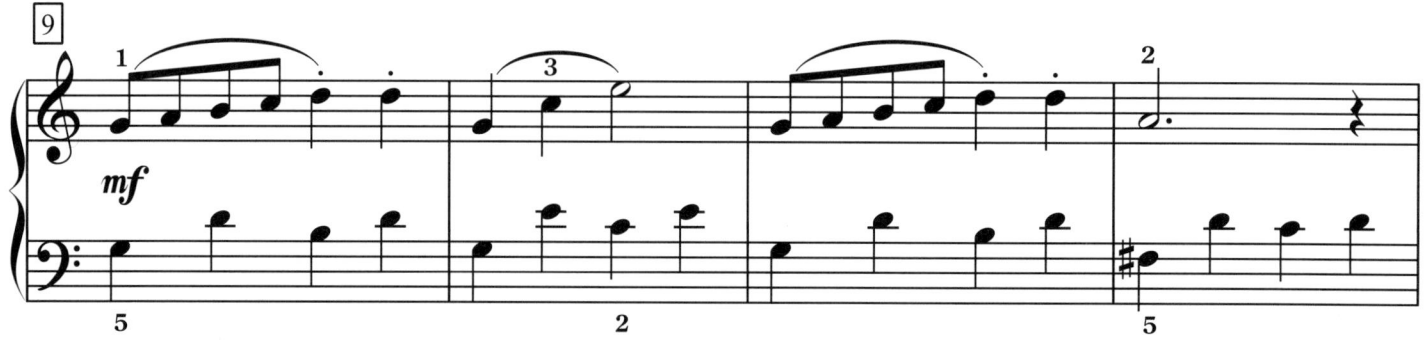

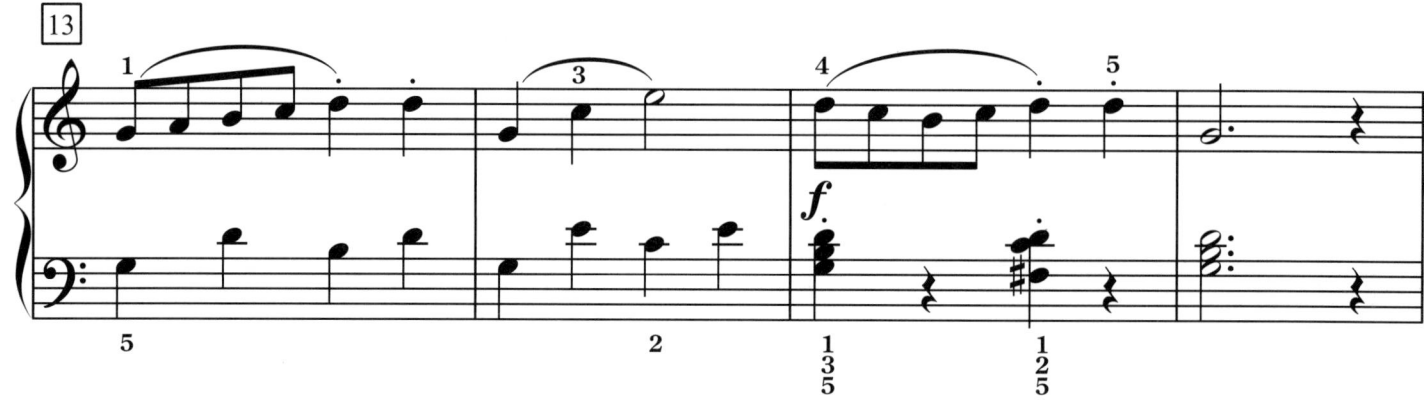

Accompaniment Patterns 25

DEVELOPMENT
Second Theme (inverted)

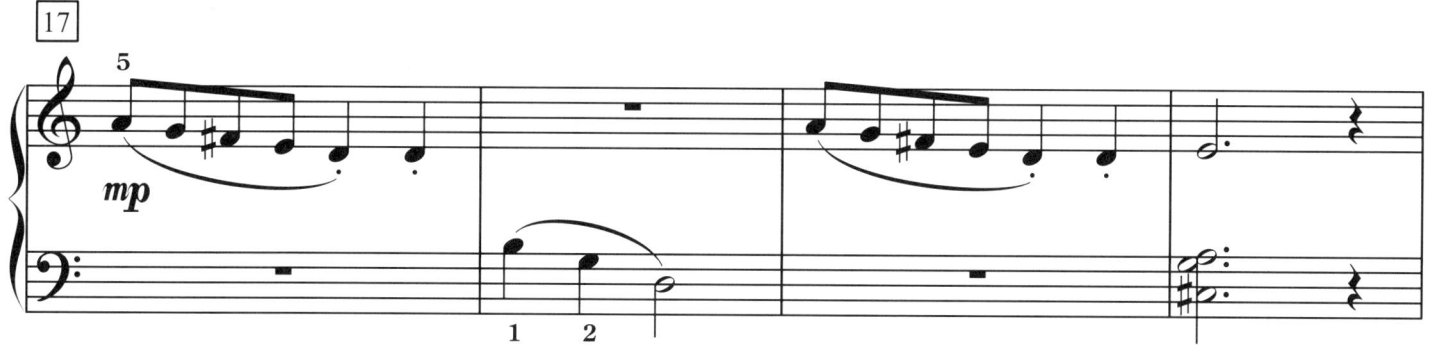

RECAPITULATION
First Theme: C Major

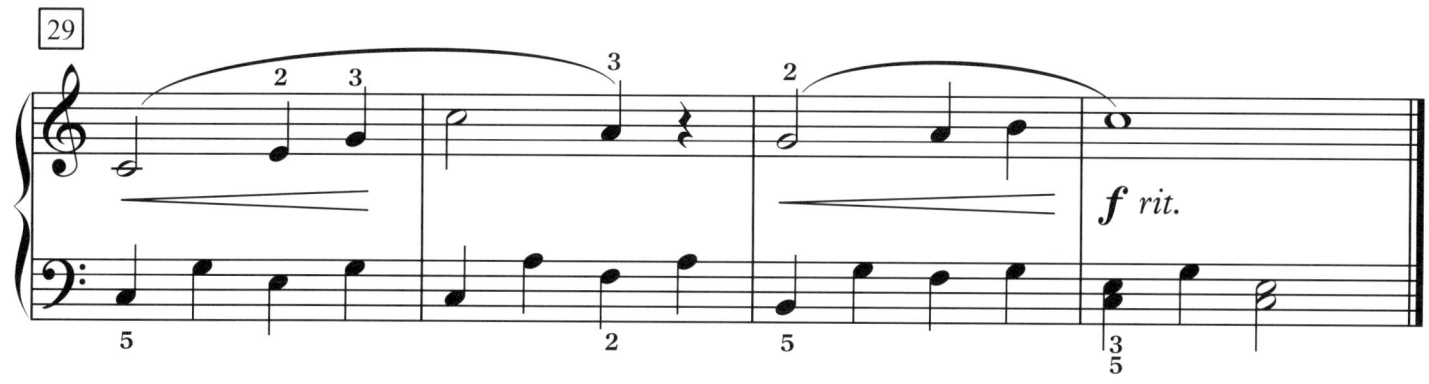

GP692

Music Box Waltz
A Viennese Waltz*

Allegro grazioso (gracefully)

*The Viennese Waltz is the original form of the waltz. It was the first ballroom dance performed in the closed hold or "waltz" position. The Viennese Waltz is implicitly faster than the Slow Waltz.

THEORY

Major Sharp Key Signatures

The sharps in key signatures are always in the same order. Memorize the order of sharps.

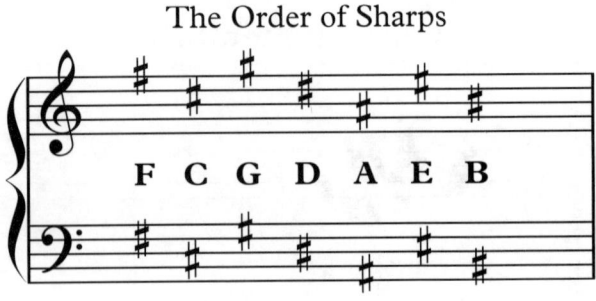

The Order of Sharps

F C G D A E B

1. Trace the order of sharps in the first measure, then draw the order of sharps two more times.

There are seven Major keys that have sharps in the key signature: G, D, A, E, B, F♯, and C♯.
To discover the name of any Major sharp key signature:

- Name the last sharp (to the right) in the key signature.

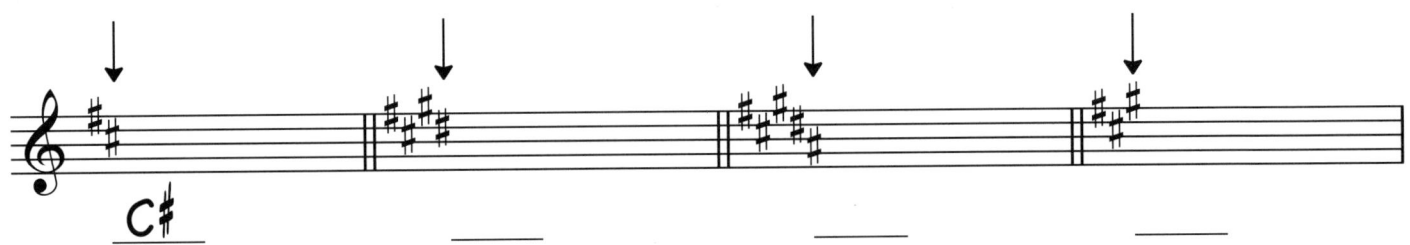

C♯ _____ _____ _____

- Name the note a half step higher than the last sharp in the key signautre.
  This note, also called the **key note,** is the name of the Major sharp key.

___D___ Major   _____ Major   _____ Major   _____ Major

GP692

Accompaniment Patterns 29

2. Name each Major key signature.

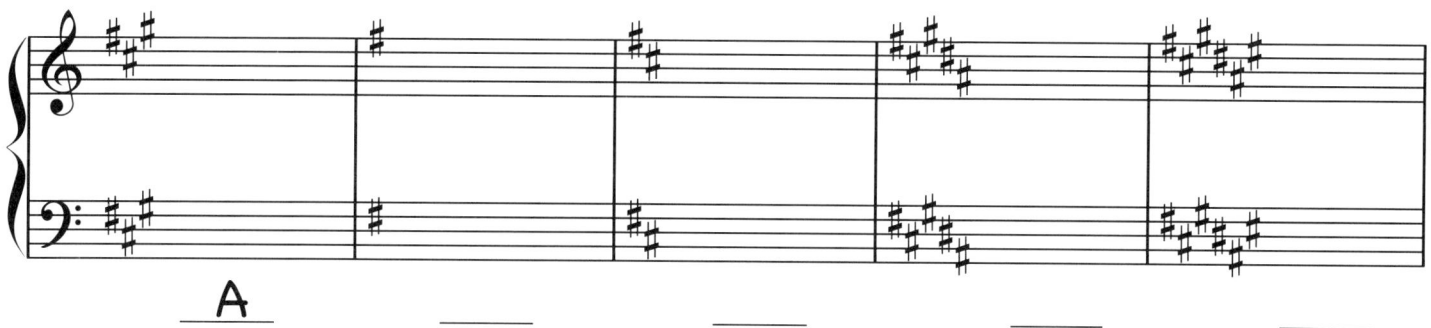

A _____   _____   _____   _____   _____

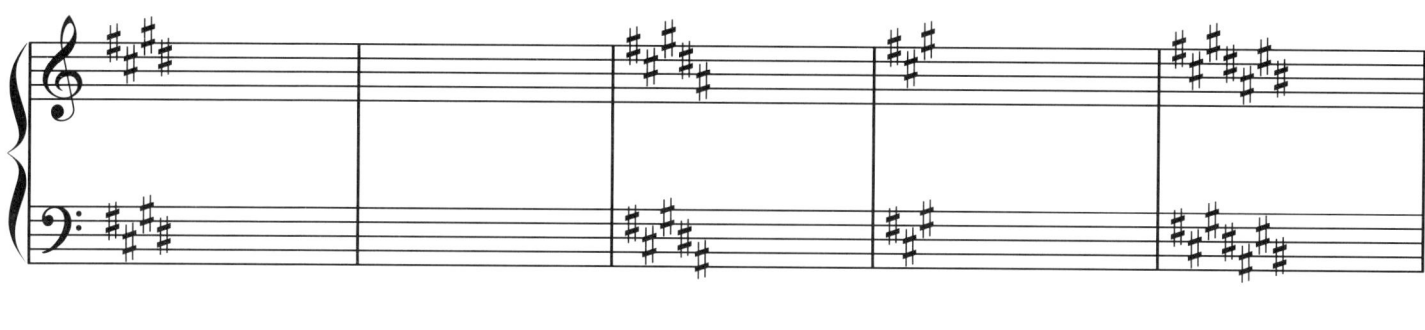

_____   _____   _____   _____   _____

To write the key signature for any Major sharp key:

- Name the note one half step below the key note.

- Write the order of sharps up to and including the sharp that is a half step below the key note.

D Major

Key note

Sharp half step below key note

3. Write each Major key signature.

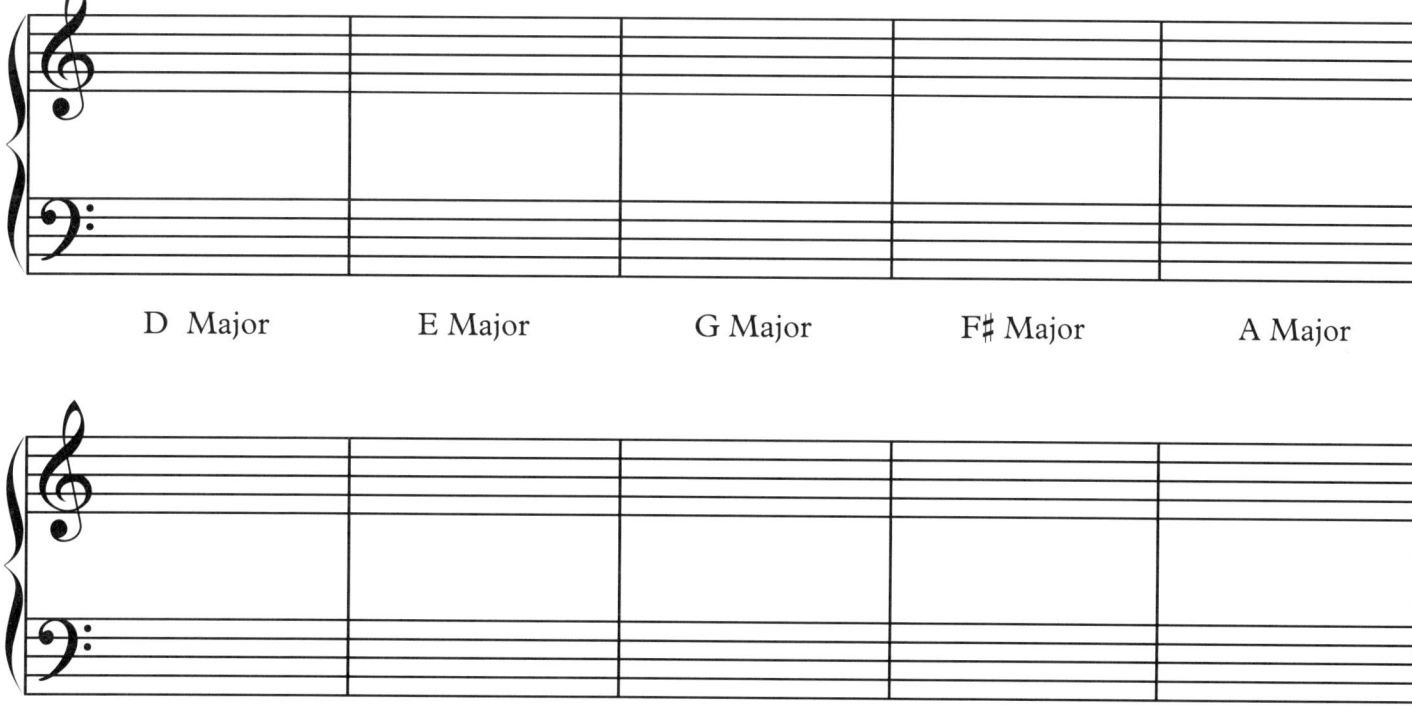

D Major   E Major   G Major   F♯ Major   A Major

C Major   C♯ Major   B Major   D Major   E Major

GP692

TECHNIC

1. Major scales and chord progressions review.

2. In the following etudes, the right hand plays broken chords extending to the octave, while the left hand plays arpeggio *(Etude I)* and split chord *(Etude II)* accompaniment patterns.

Etude I

Etude II

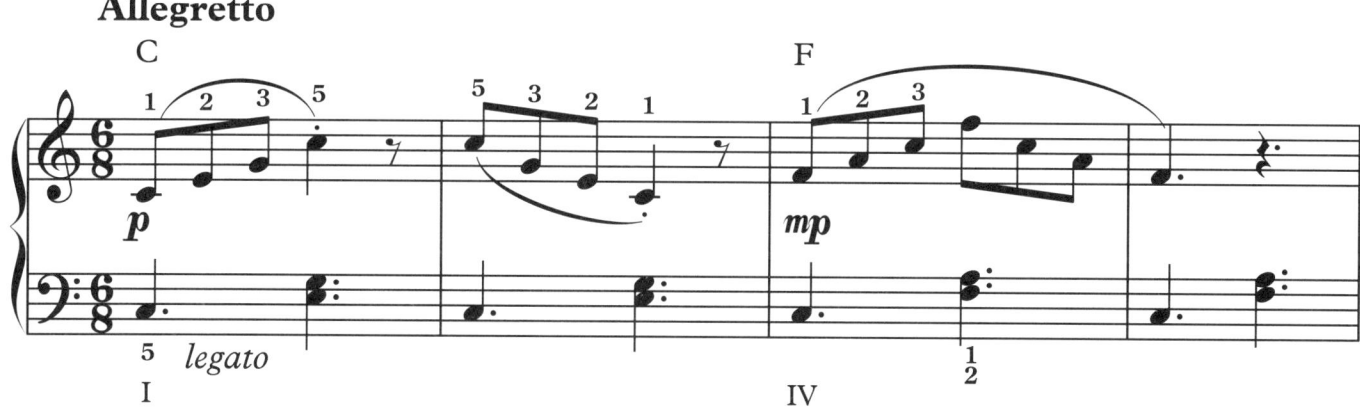

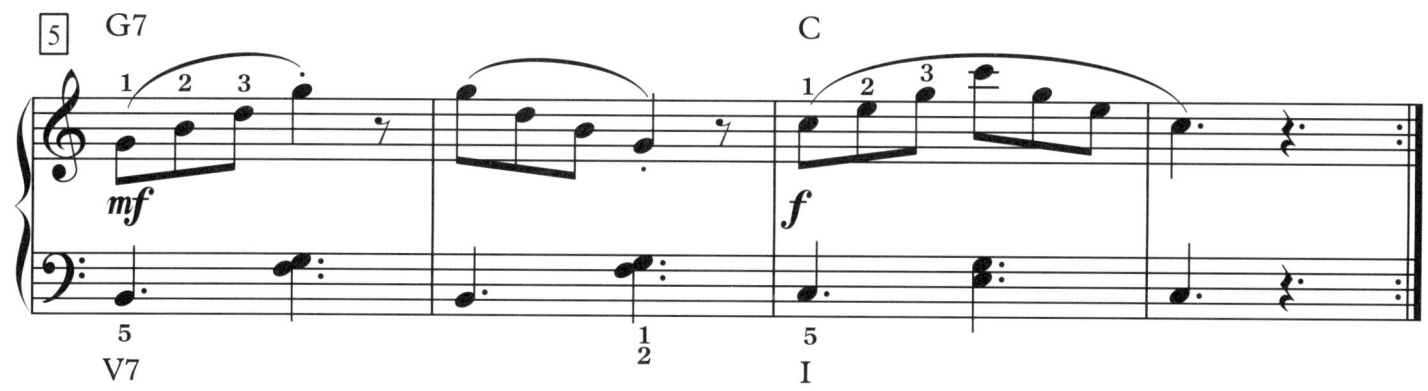

UNIT 3
A MINOR, D MINOR, E MINOR

Relative Minor Scales and Key Signatures

Every Major scale has a **relative minor** scale with the same key signature.

A minor is the relative to **C Major**: both keys have no sharps or flats in the key signature.

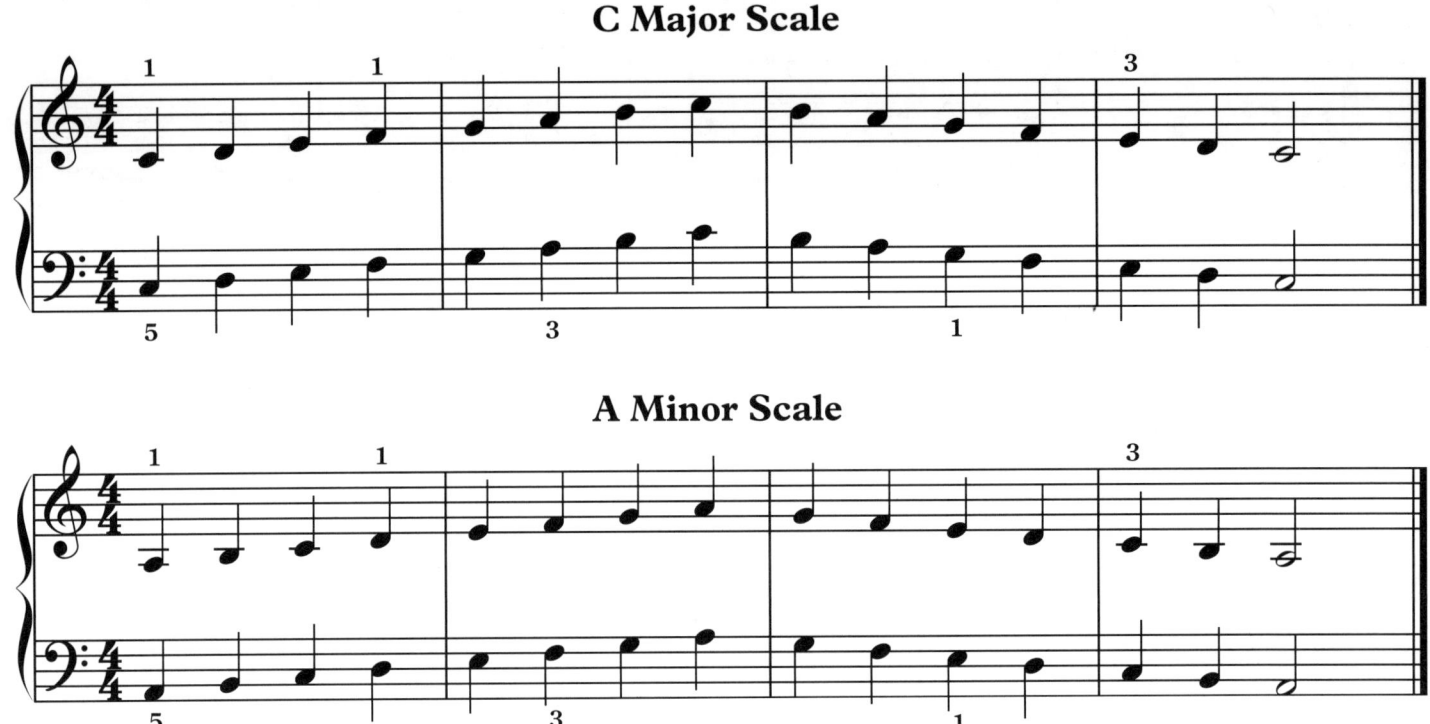

There are two ways to discover the relative minor to any Major key.

1. The first degree of any minor key is three half steps below the first degree of its relative Major.

2. The sixth degree of any Major scale is the first degree of its relative minor.

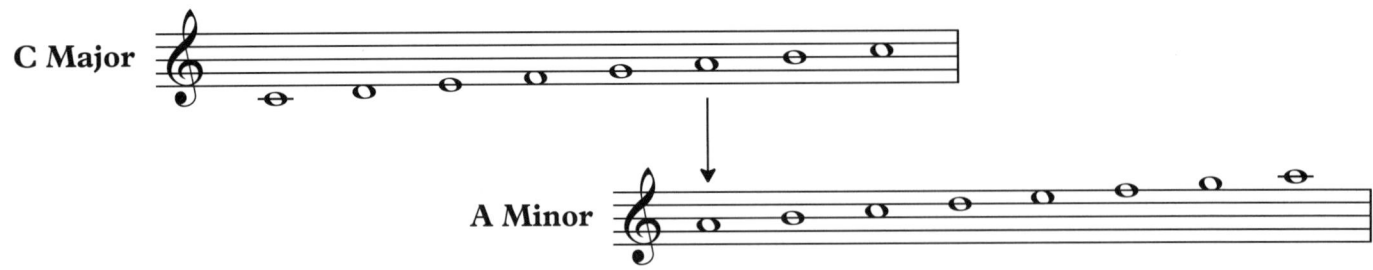

Forms of Minor Scales

There are three forms of minor scales: **Natural**, **Harmonic**, and **Melodic**.

The **natural** form follows the key signature exactly; none of the notes are altered.

A Natural Minor Scale

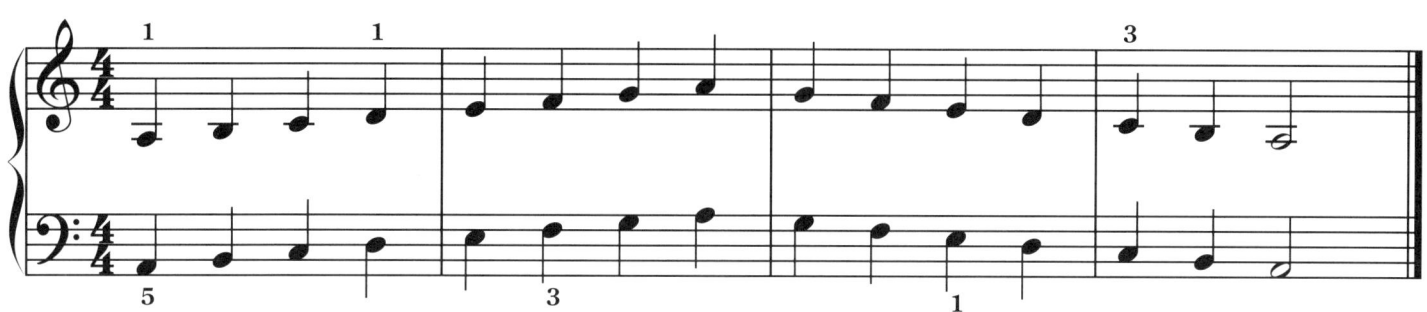

In the **harmonic** form, the seventh degree of the scale is raised one half step.
This form is used for chords, i.e. harmonies.

A Harmonic Minor Scale

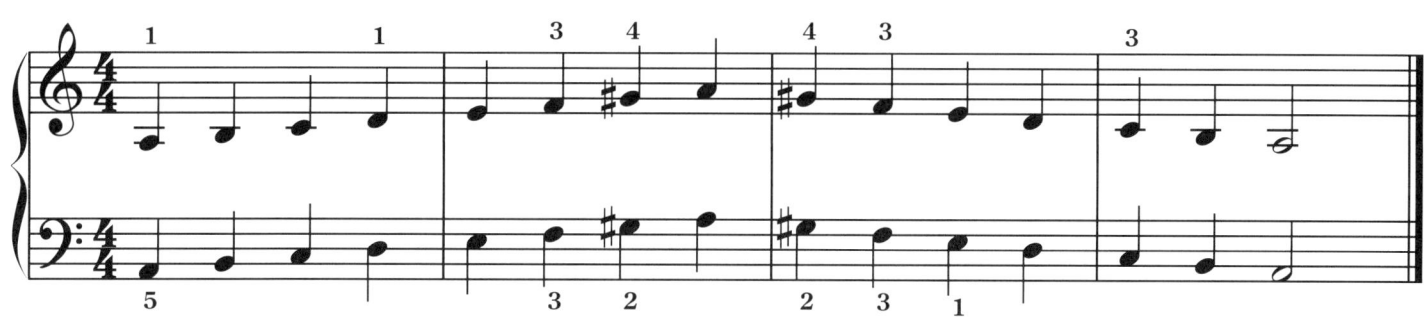

In the **melodic** form, the sixth and seventh degrees are raised ascending, then lowered descending.
This form is used for melodies.

A Melodic Minor Scale

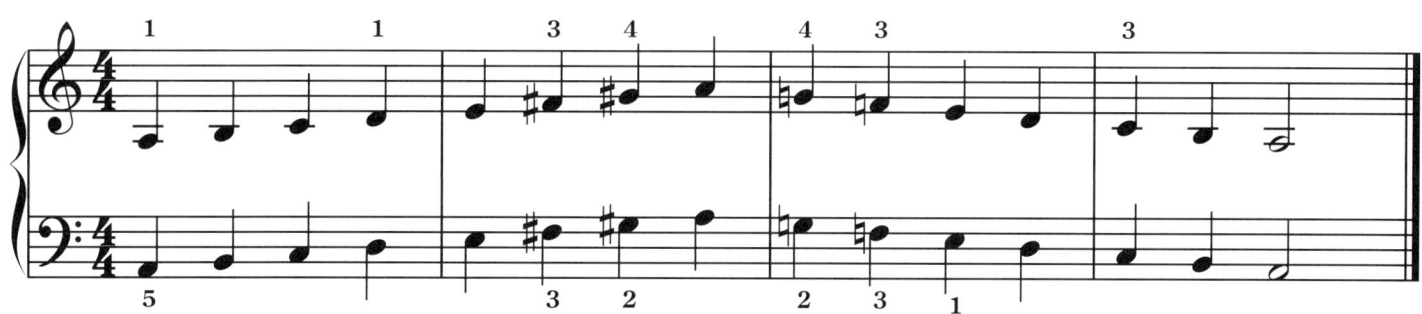

Primary Chords in Minor Keys

The **harmonic** form is used for primary chords in minor keys.
The **i** and **iv** chords are minor.* The **V** chord is Major because of the raised seventh degree.

Primary Chords in A Minor

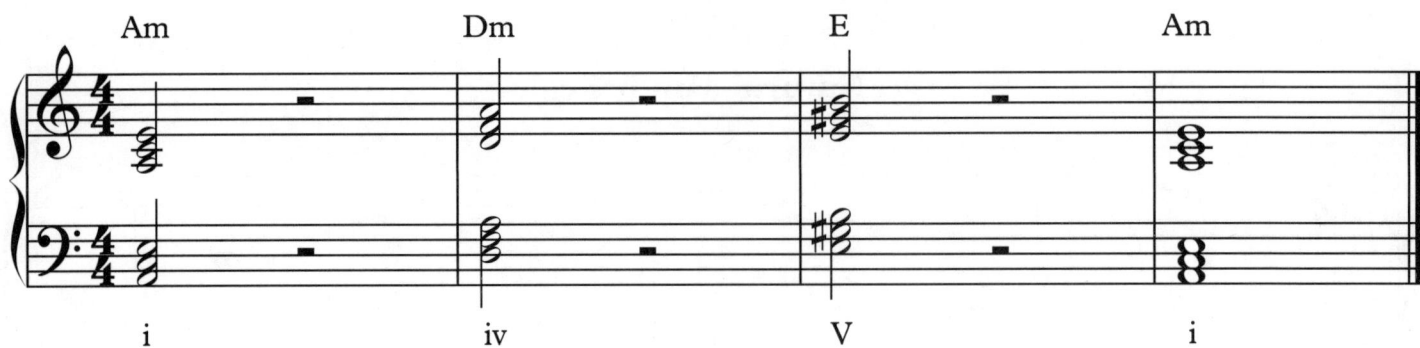

*Lower case Roman numerals are used for minor chords.

Primary Chord Progression in A Minor

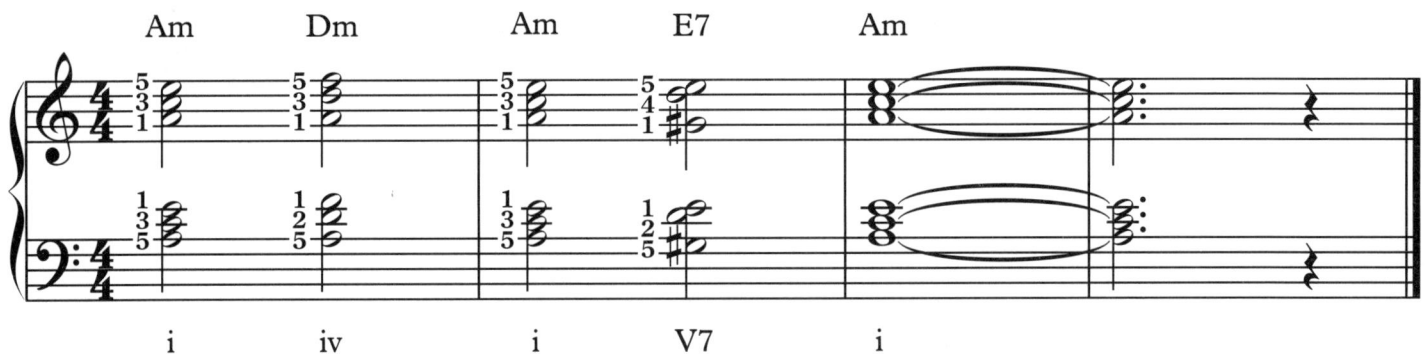

Bold and Brave

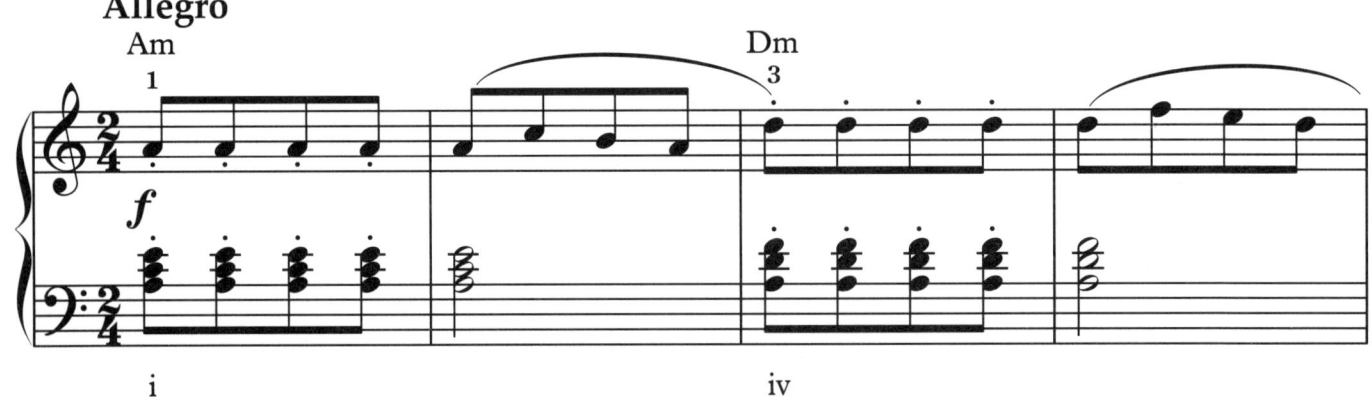

A Minor, D Minor, E Minor — 35

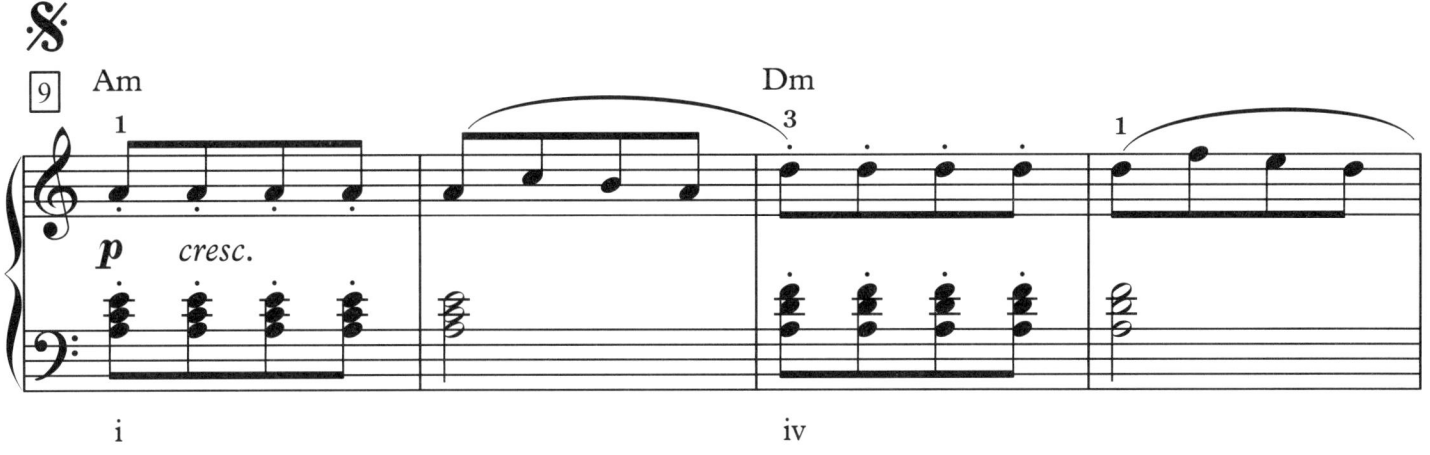
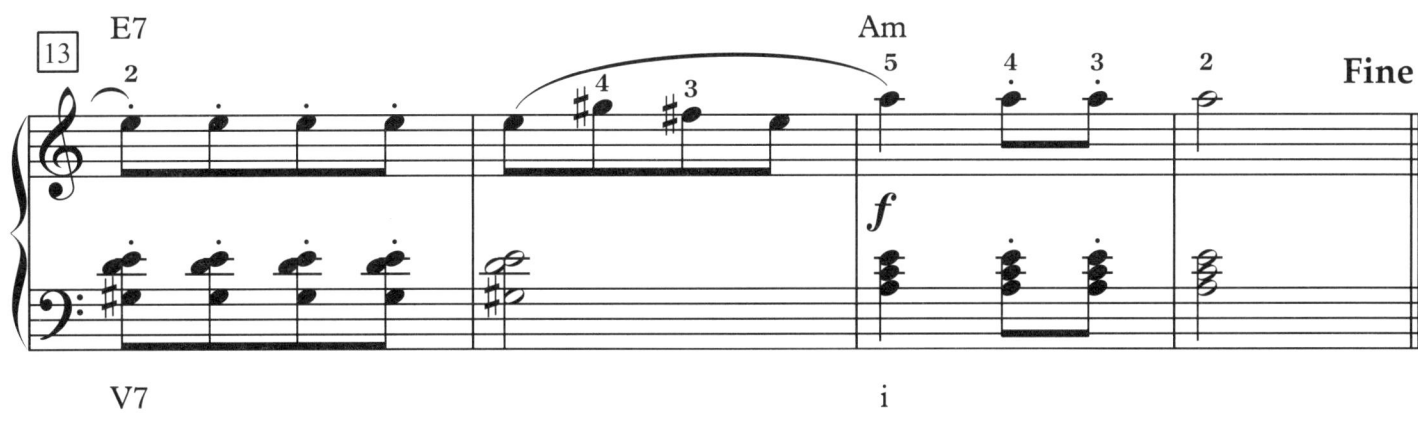
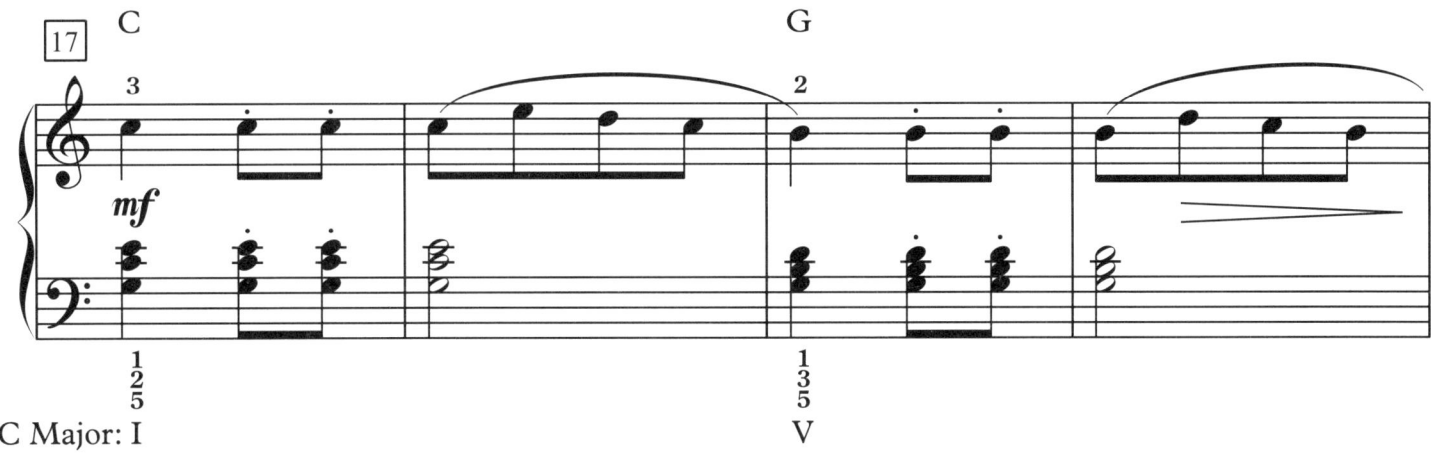
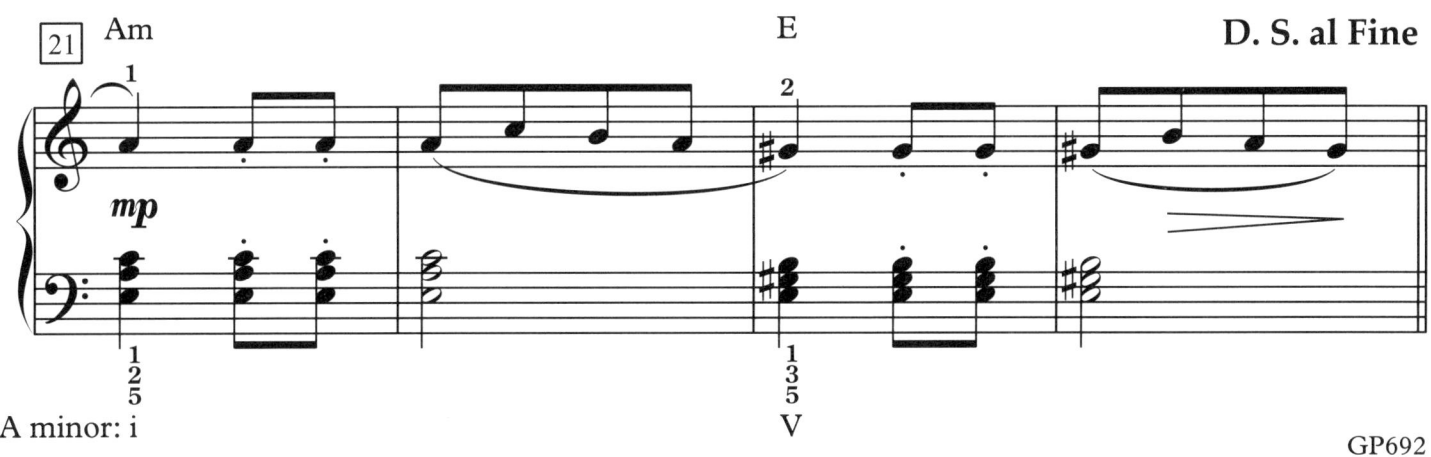

D Minor Scales and Chords

D minor is relative to **F Major**. Both keys have one flat, B♭, in the key signature.

D Harmonic Minor Scale

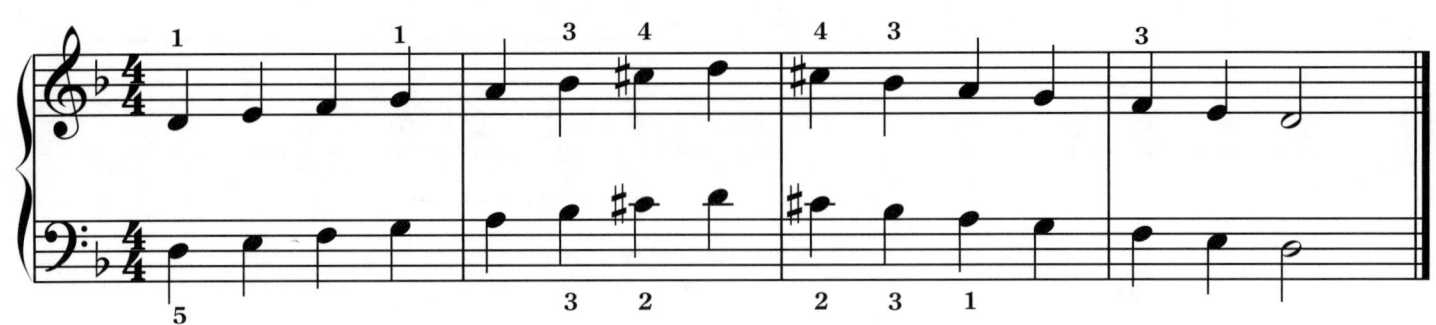

D Melodic Minor Scale

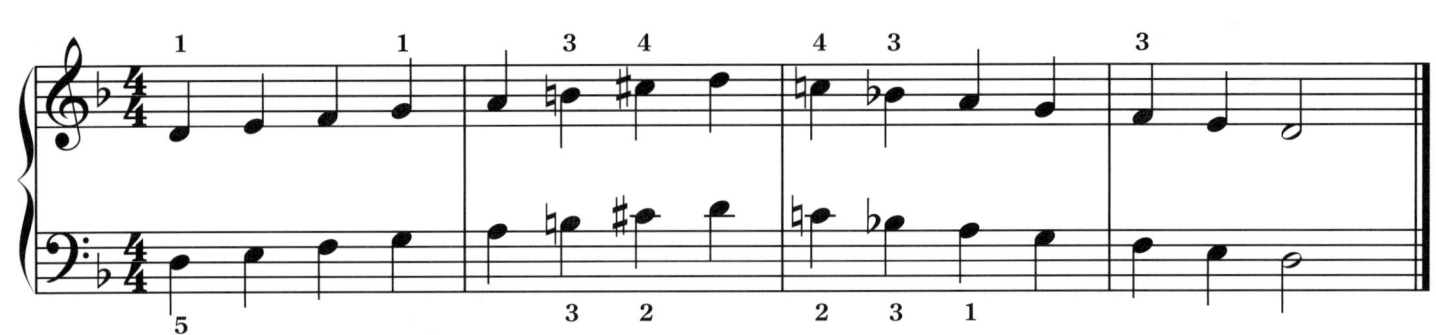

Primary Chords in D Minor

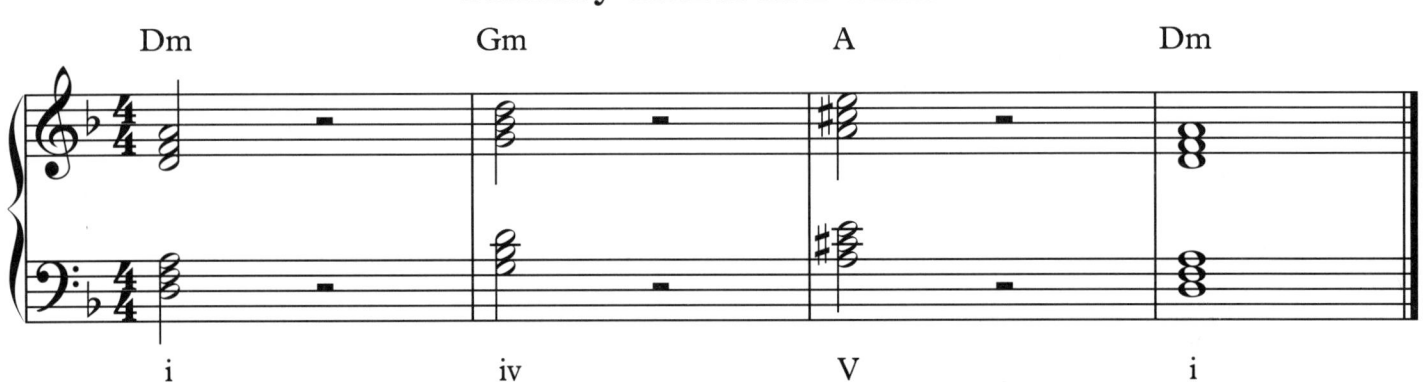

Primary Chord Progression in D Minor

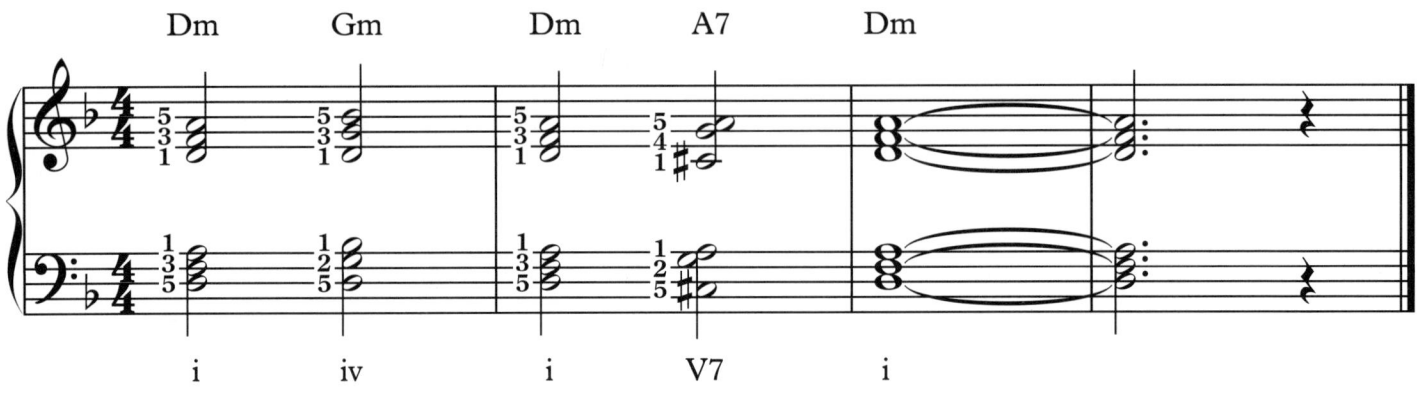

A Minor, D Minor, E Minor 37

Lament

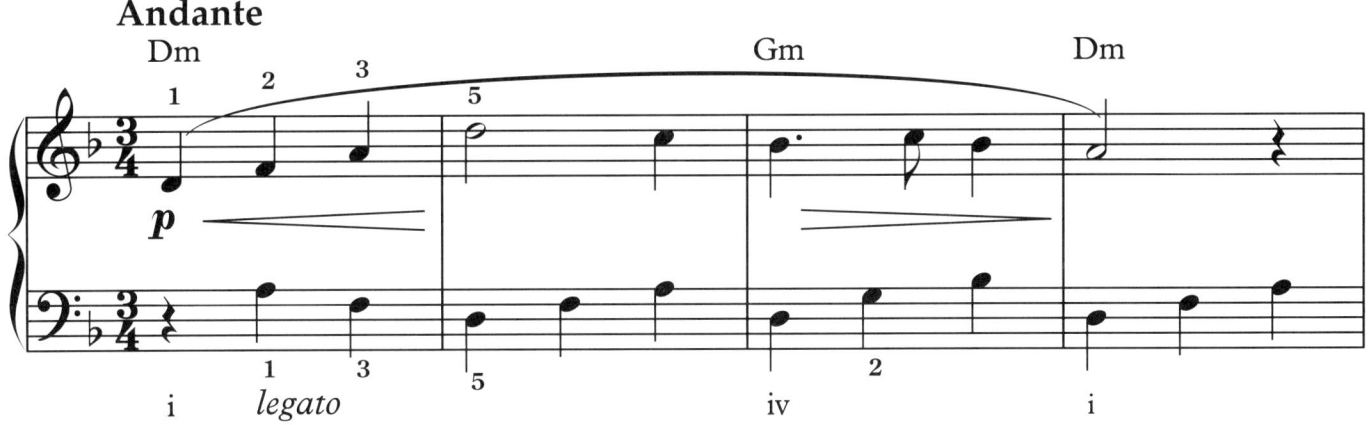
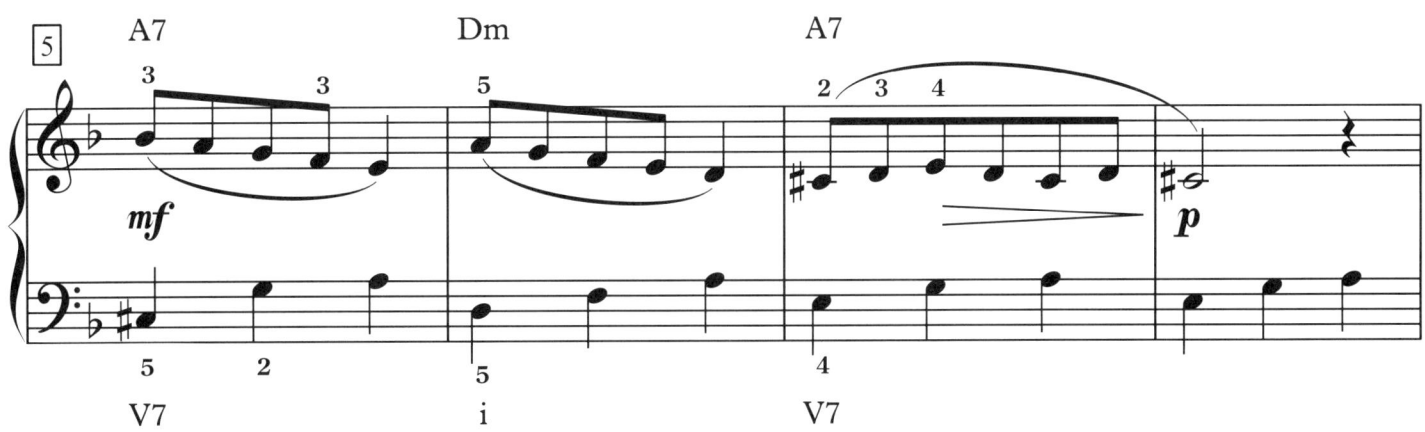
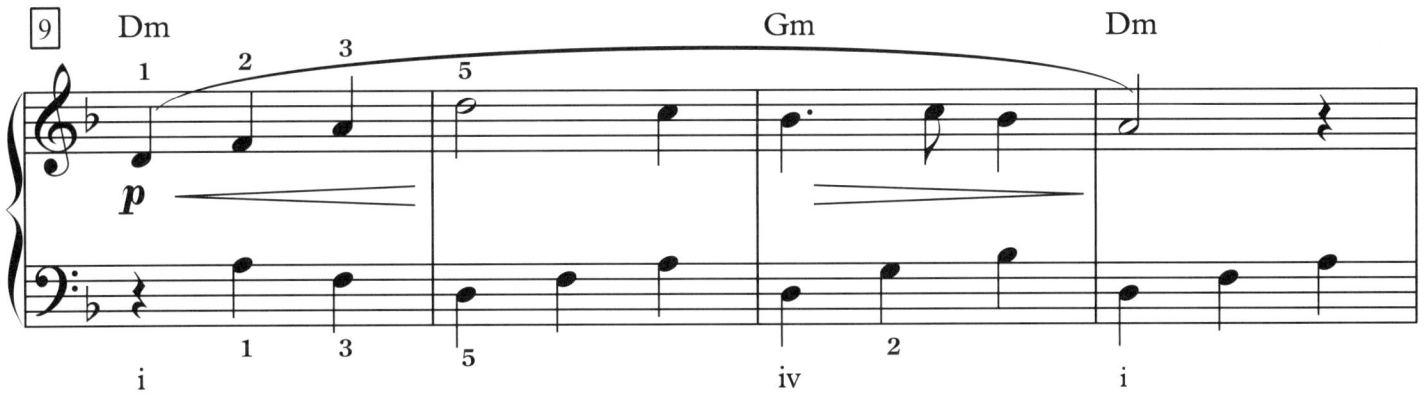
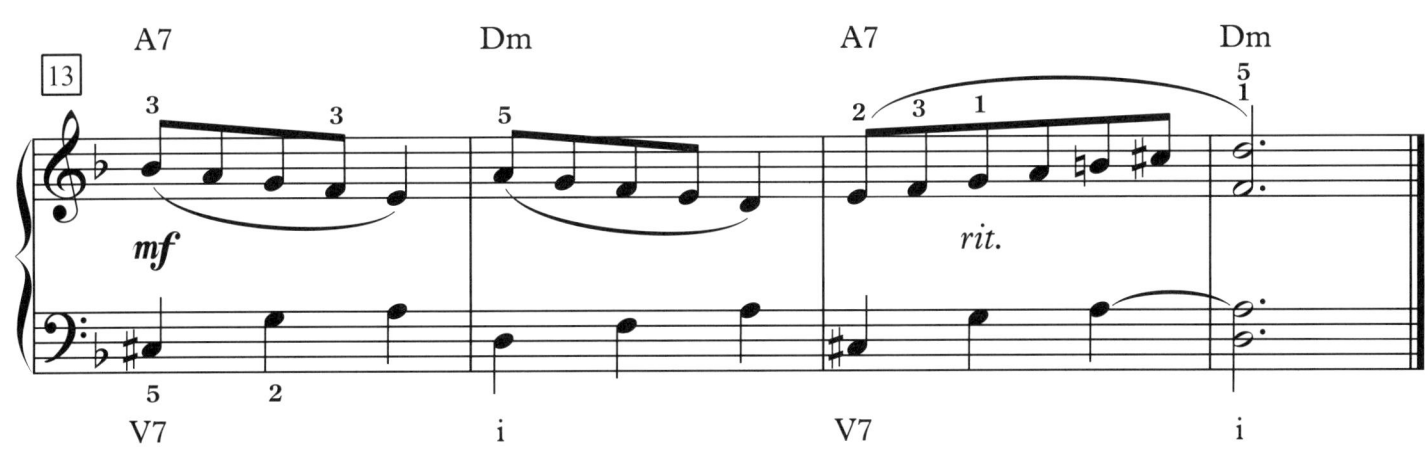

E Minor Scales and Chords

E minor is relative to **G Major**. Both keys have one sharp, F♯, in the key signature.

E Harmonic Minor Scale

E Melodic Minor Scale

Primary Chords in E Minor

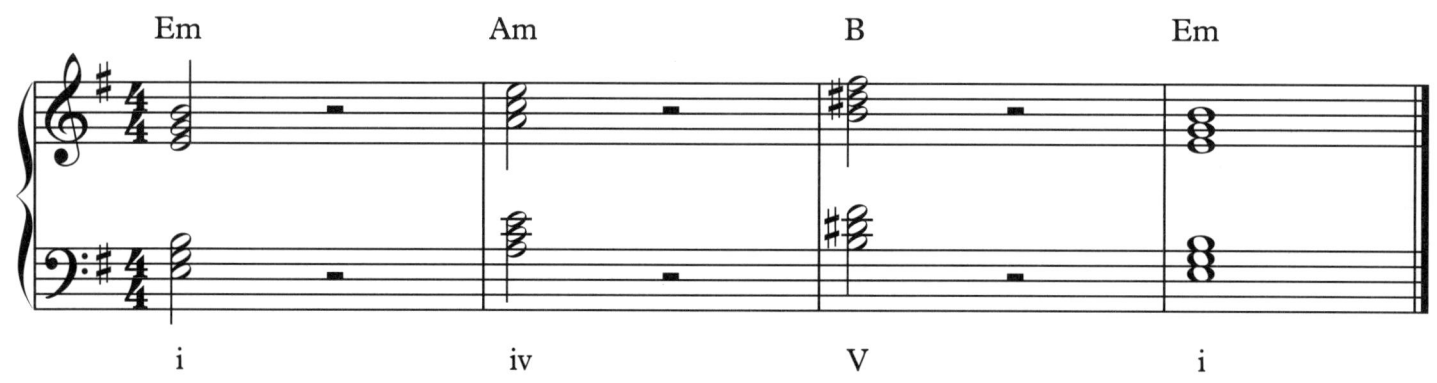

Primary Chord Progression in E Minor

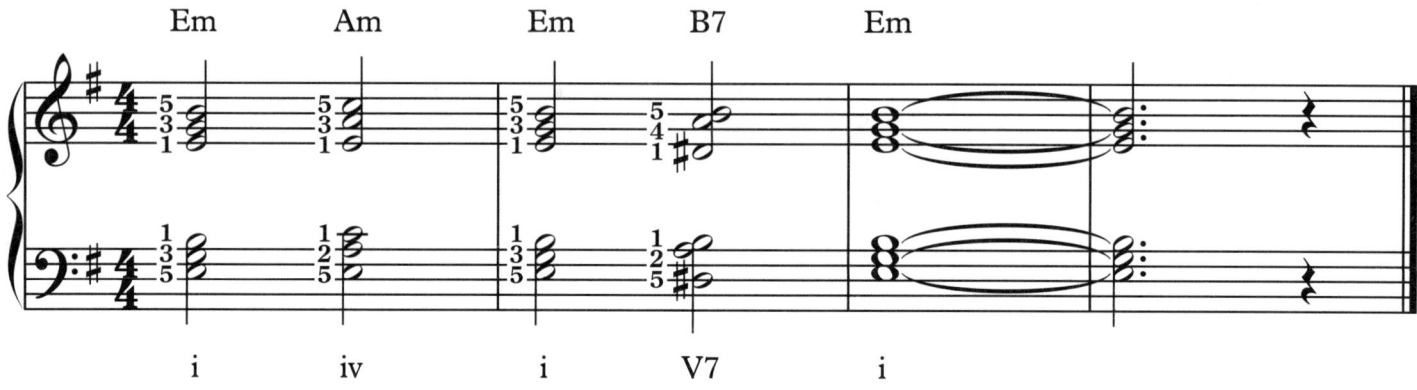

A Minor, D Minor, E Minor 39

This piece has three sections: section **A**, from measures 1-8, and section **B**, from measures 9-16, and then a repeat of section **A**. Music with three sections is in **ABA** or **ternary** form.

Tarantella

***sforzando**: a sudden strong accent.

GP692

THEORY

1. Change this A natural minor scale to harmonic minor by raising the seventh degree a half step.

2. Change this A natural minor scale to melodic minor by raising the sixth and seventh degrees a half step ascending, then lowered descending.

The harmonic minor scale is used when forming primary chords in minor keys.
The raised seventh degree makes the **V7** chord the same in A minor as in A Major.
In minor keys, **i** and **iv** are minor chords. Lower case Roman numerals are used for minor chords.

Primary Chords in A Minor   **Primary Chord Progression**

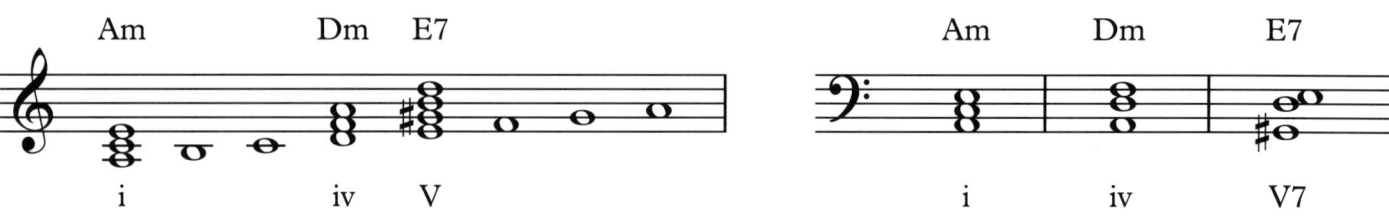

3. Draw this primary chord progression. Use whole notes.

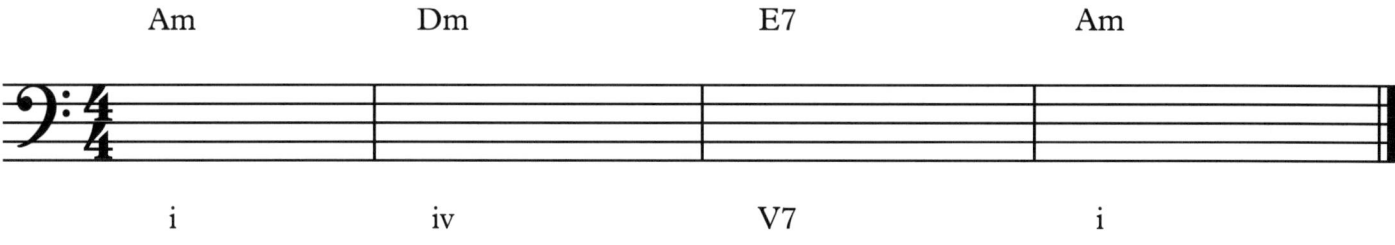

4. Harmonize each measure of this melody with i, iv, or V7. Use whole notes.
   Write Roman numerals below the staff, and chord names above the staff.
   Play what you have written.

5. Change this D natural minor scale to harmonic minor by raising the seventh degree a half step.

6. Change this D natural minor scale to melodic minor by raising the sixth and seventh degrees a half step step ascending, then lowered descending.

The harmonic minor scale is used when forming primary chords in minor keys.
The raised seventh degree makes the **V7** chord the same in D minor as in D Major.
In minor keys, **i** and **iv** are minor chords.

Primary Chords in D Minor

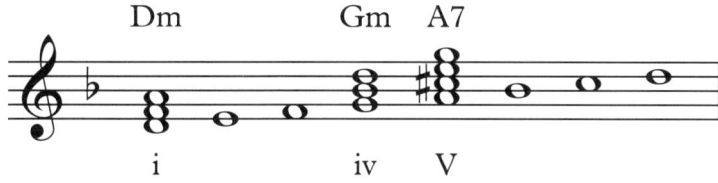

Primary Chord Progression

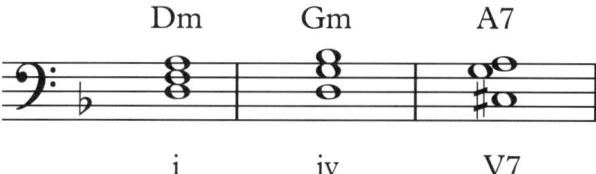

7. Draw this primary chord progression. Use half notes.

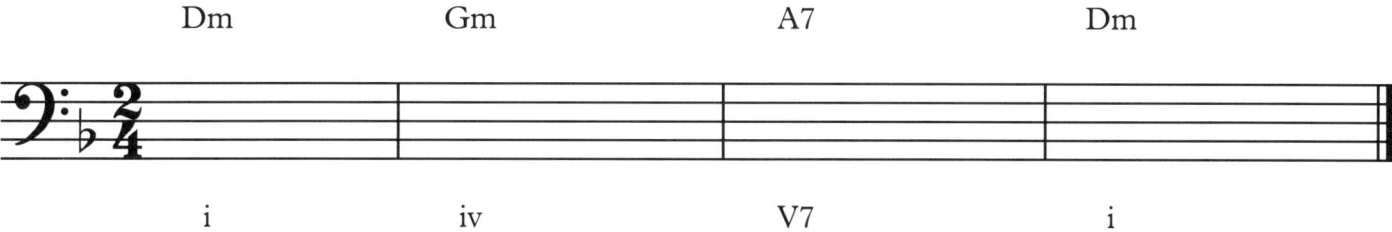

8. Harmonize each measure of this melody with i, iv, or V7. Use half notes.
   Write Roman numerals below the staff, and chord names above the staff.
   Play what you have written.

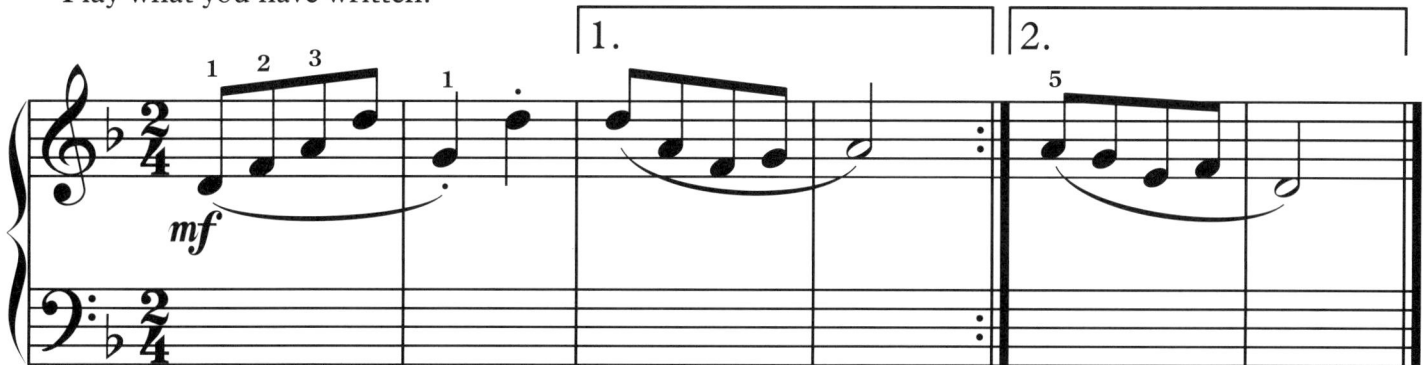

9. Change this E natural minor scale to harmonic minor by raising the seventh degree a half step.

10. Change this E natural minor scale to melodic minor by raising the sixth and seventh degrees a half step step ascending, then lowered descending.

The harmonic minor scale is used when forming primary chords in minor keys.
The raised seventh degree makes the **V7** chord the same in E minor as in E Major.
In minor keys, **i** and **iv** are minor chords.

Primary Chords in E Minor   ### Primary Chord Progression

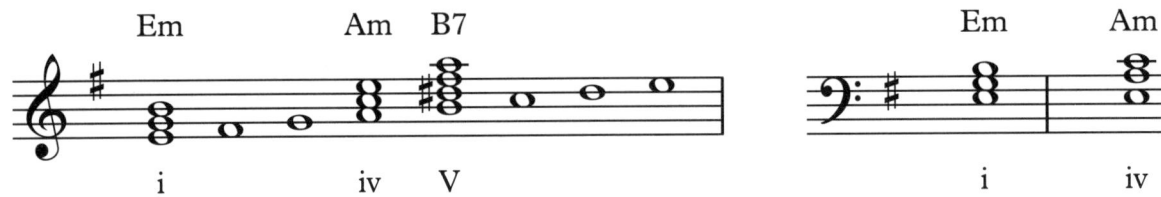

11. Draw this primary chord progression. Use dotted half notes.

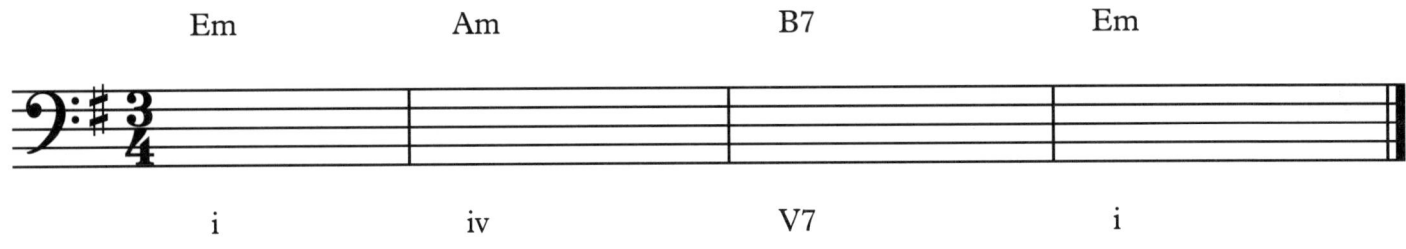

12. Harmonize each measure of this melody with i, iv, or V7. Use dotted half notes.
    Write Roman numerals below the staff, and chord names above the staff.
    Play what you have written.

TECHNIC
Velocity Etude

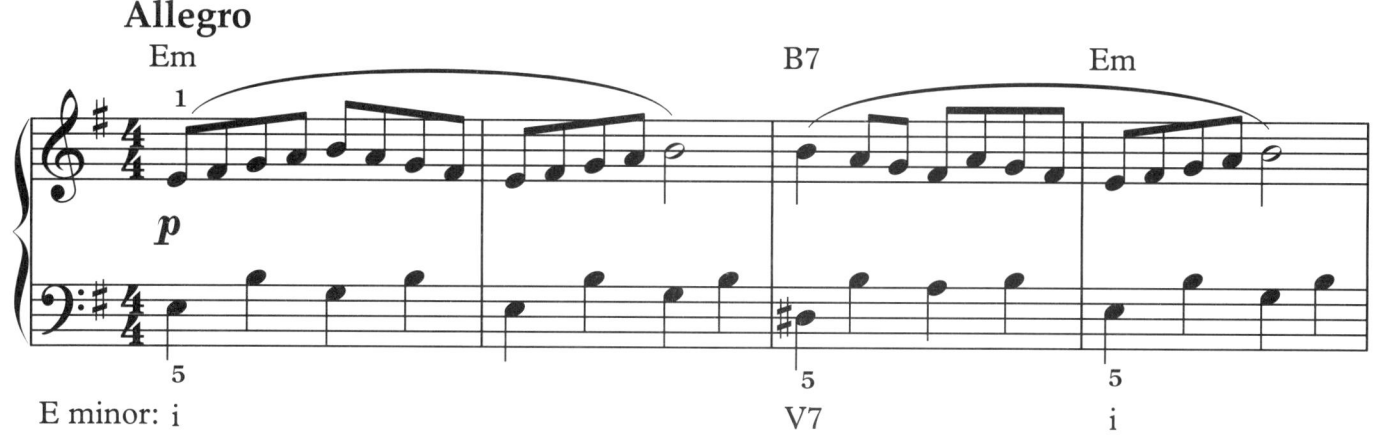

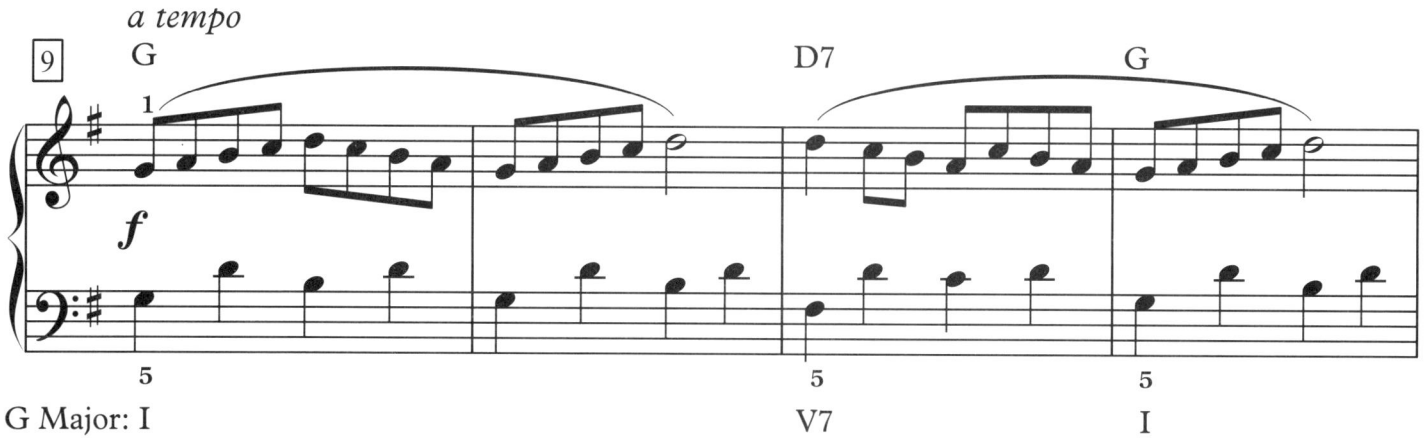
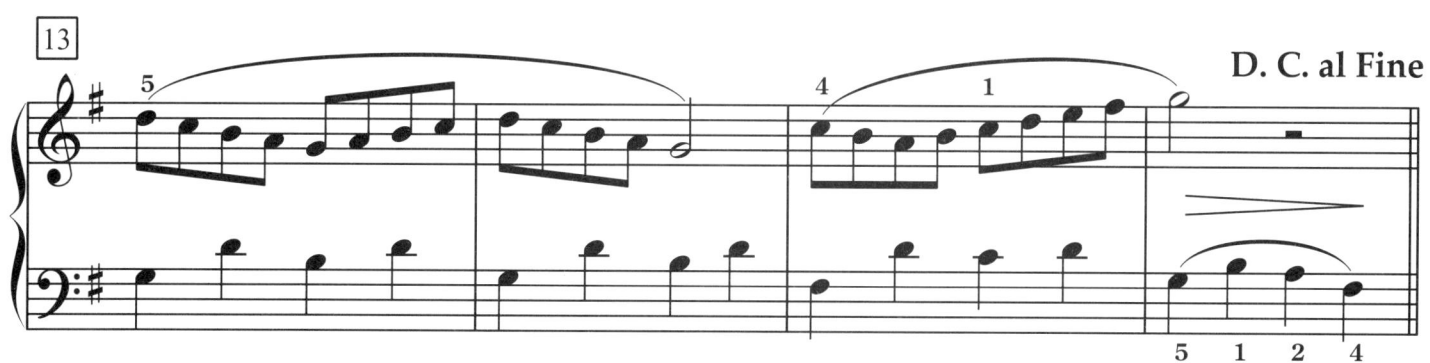

UNIT 4
TRIADS AND INVERSIONS; TRIPLET

Notes of a triad are called the root, 3rd, and 5th. The root gives a triad its letter name.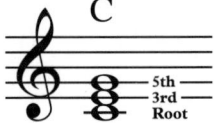

A triad is in **root position** when the root is the lowest note.

A triad is in an **inversion** when the 3rd or 5th is the lowest note.

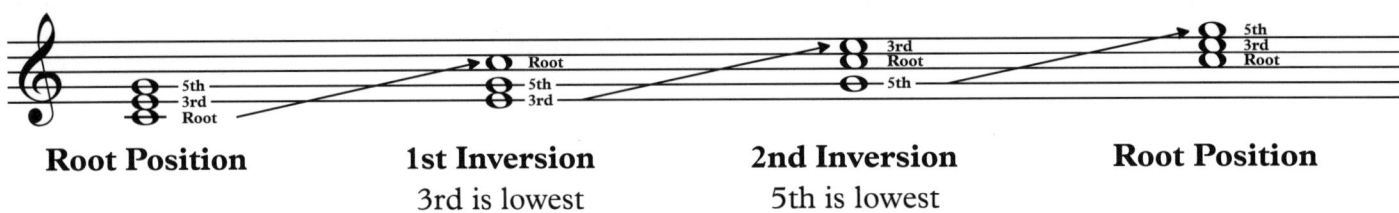

Inversions may be created by moving the bottom note to the top.

C Major Triad and Inversions

Play this C Major triad in root position and inversions.
Observe the fingering, particularly when to use finger 2.

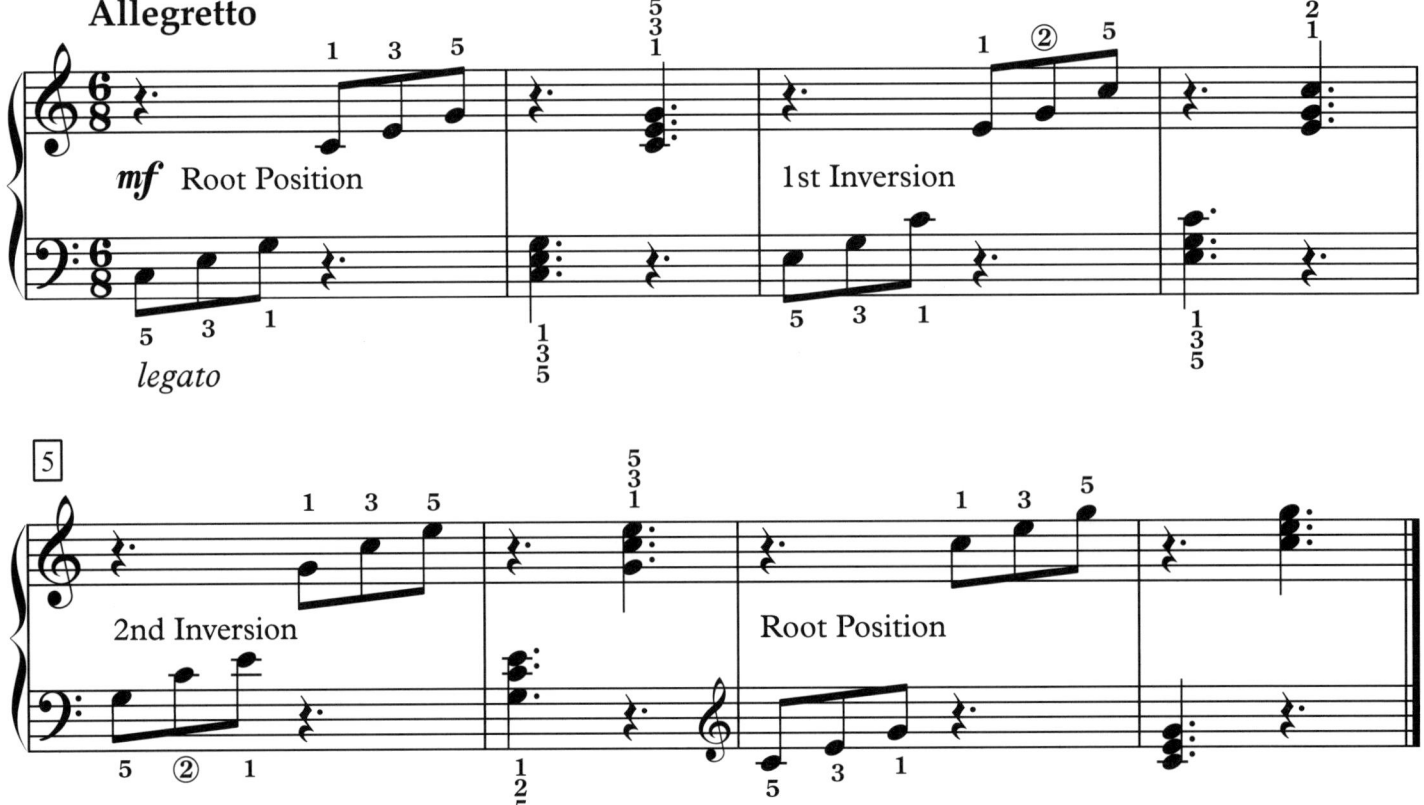

Transpose to G Major and A minor triads.

Triadic Fanfare

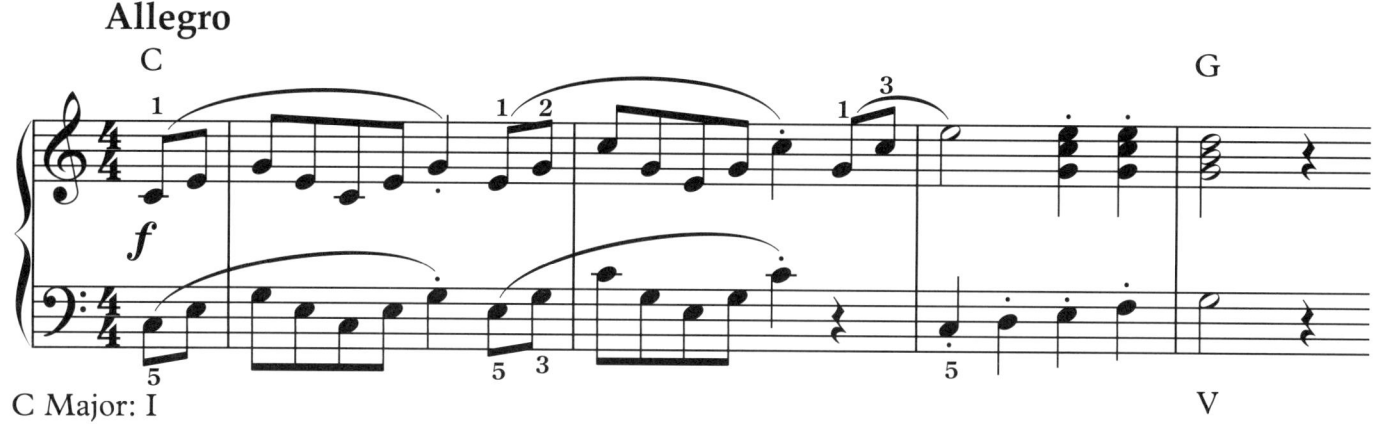

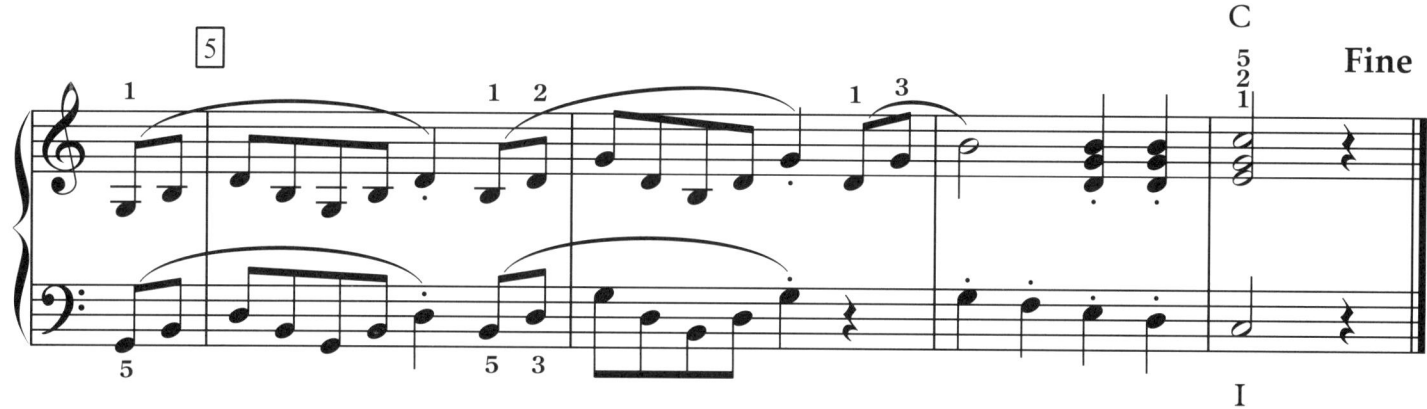

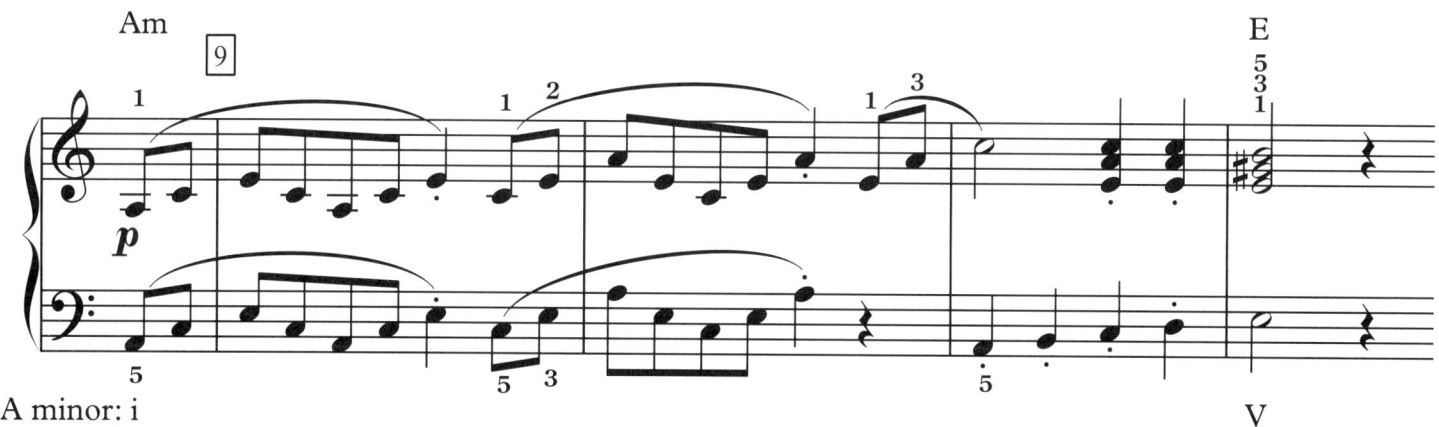

Royal Arrival

Marcia moderato (moderate march tempo)

2nd Inversion Boogie

Molto allegro

48 ■ Unit 4

Three eighth notes with an Italic *3* close to the beam is called a **triplet**. It means that three eighth notes equal one quarter note, rather than two.

The music below is the *Tarantella* from page 39, rewritten in 2/4 and using triplets.

Tarantella

Once a pattern has been established, the *3* is often omitted.

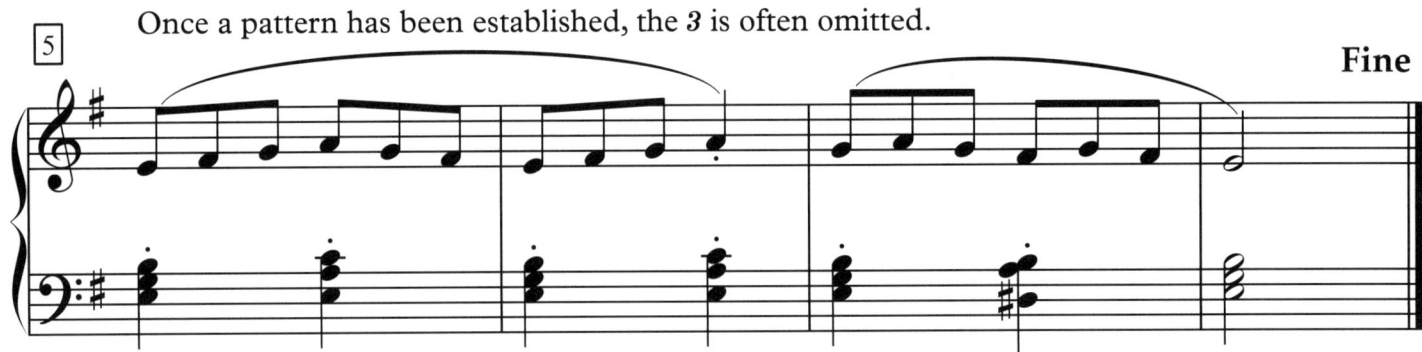

The *3* is usually placed close to the beam.

Notice the difference between the finger number 3 and the Italic *3* for triplets.

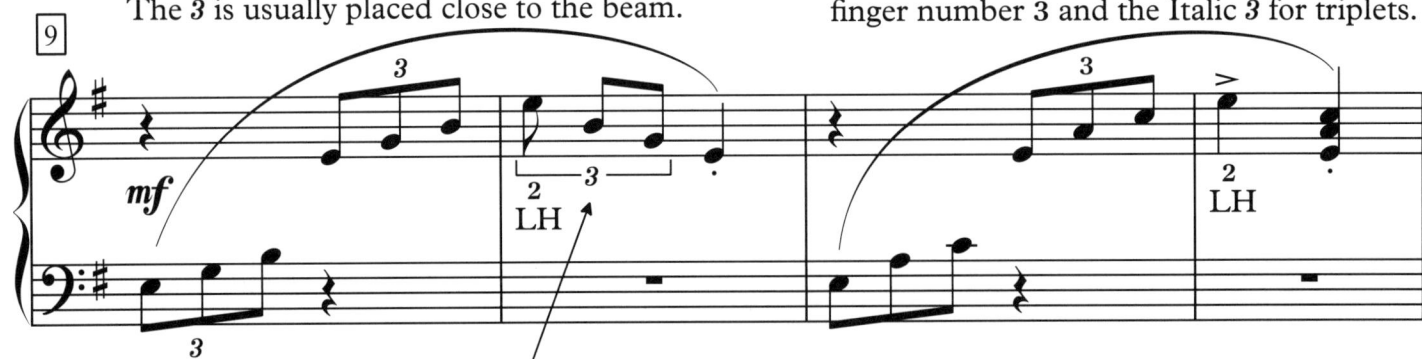

When the *3* is moved to the note-head side to avoid confusion with finger numbers, it is placed in the center of a bracket.

GP692

Triads and Inversions; Triplet 49

This piece has two sections: section **A**, from measures 1-8, and section **B**, from measures 9-16.
A piece with two sections is in **AB** or **binary** form.

George Philipp Telemann was a German composer and director of music at churches in Hamburg.
He was a friend of J. S. Bach.

THEORY

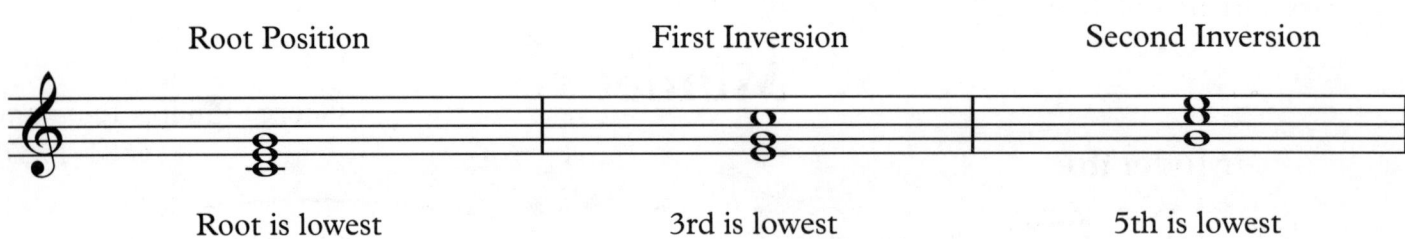

1. Draw the inversions of each root position triad.

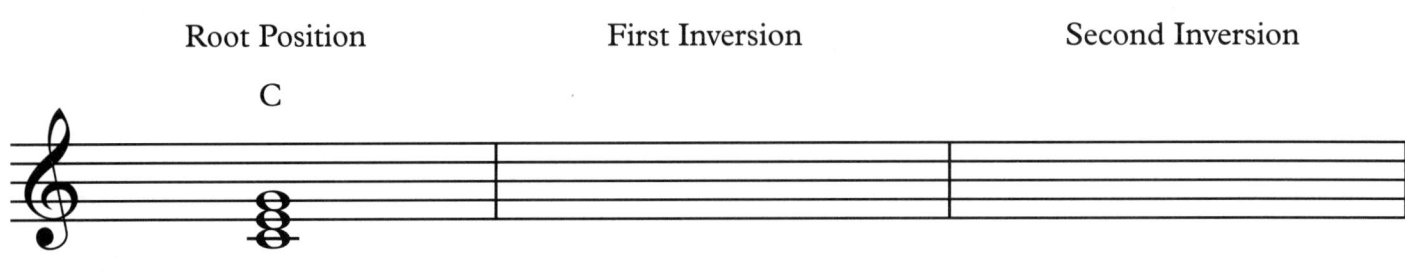

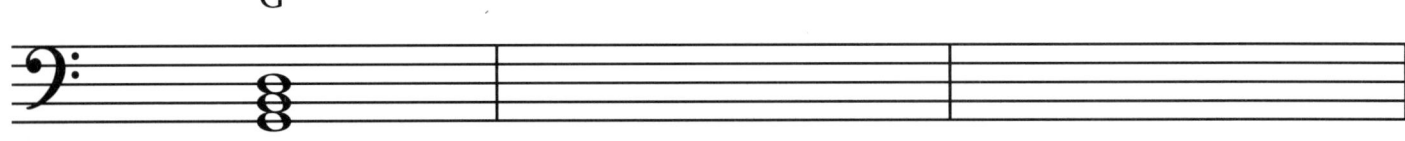

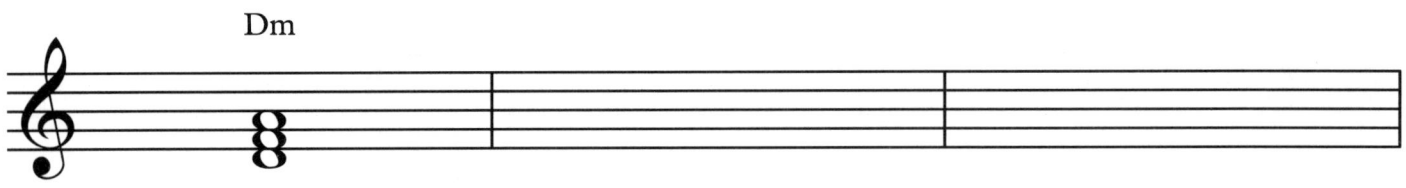

Triads and Inversions; Triplet — 51

Inversions may be recognized by identifying the intervals measured from the lowest note.

First inversion triads have the intervals of a 6th and a 3rd. The root is on top.
A triad in first inversion is also called a **6-3 chord**.

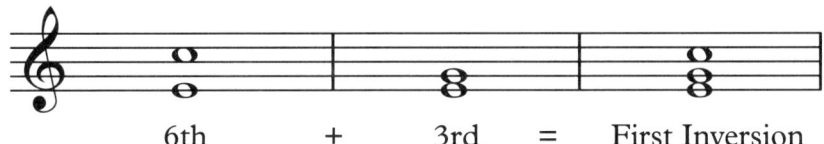

6th + 3rd = First Inversion

2. These triads are all in first inversion with the root on top. Write the name of each triad.

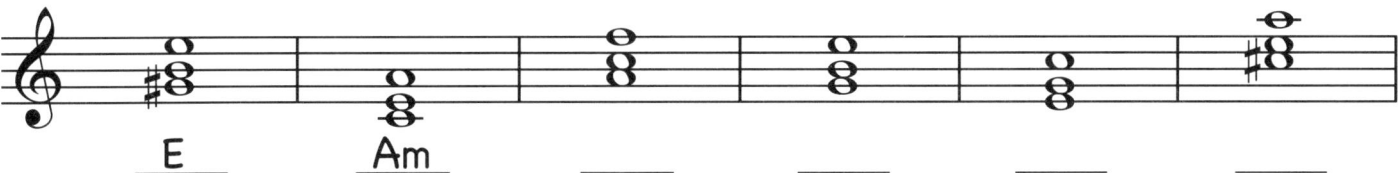

E   Am   ___   ___   ___   ___

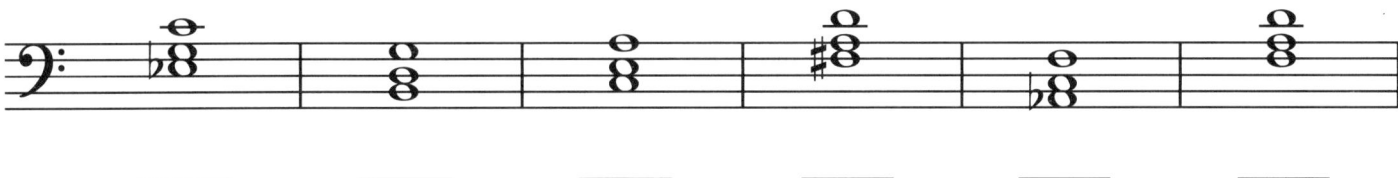

___   ___   ___   ___   ___   ___

Second inversion triads have the intervals of a 6th and a 4th. The root is in the middle.
A triad in second inversion is also called a **6-4 chord**.

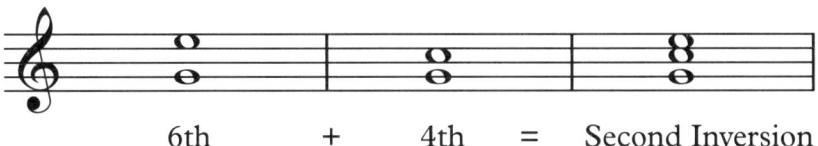

6th + 4th = Second Inversion

3. These triads are all in second inversion with the root in the middle. Write the name of each triad.

G   Dm   ___   ___   ___   ___

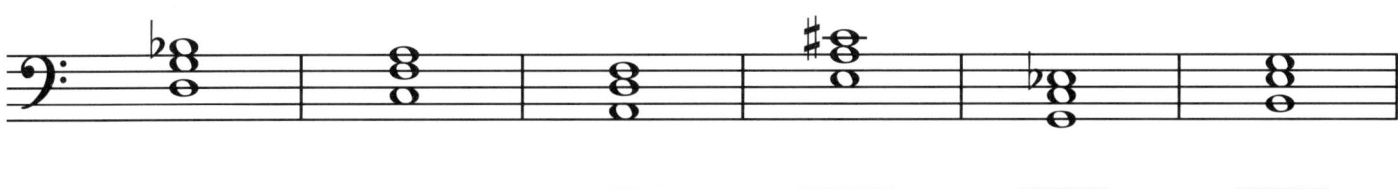

___   ___   ___   ___   ___   ___

TECHNIC

1. C Major triad and inversions, broken and blocked, descending.

Transpose to G Major and A minor triads.

2. Primary triads in C Major with inversions, blocked.

3. Primary triads in C Major with inversions, broken.

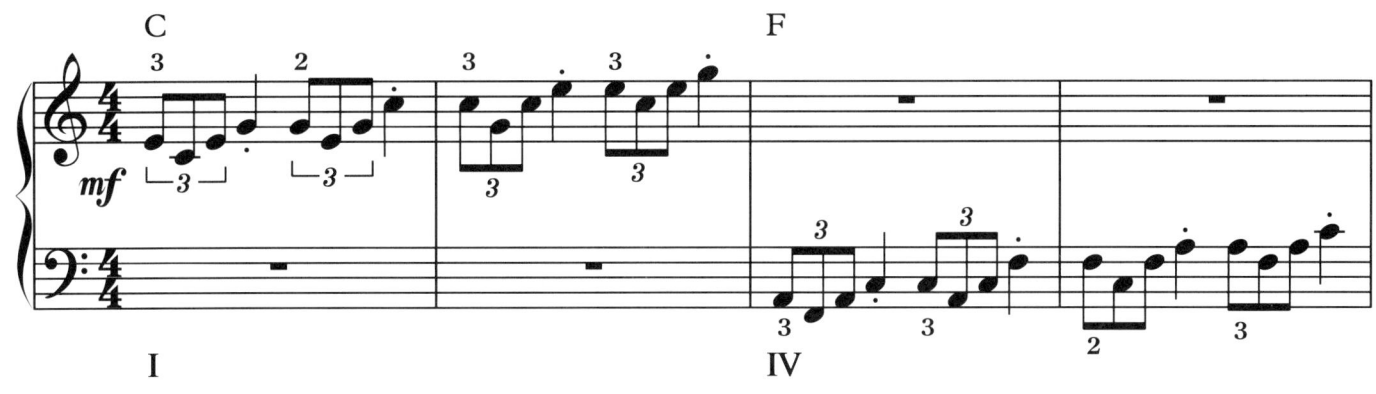

4. C Major scale in contrary motion.

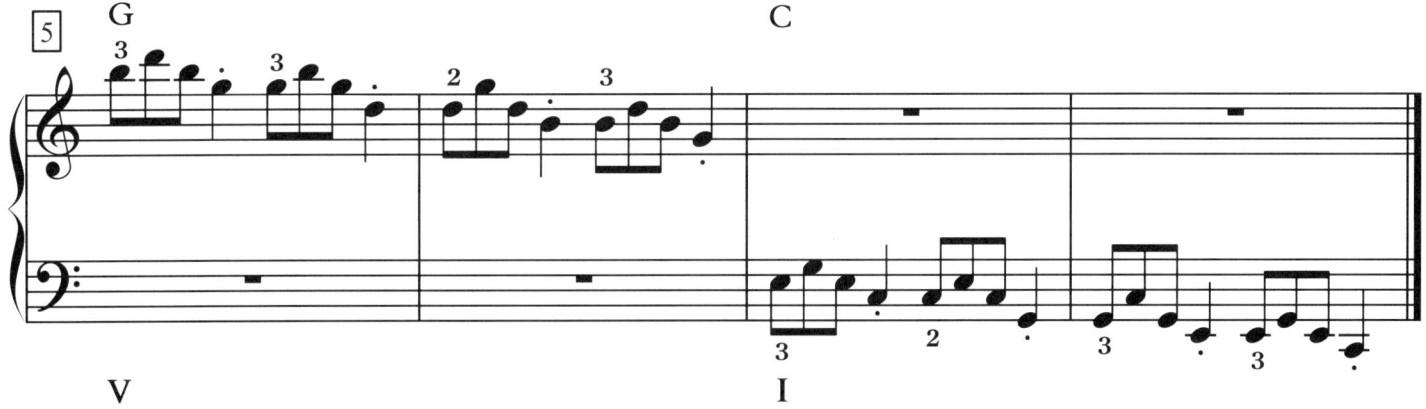

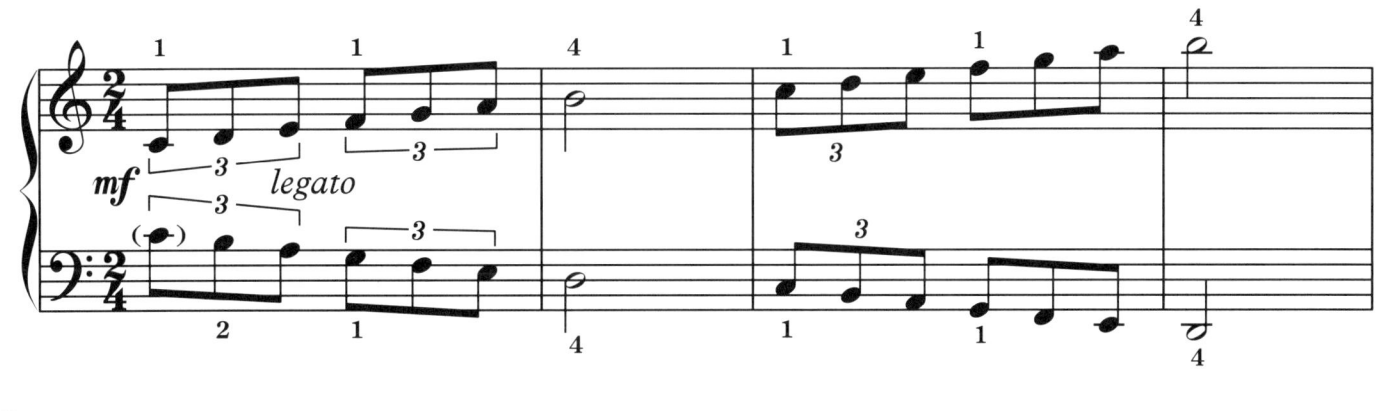

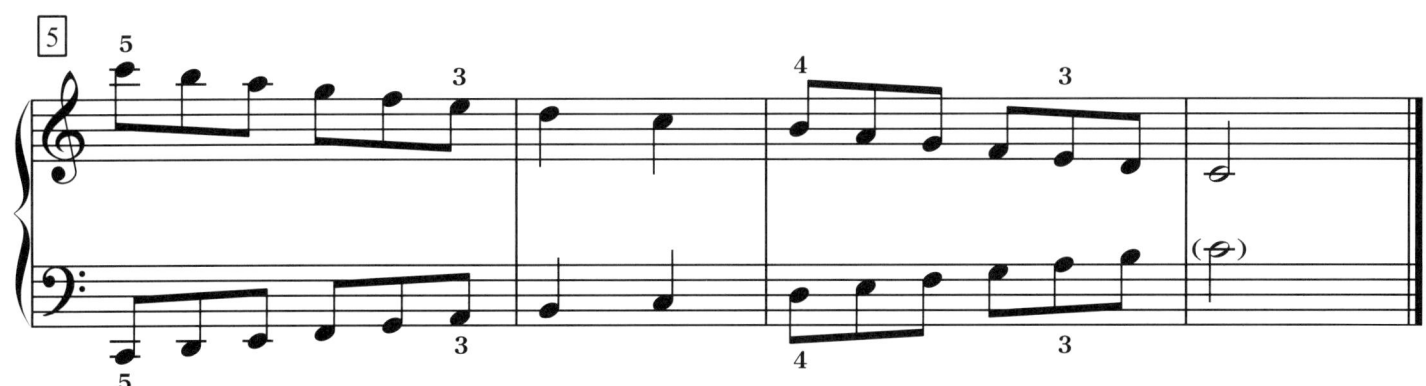

UNIT 5
LEGATO PEDALING; CHROMATIC SCALE

The **damper pedal** (right pedal) is used to connect, as well as sustain, sound.
The exercises on this page will help develop the timing and technique for legato (connected) pedaling.

1. Depress the pedal on count 2, release it on count 1.

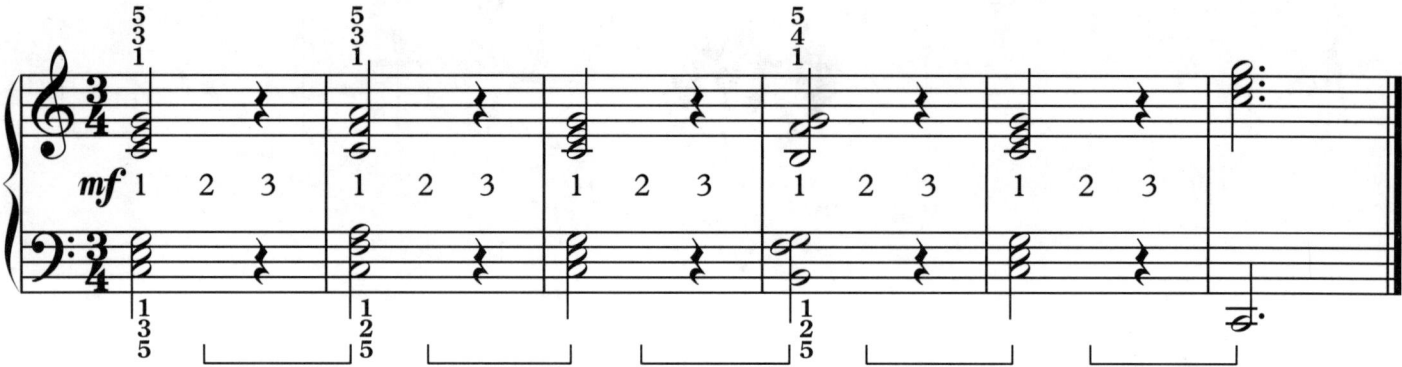

2. Change the pedal (release, then immediately depress) on count 2.

3. Change the pedal on count 1.

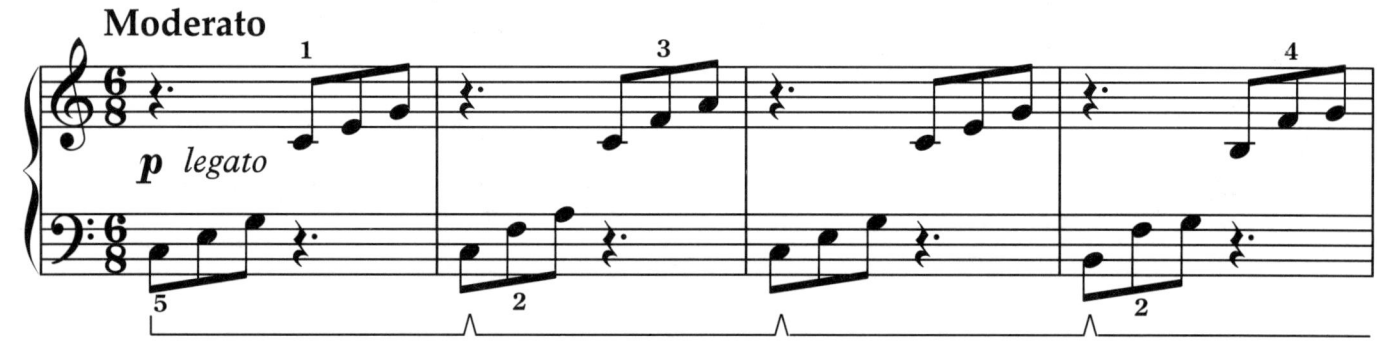

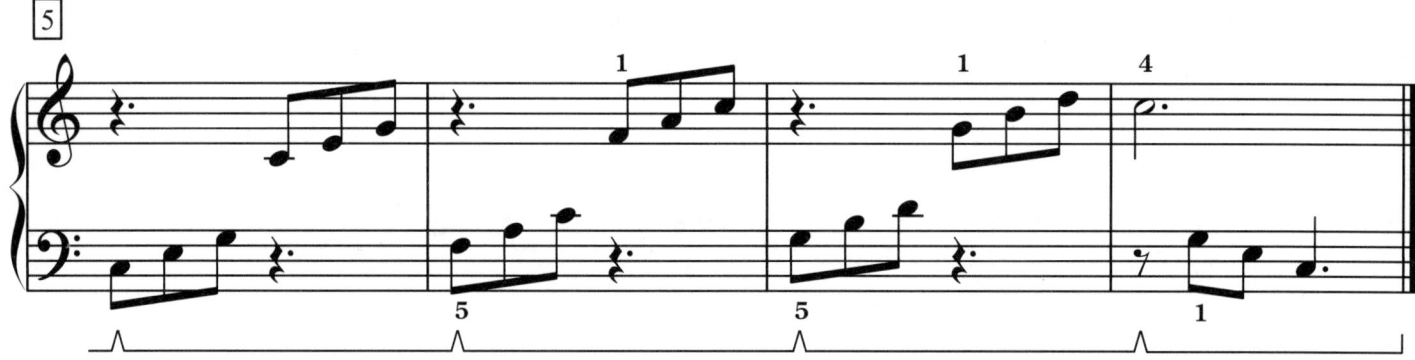

The Shepherd's Flute

Tat'iana Salutrinskaya was born in Tambov, Russia, and studied composition at the Moscow Conservatory of Music. She wrote music for piano students.

Tat'iana Salutrinskaya
(Dates unknown)

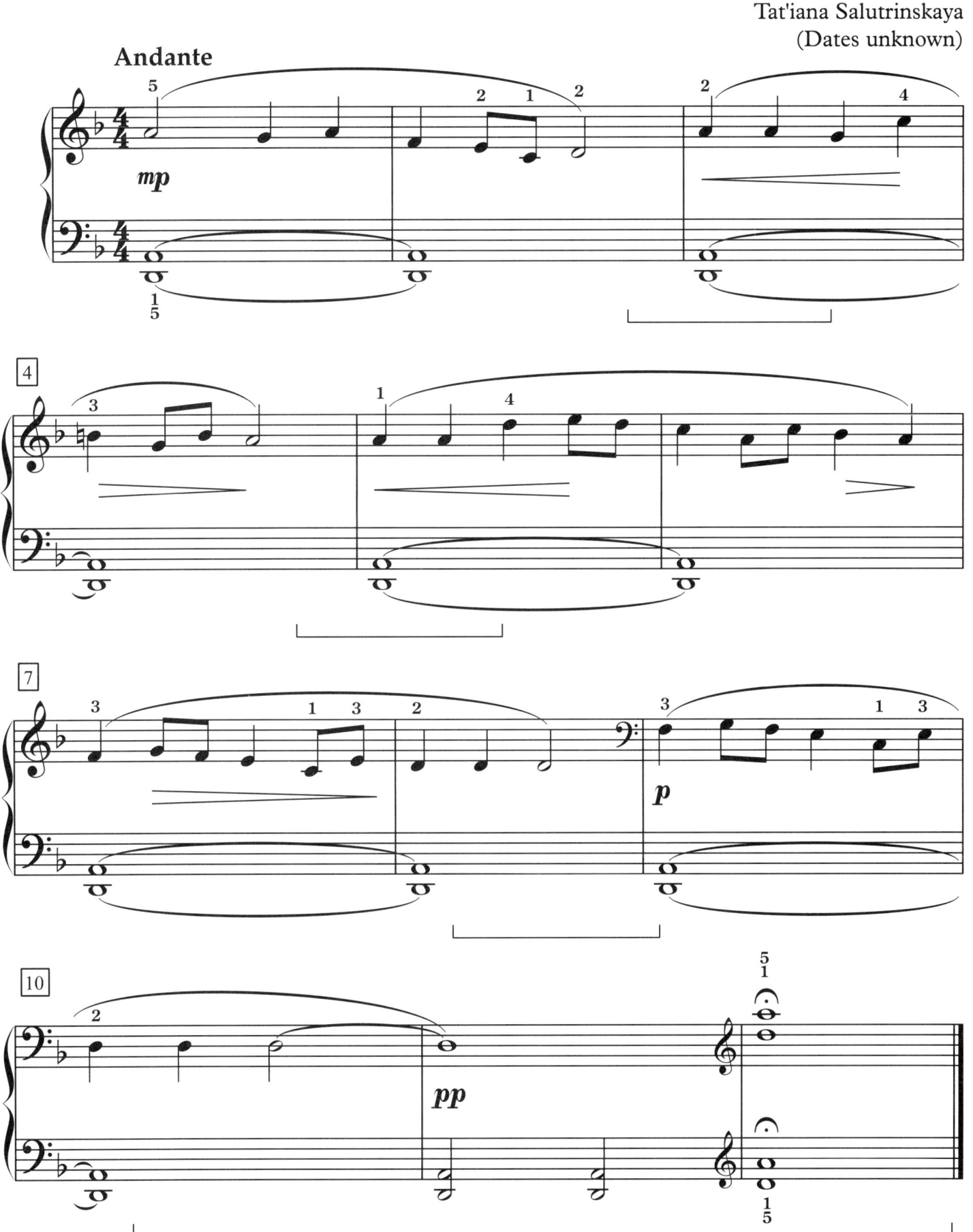

Solemn Occasion

Sakura
(Cherry Blossoms)

Japanese Folk Melody

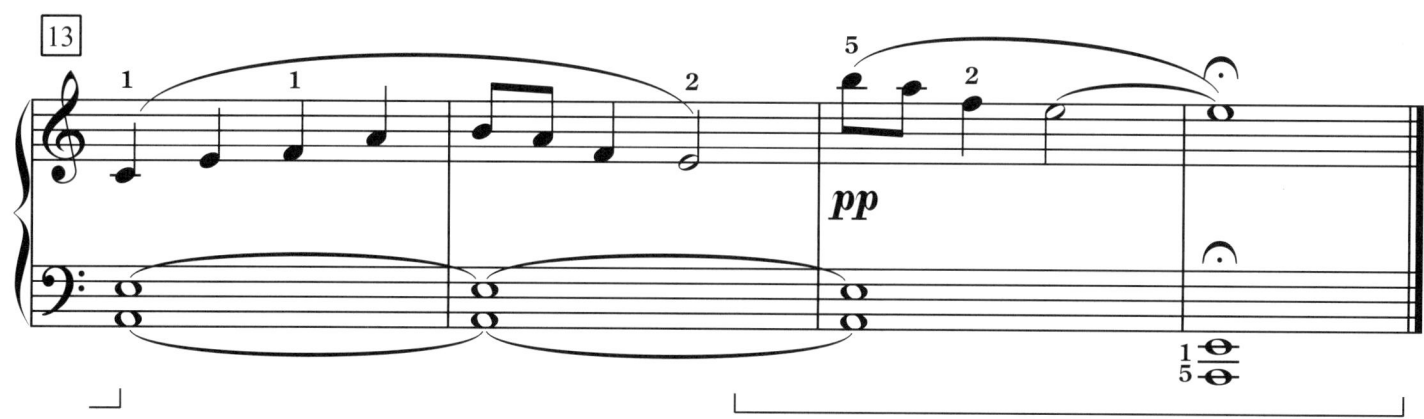

Chromatic Scale

The **chromatic scale** is formed entirely of half steps. It can begin on any note.
The fingering patterns for chromatic scales are different from those for Major and minor scales.

1. Use finger 3 on black keys, and finger 1 on white keys.

2. Use finger 2 when there are consecutive white keys.

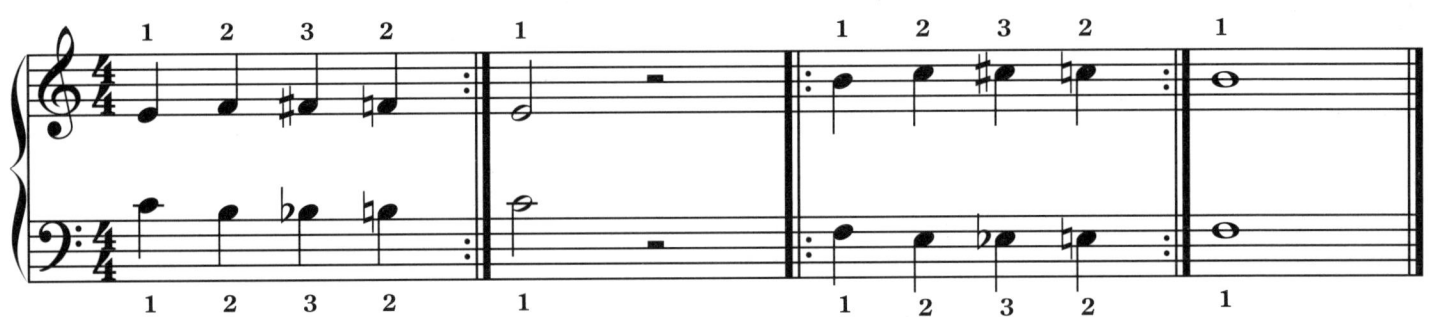

3. Put it together.

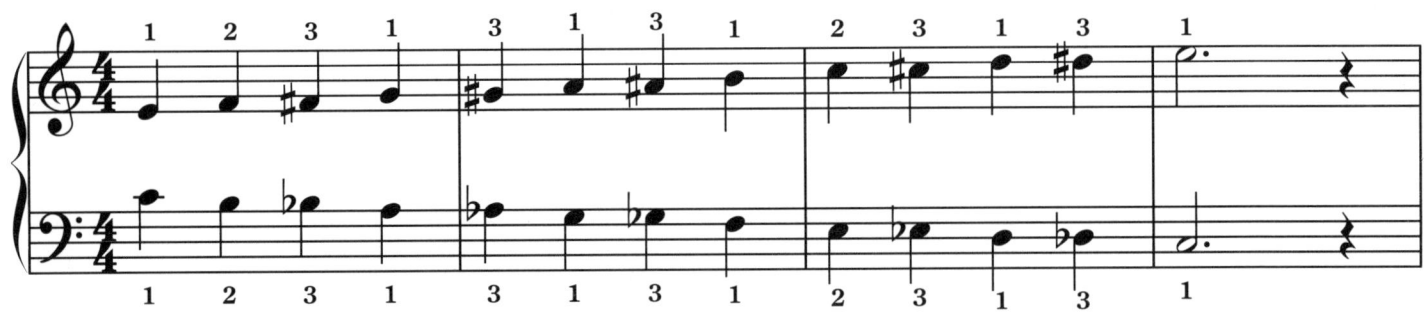

*Sharps are used for the ascending chromatic scales, and flats for descending.

GP692

Legato Pedaling; Chromatic Scale | 59

Dashing Through the Day

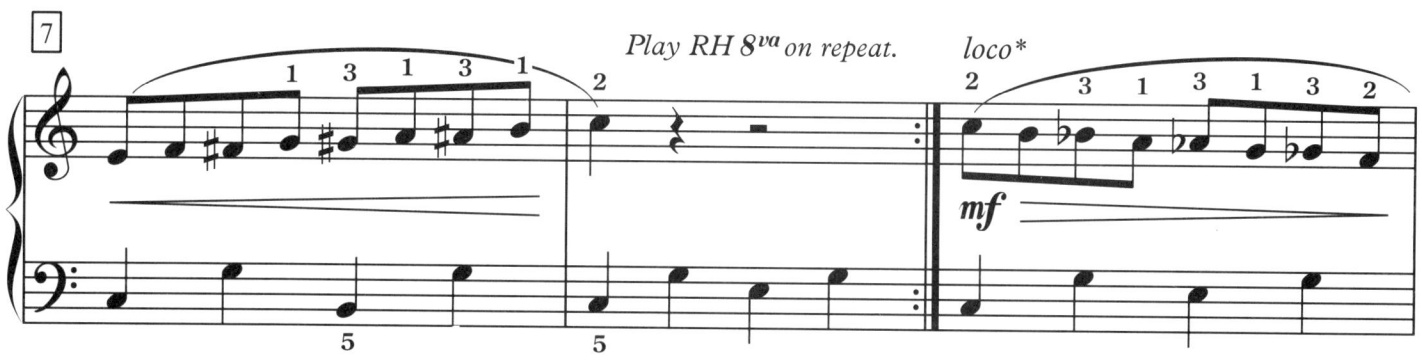

*Not 8va. Literally "at place."

GP692

THEORY

Intervals of the Scale

The intervals of the C Major scale are shown below.
Each interval is formed from the **tonic** (first degree) of the scale.
There are two types, or **qualities** of intervals formed this way.

1. **Major**: 2nd, 3rd, 6th, and 7th.
2. **Perfect**: 4th, 5th, and octave.

These intervals are the same for any Major scale.

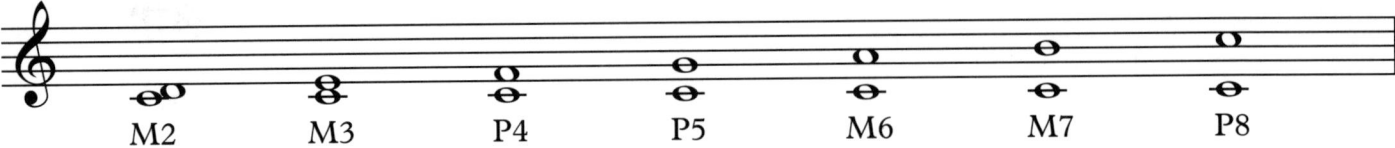

1. Name these intervals of the D Major scale. Play them.

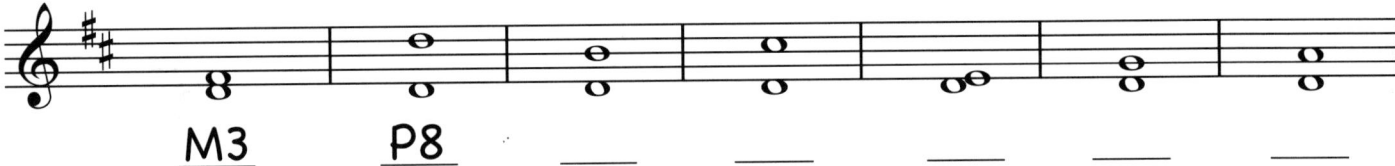

M3   P8   ___   ___   ___   ___   ___

2. Name these intervals of the G Major scale. Play them.

___   ___   ___   ___   ___   ___   ___

3. Name these intervals of the F Major scale. Play them.

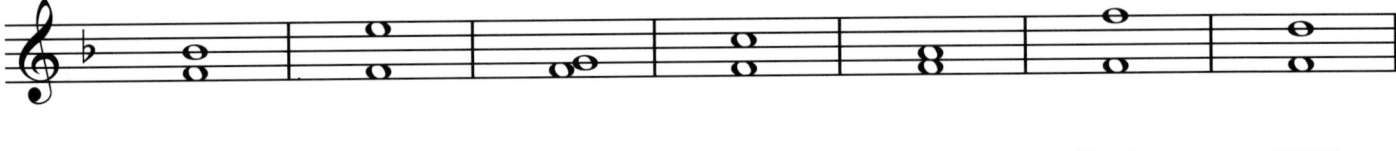

___   ___   ___   ___   ___   ___   ___

4. Name these intervals of the A Major scale. Play them.

___   ___   ___   ___   ___   ___   ___

GP692

Major intervals become minor when the top note is lowered a half step.

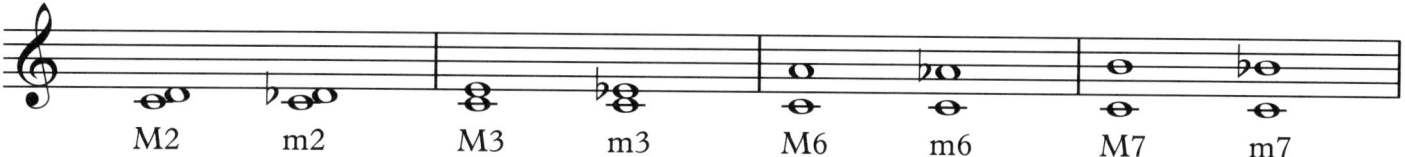

5. Draw the minor interval after each Major interval. Observe the key signature and use a flat or natural sign as needed. Play these intervals.

Key of D Major

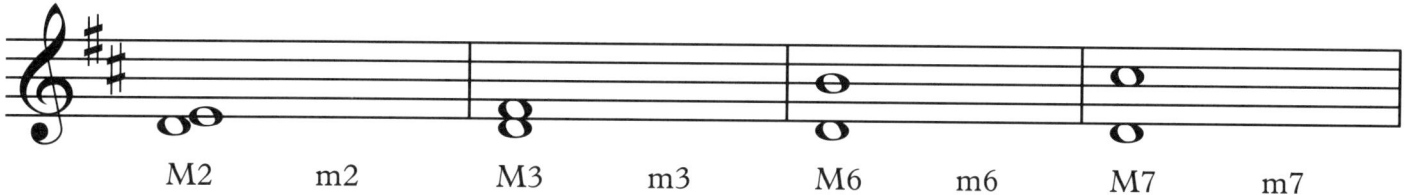

Key of G Major

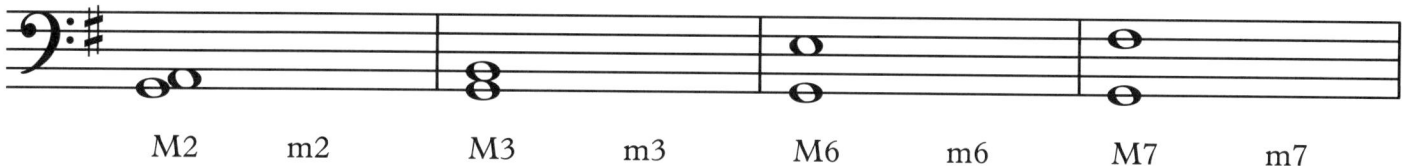

6. Name each interval. Play them.

Key of F Major

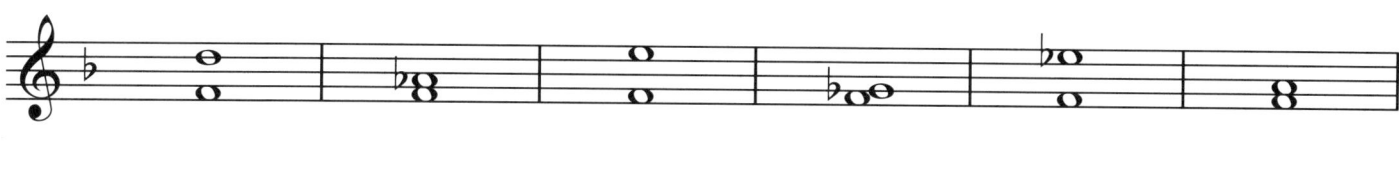

Key of C Major

Signs and Terms Review

6. Match each sign with its term. Then, write the meaning of each term.

   a. > ____ crescendo (*cresc.*) _____

   b. ◁══ ____ fermata _____

   c. ══▷ ____ diminuendo (*dim.*) _____

   d. 𝄐 ____ accent _____

7. Arrange these tempo terms from slowest to fastest.

   Allegro Andante Allegretto Moderato

   _____ _____ _____ _____

8. Write the meaning of each tempo term.

   Andante _____   Allegretto _____

   Moderato _____   Allegro _____

   Vivace _____   A tempo _____

9. Match each term with its meaning.

   a. Binary form   ____ A three-note chord

   b. Waltz bass   ____ [music notation]

   c. Triad   ____ A piece with two sections

   d. Alberti bass   ____ [music notation]

TECHNIC

1. Chromatic scale from E to C. Practice hands separately first.

2. Chromatic scale from C to C. Practice hands separately first.

UNIT 6
B♭ MAJOR, G MINOR

B♭ Major Scale and Key Signature

The key signature for B♭ Major has two flats: B♭ and E♭.

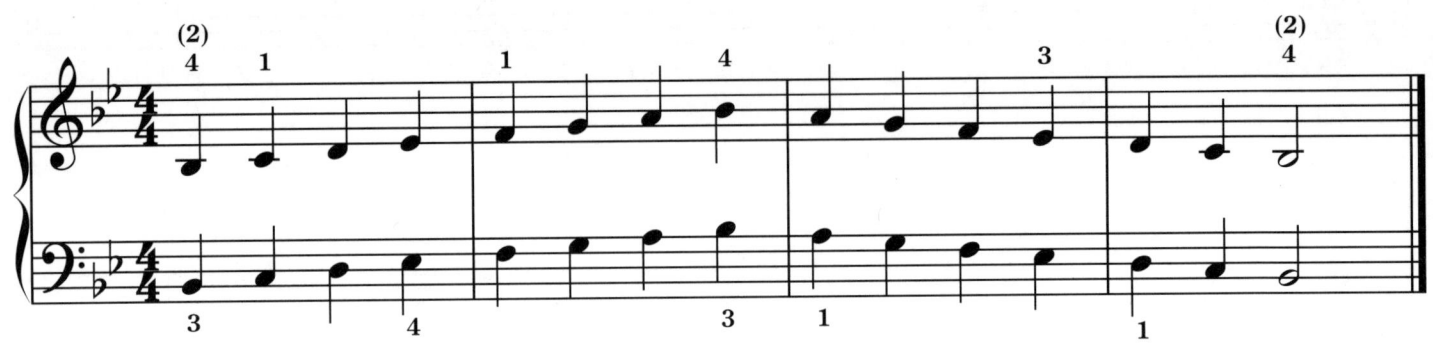

Primary Triads in B♭ Major

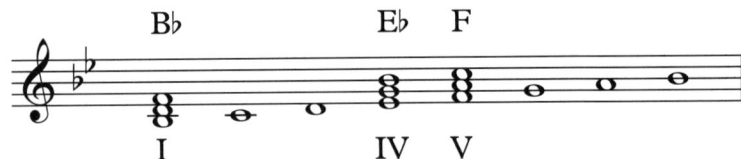

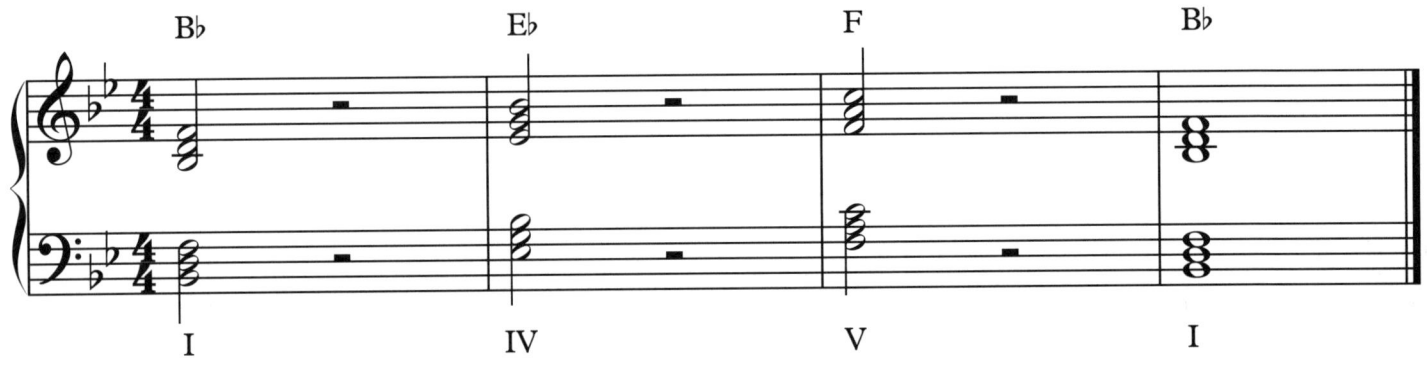

Primary Chord Progression

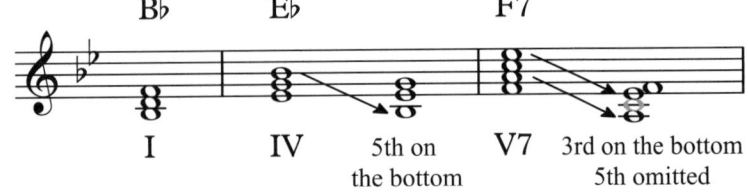

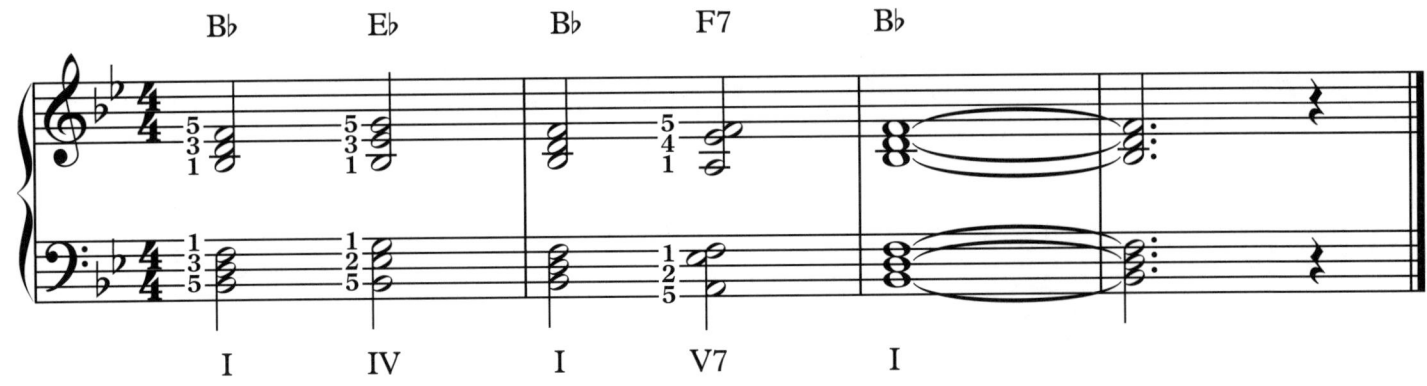

GP692

Reading in B♭ Major

I.

Allegro

II.

Moderato

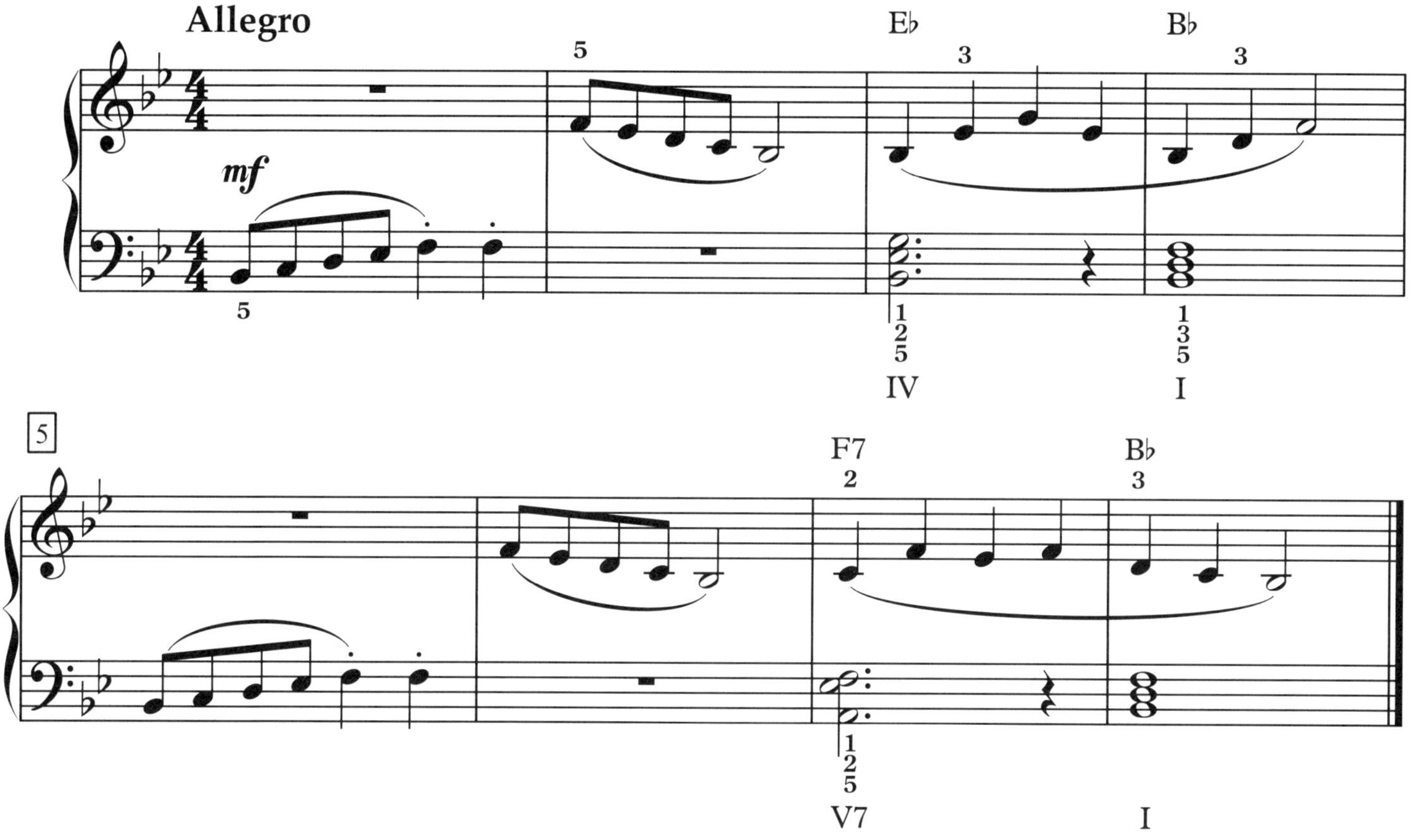

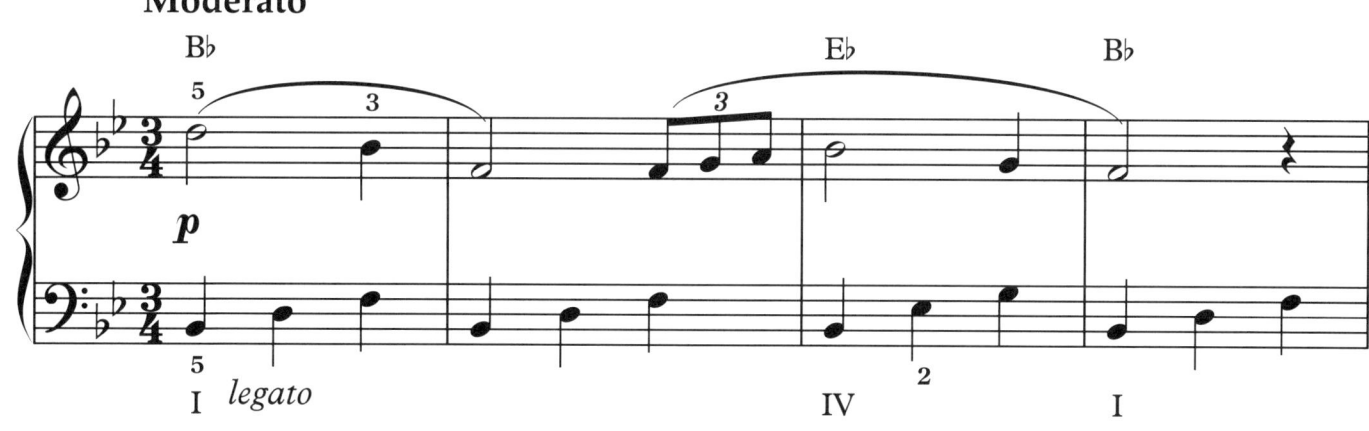

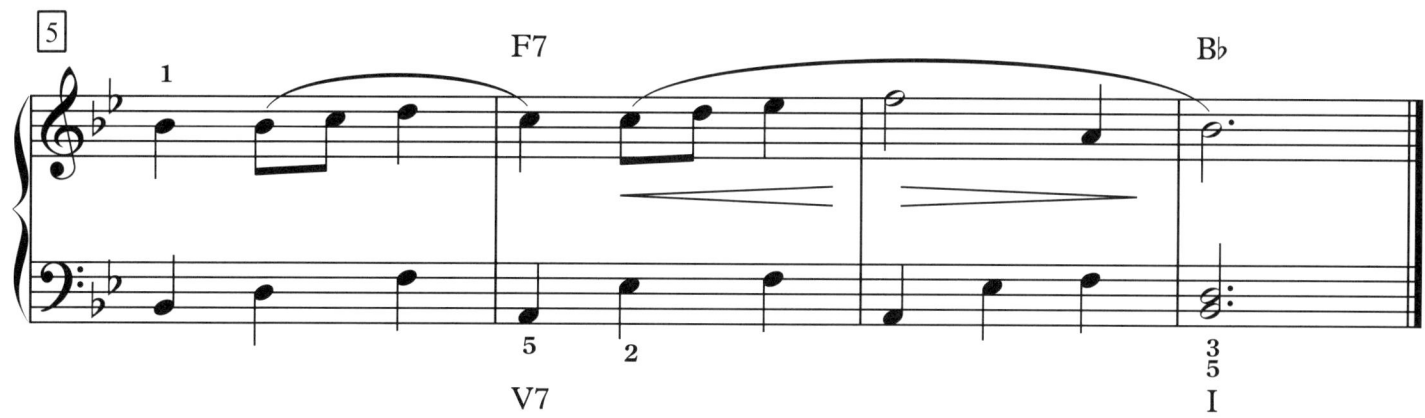

American composer **William Walker** (1809-1875) set verses by John Newton to the "New Britain" tune, creating the song we know today as "Amazing Grace."

Amazing Grace

Traditional English Melody
"New Britain"

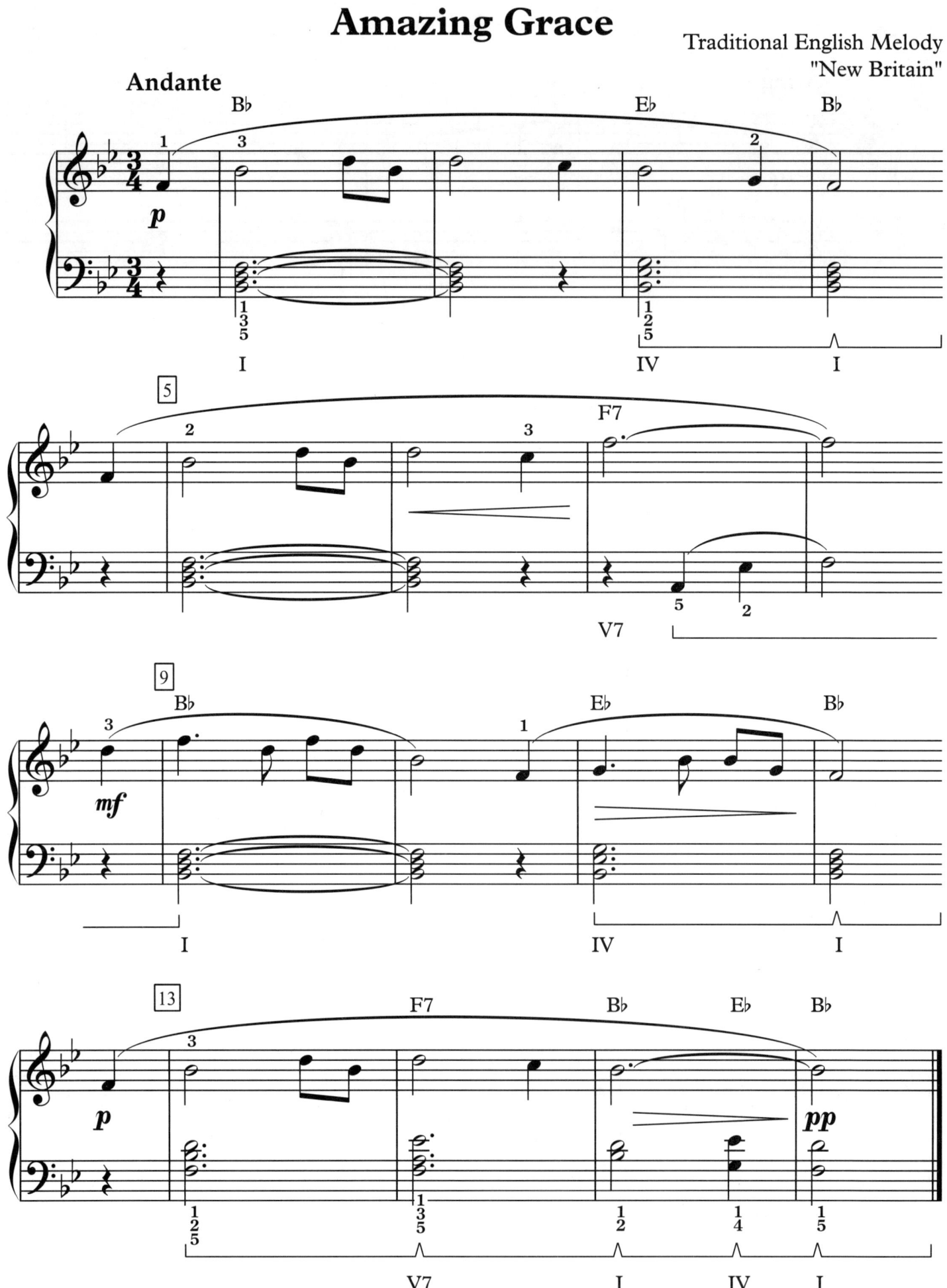

Cornelius Gurlitt was a prodigous German composer of many songs, operas, and symphonies, but is now remembered mostly for his vast quantity of excellent pieces for piano students.

Hunting Song
Op. 82, No. 42

Cornelius Gurlitt
(1820-1901)

G Minor Scales and Chords

G minor is relative to **B♭ Major**. Both keys have two flats in the key signature, B♭ and E♭.

G Harmonic Minor Scale

G Melodic Minor Scale

Primary Chords in G Minor

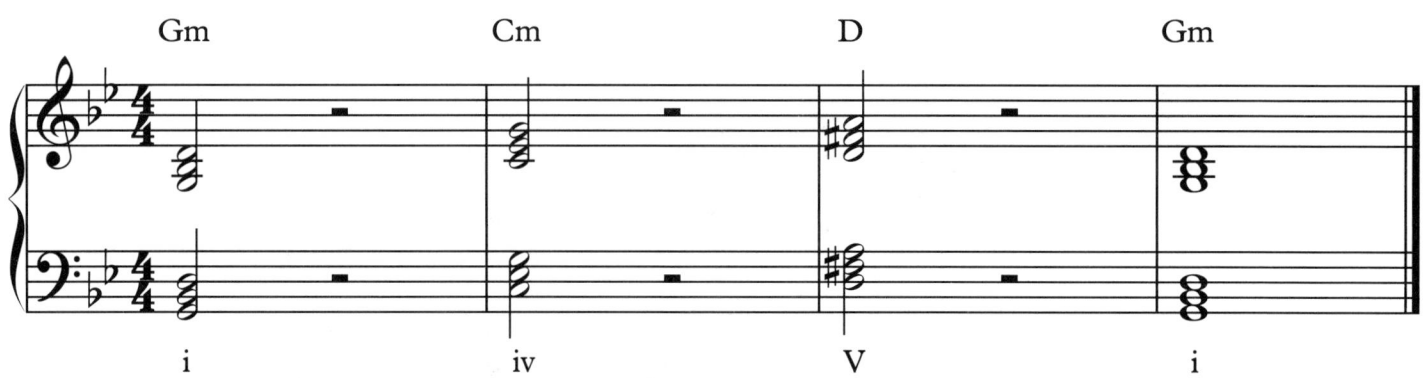

Primary Chord Progression in G Minor

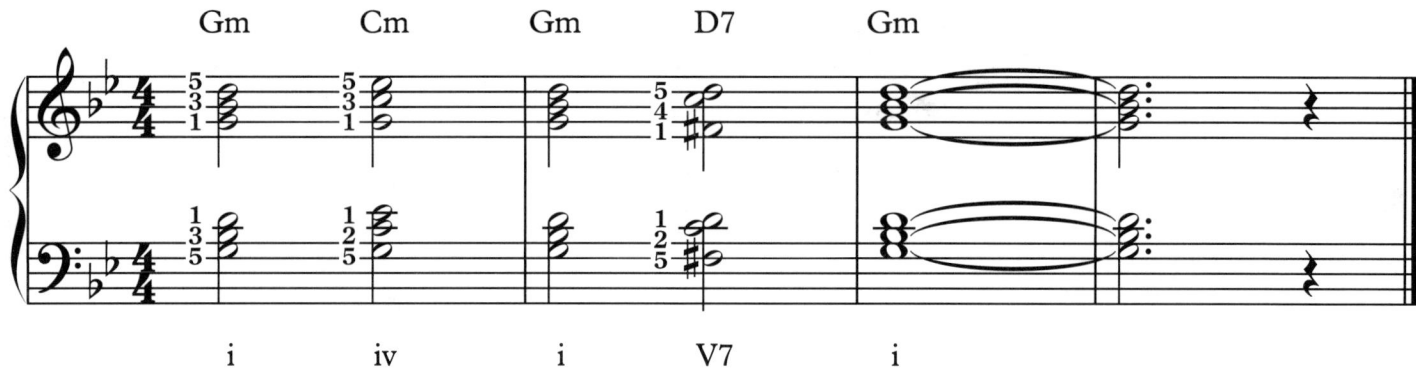

Bb Major, G Minor 69

Fritz Spindler was a German pianist and composer. Although his many compositions include salon pieces, chamber music, and symphonies, he is remembered mostly for his piano pieces.

Song without Words

Fritz Spindler
(1817-1905)

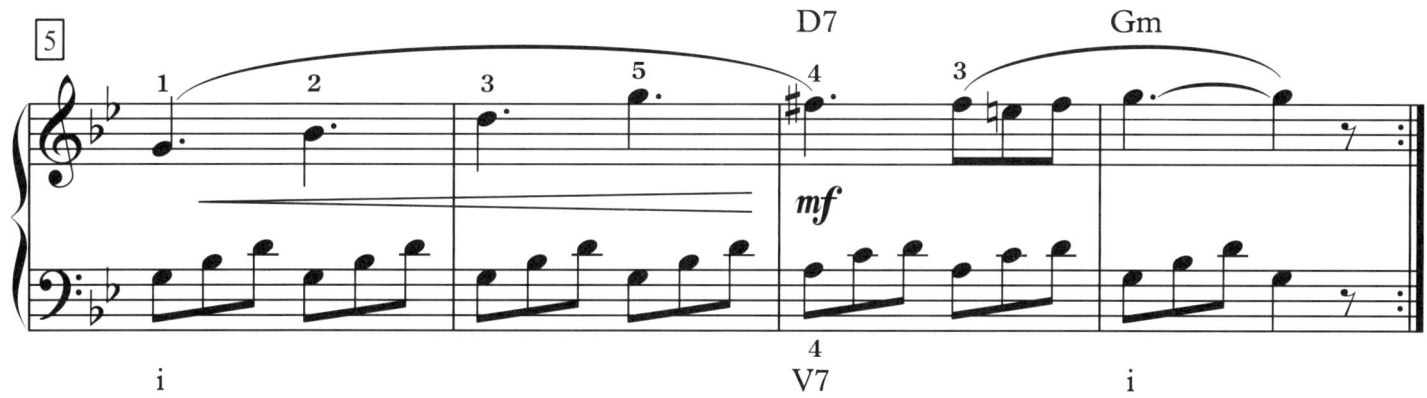
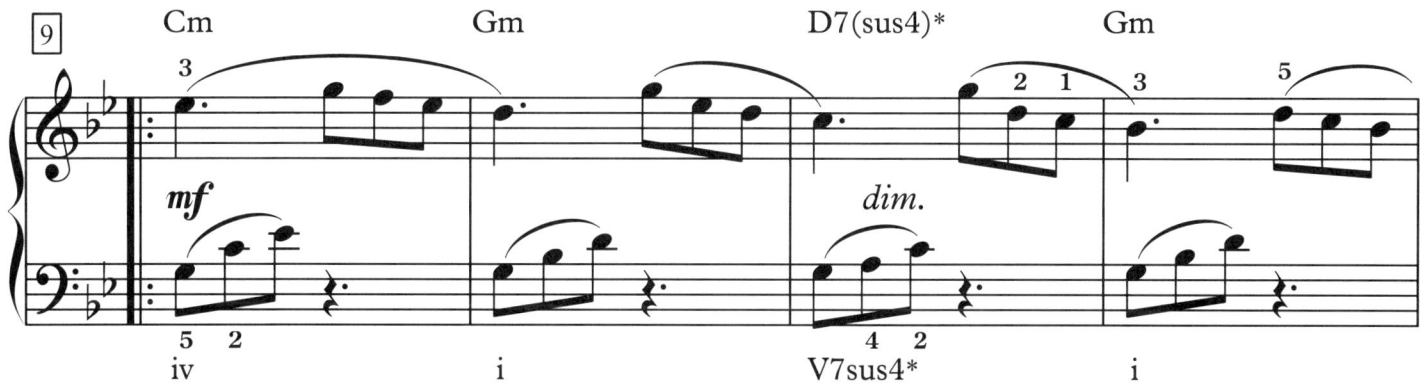
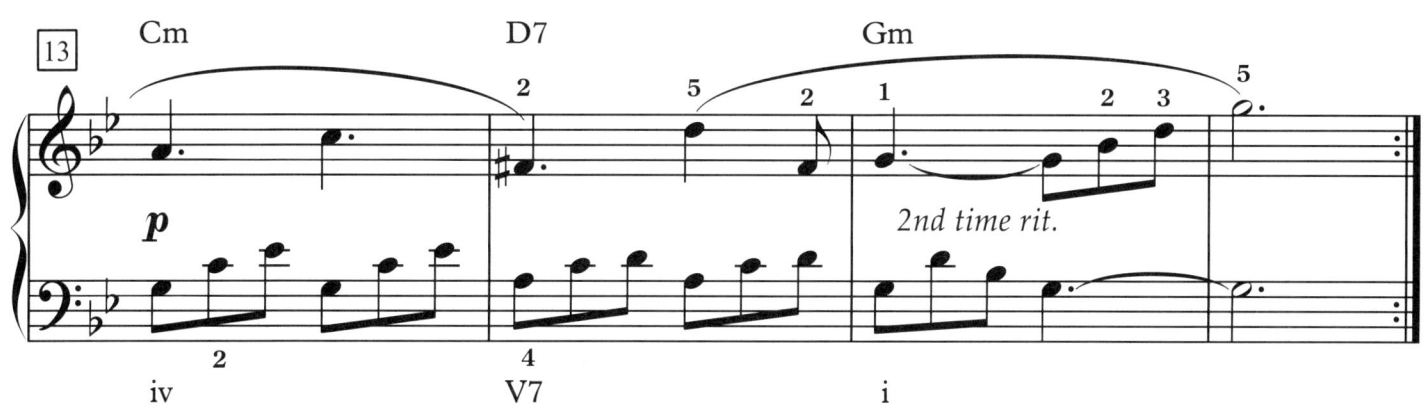

*In a **sus4** chord, the 3rd has been omitted and replaced with the note a 4th above the root.

THEORY

B♭ Major Key Signature

The key signature for B♭ Major has two flats: B♭ and E♭.

1. Trace the first key signature, then draw two more.

Primary Chords in B♭ Major   ## Primary Chord Progression

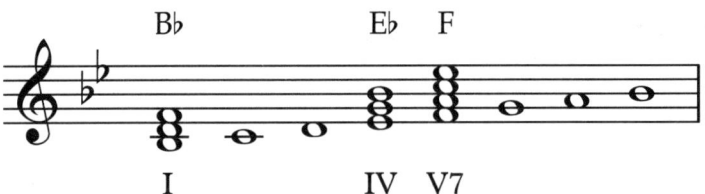   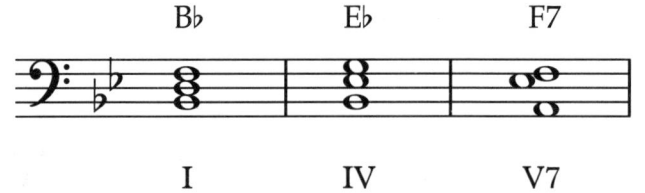

2. Draw this primary chord progression. Use whole notes.

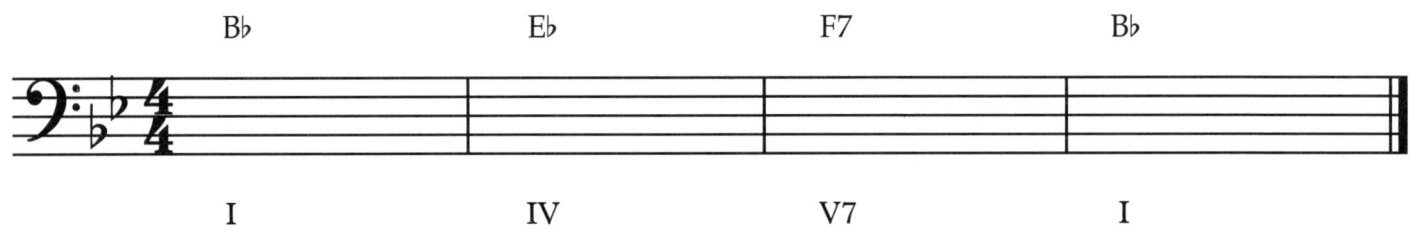

3. Harmonize each measure of this melody with I, IV, or V7. Use dotted half notes.
   Write Roman numerals below the staff, and chord names above the staff.
   Play what you have written.

G Minor Scales

4. Change this G natural minor scale to harmonic minor by raising the seventh degree a half step.

5. Change this G natural minor scale to melodic minor by raising the sixth and seventh degrees a half step step ascending, then lowered descending.

Primary Chords in G Minor **Primary Chord Progression**

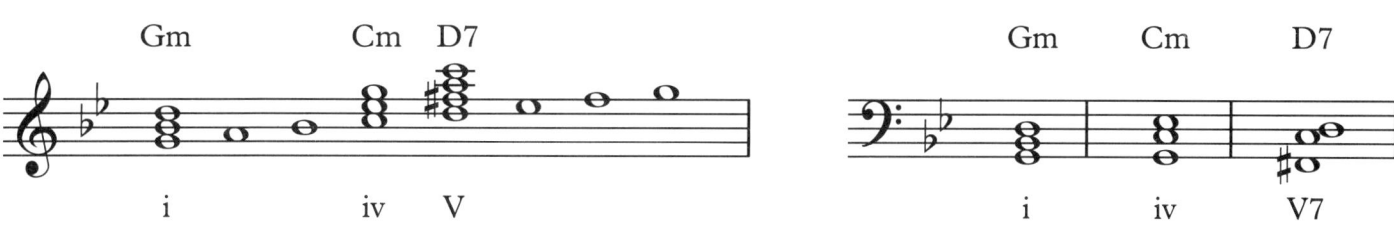

6. Draw this primary chord progression. Use whole notes.

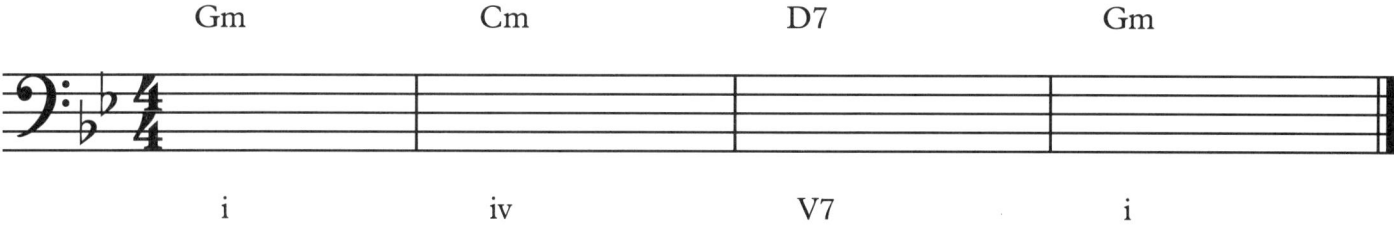

7. Harmonize each measure of this melody with i, iv, or V7. Use whole notes.
   Write Roman numerals below the staff, and chord names above the staff.
   Play what you have written.

TECHNIC

1. Primary Triads in B♭ Major.

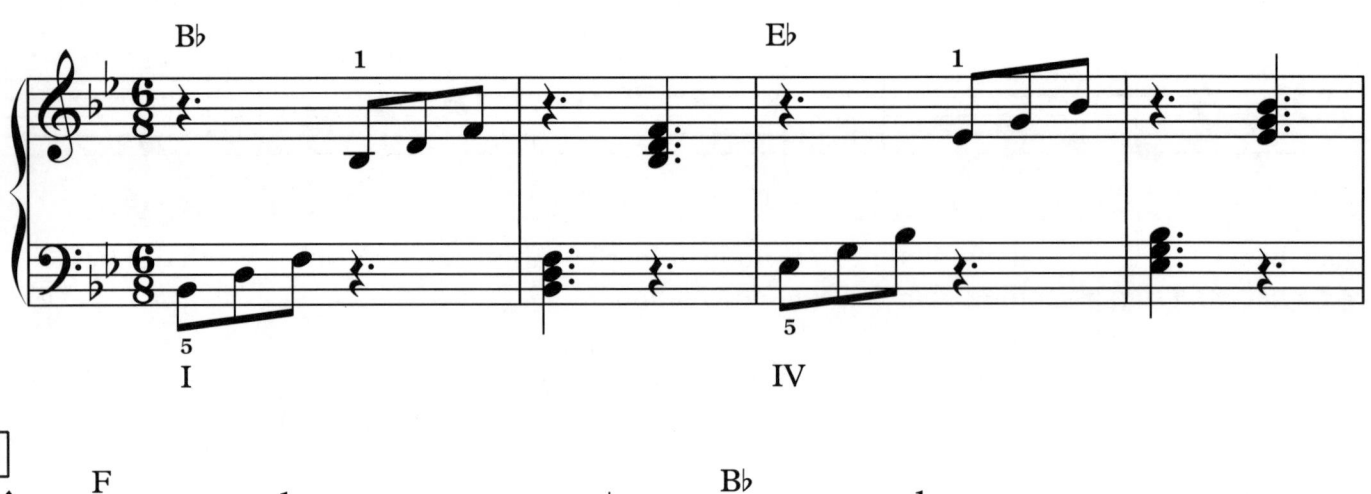

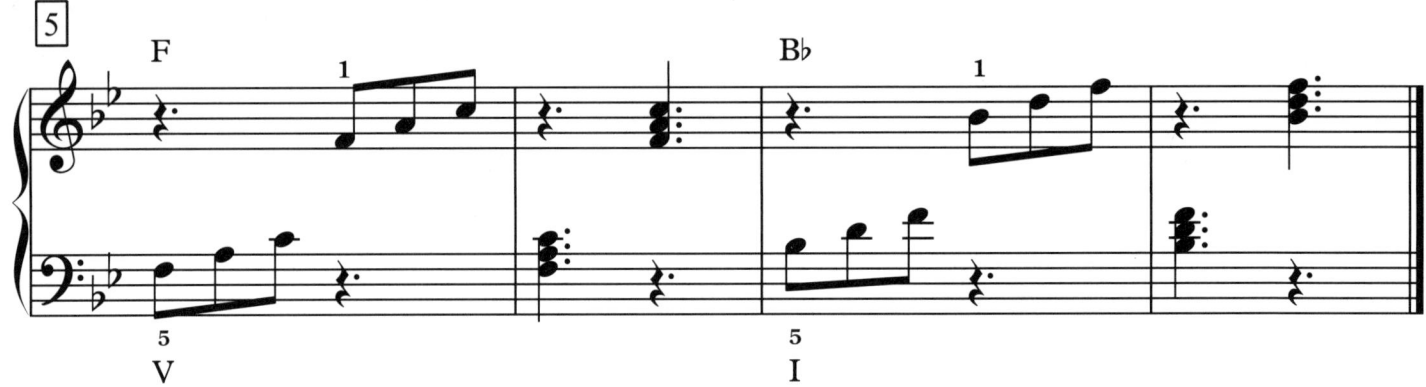

2. Primary Triads in G Minor.

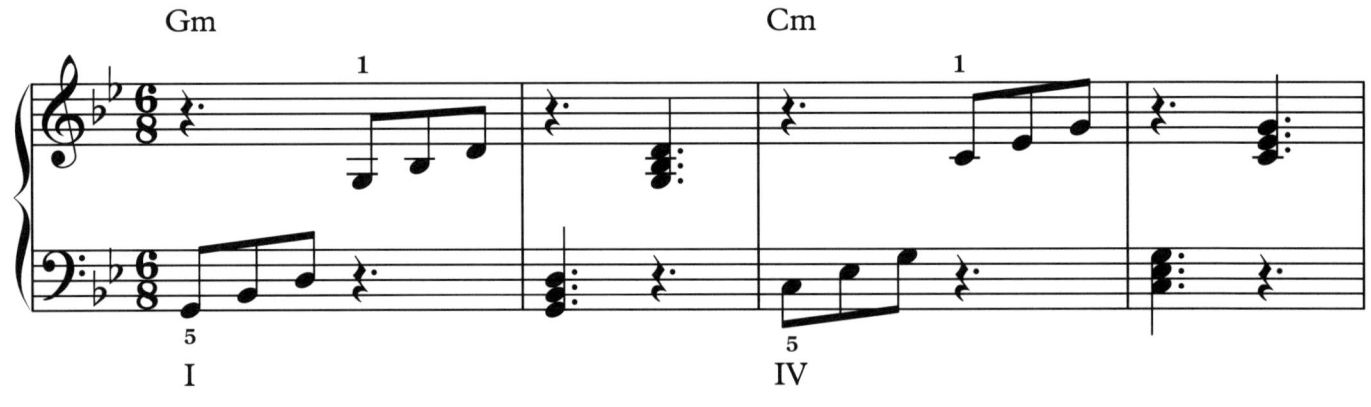

3. In this etude, the **A** section (meas. 1-8) is in the key of G minor. However, the **B** section (meas. 9-16) modulates to the relative key of B♭ Major, returning gradually to G minor in measures 15 and 16.

Etude
Op. 300, No. 71

Louis Köhler
(1820-1886)

UNIT 7
TIME SIGNATURE 2/2; DIMINISHED AND AUGMENTED TRIADS

Time Signature 2/2

2 means two beats in each measure.
2 means the 𝅗𝅥 receives one beat.

This time signature may also be called **cut time**.

Musette

Follow these practice steps to learn to play *Musette* in cut time.

1. Start by playing and counting four beats per measure, with the metronome at ♩=60.
2. Gradually increase the tempo until you can play easily at ♩=120.
3. Now play at 𝅗𝅥=60 (same tempo as ♩=120), counting two beats per measure.

Félix Le Couppey
(1811-1887)

GP692

Time Signature 2/2; Dim. and Aug. Triads 75

Félix Le Couppey was a French composer, pianist, and teacher. He wrote a piano method, as well as many elementary etudes for piano students.

A **musette** is a French bagpipe on which dance-like music, with a long-held "drone" bass (such as the left hand of this piece) could be played. It was particularly popular in the 17th and 18th centuries.

GP692

Diminished Triads

Any minor triad becomes **diminished** when the 5th is lowered a half step.
Diminished triads may be labeled with the abbreviation **dim**, or with a cricle ○.
Play these minor and diminished triads.

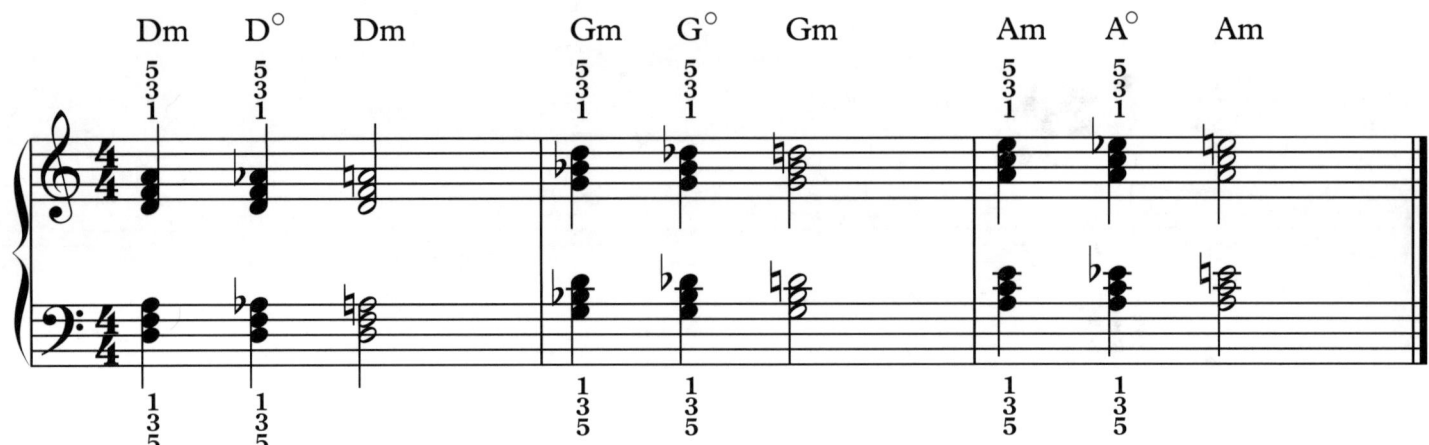

Puck

In medieval English folklore, Puck is a malicious fairy or demon. In Elizabethan lore, he was a mischievous fairy also called Robin Goodfellow, or Hobgoblin. As one of the leading characters in William Shakespeare's "Midsummer Night's Dream," Puck boasts of his pranks of changing shapes, misleading travellers at night, spoiling milk, frightening young girls, and tripping venerable old dames.

¢ means **cut time**, and is another way to write $\frac{2}{2}$.

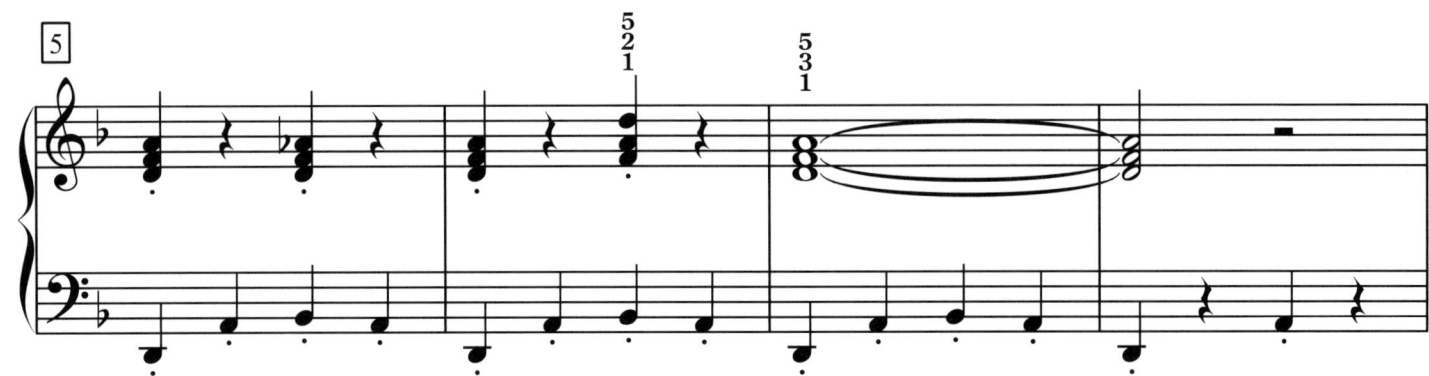

Time Signature 2/2; Dim. and Aug. Triads 77

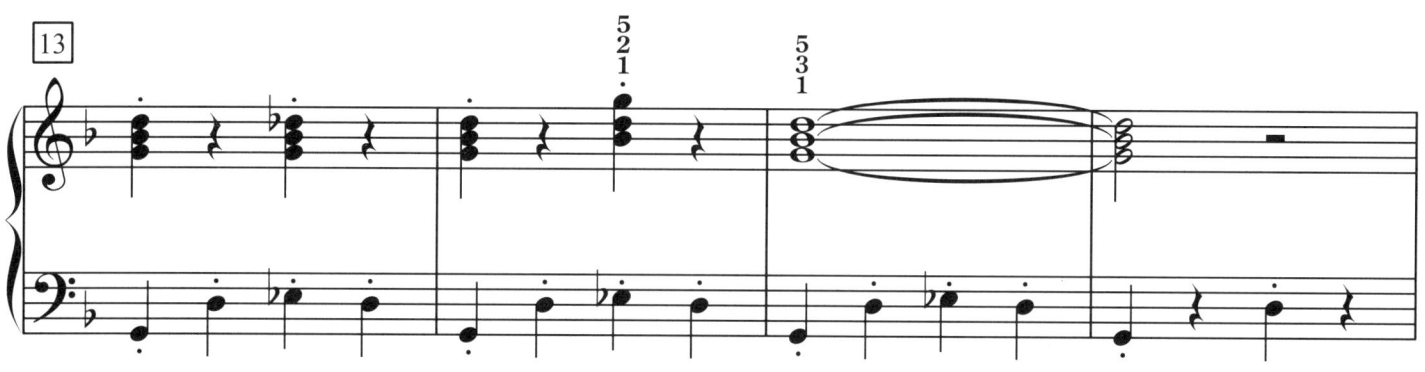
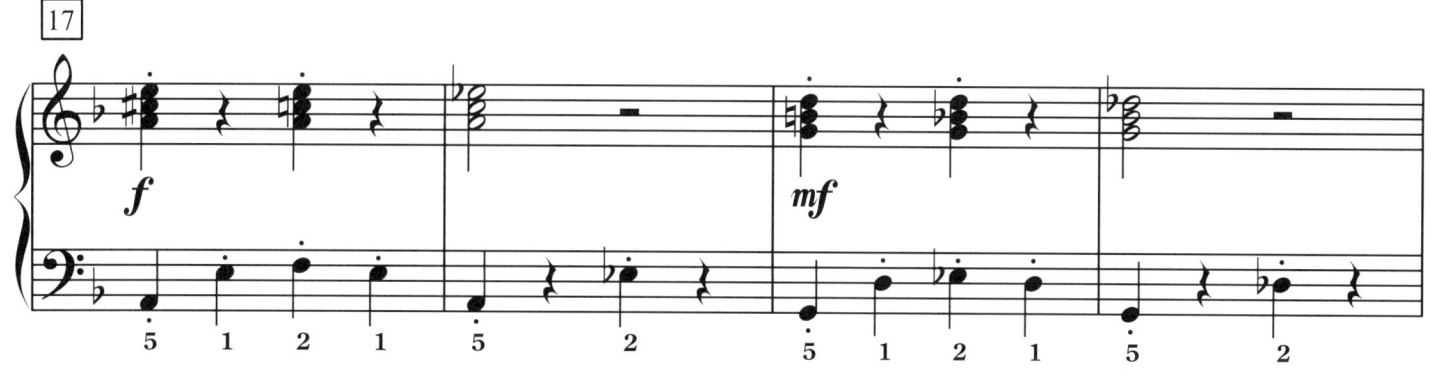

GP692

Augmented Triads

Any Major triad becomes **Augmented** when the 5th is raised a half step.
Augmented triads may be labeled with the abbreviation **Aug**, or a plus sign **+**.
Play these Major and Augmented triads.

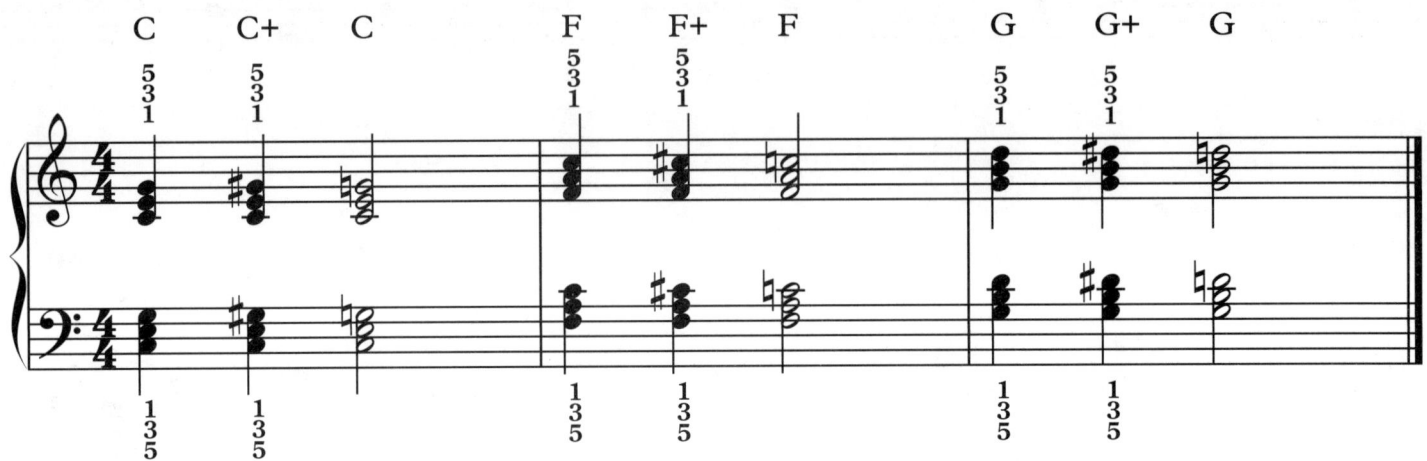

Expanding Horizons

Time Signature 2/2; Dim. and Aug. Triads ■ 79

On an Escapade

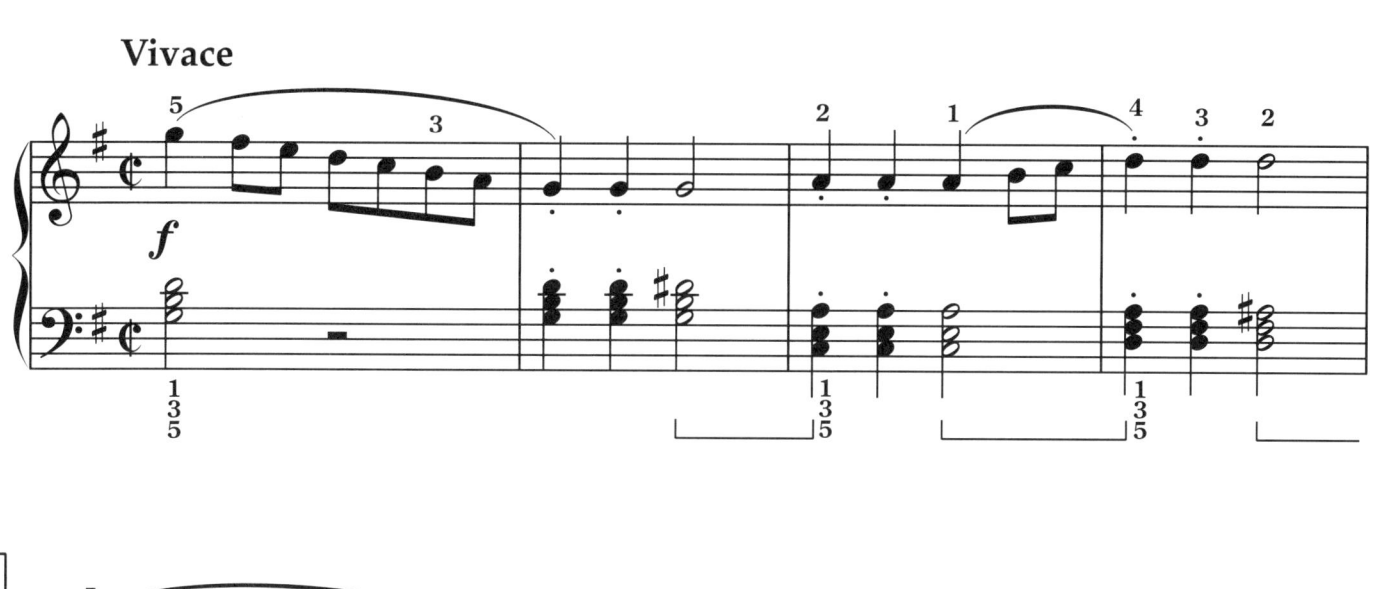
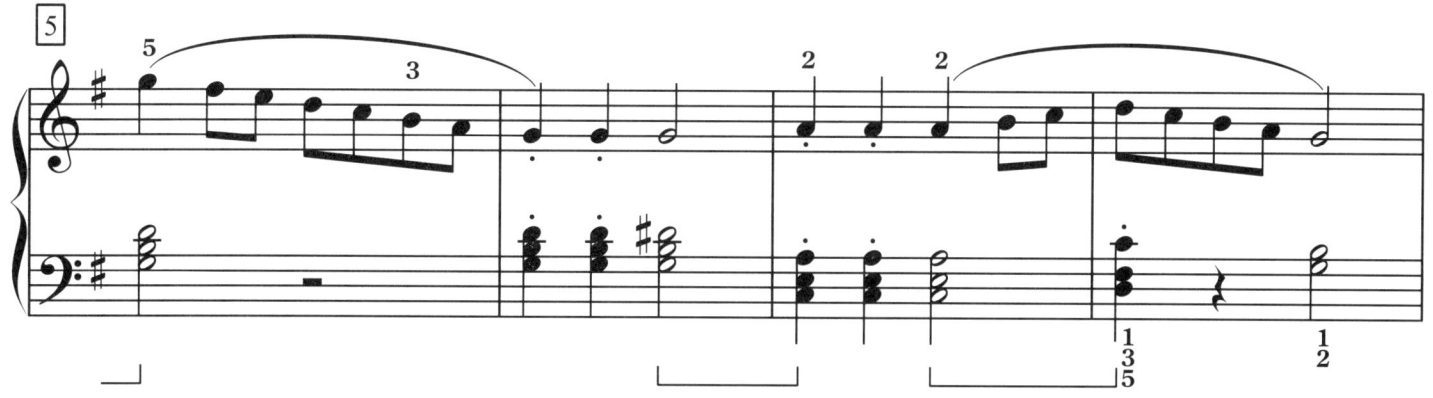
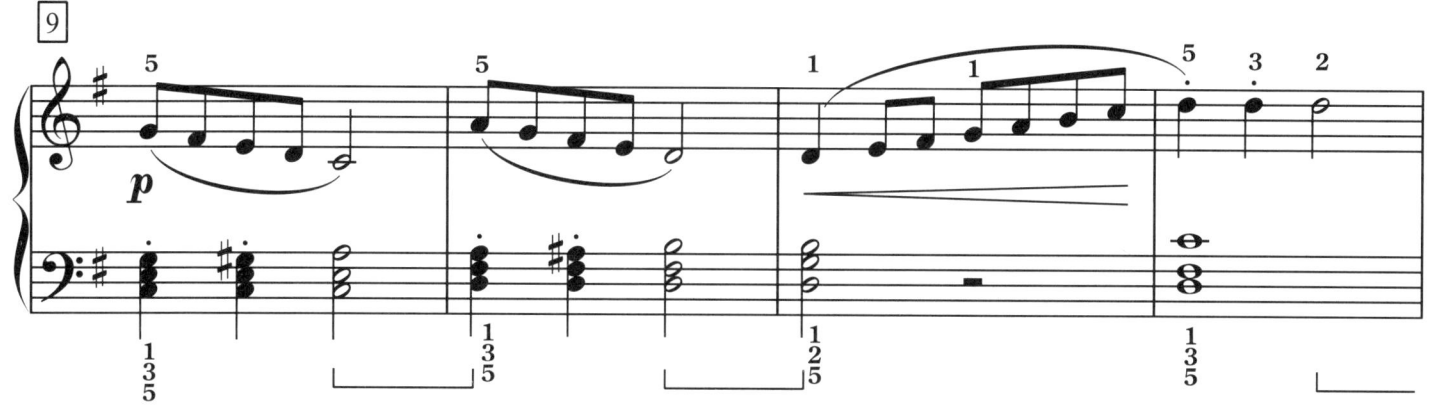
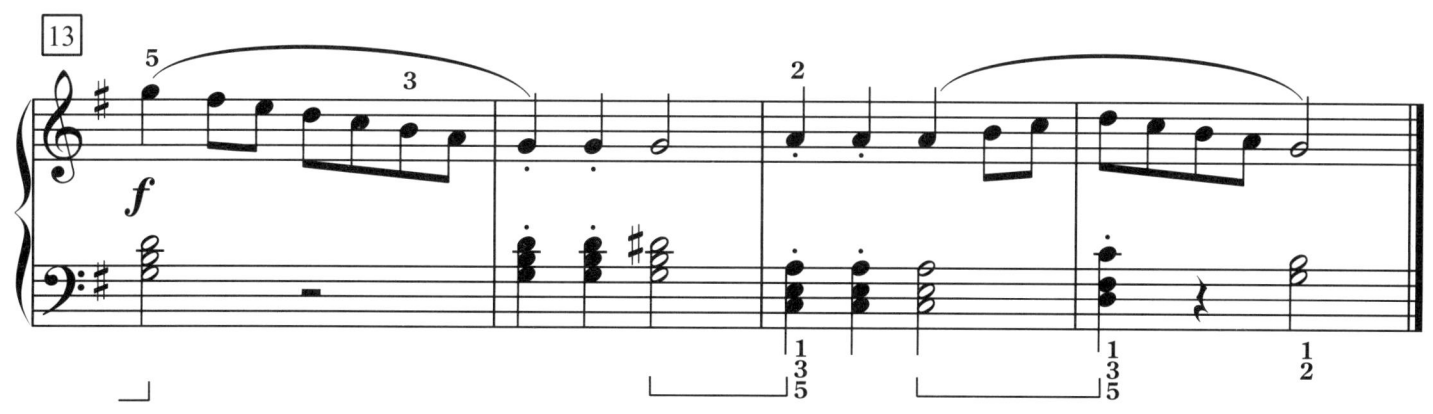

GP692

THEORY

Diminished triads are formed by lowering the 5th of a minor triad a half step.
Diminished triads may be labeled with the abbreviation **dim**, or with a circle ○.

Diminished triads in root position have the intervals of a diminished 5th and a minor 3rd.

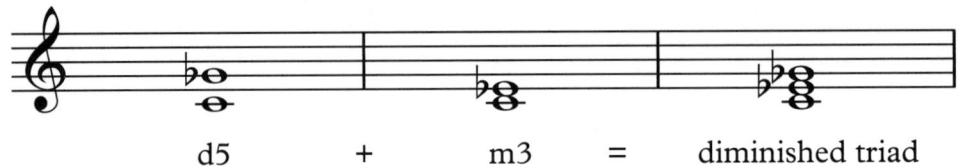

d5   +   m3   =   diminished triad

1. Draw a diminished triad after each minor triad.

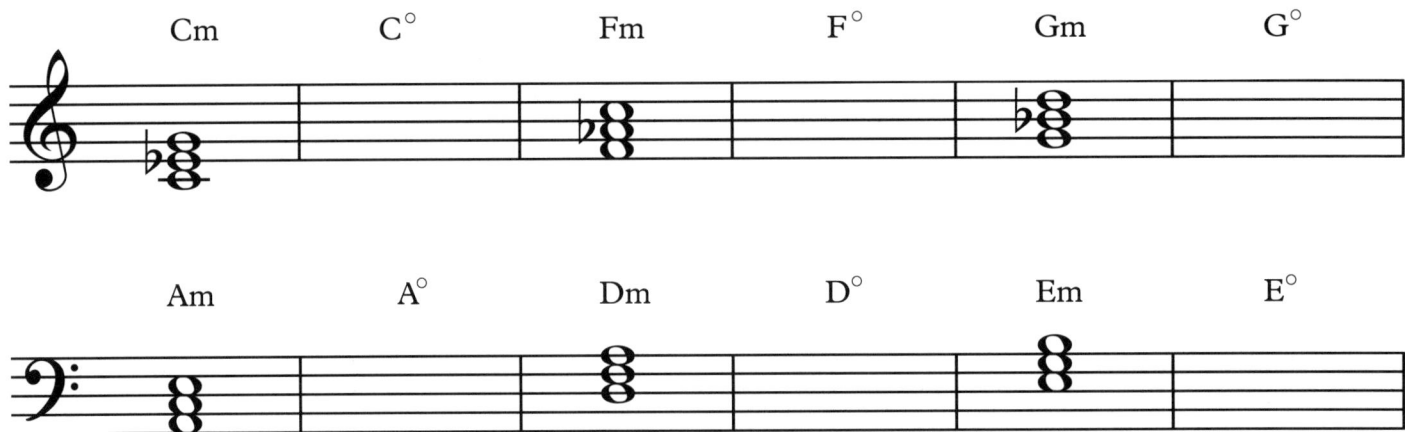

2. Draw the inversions for each root position diminished triad.

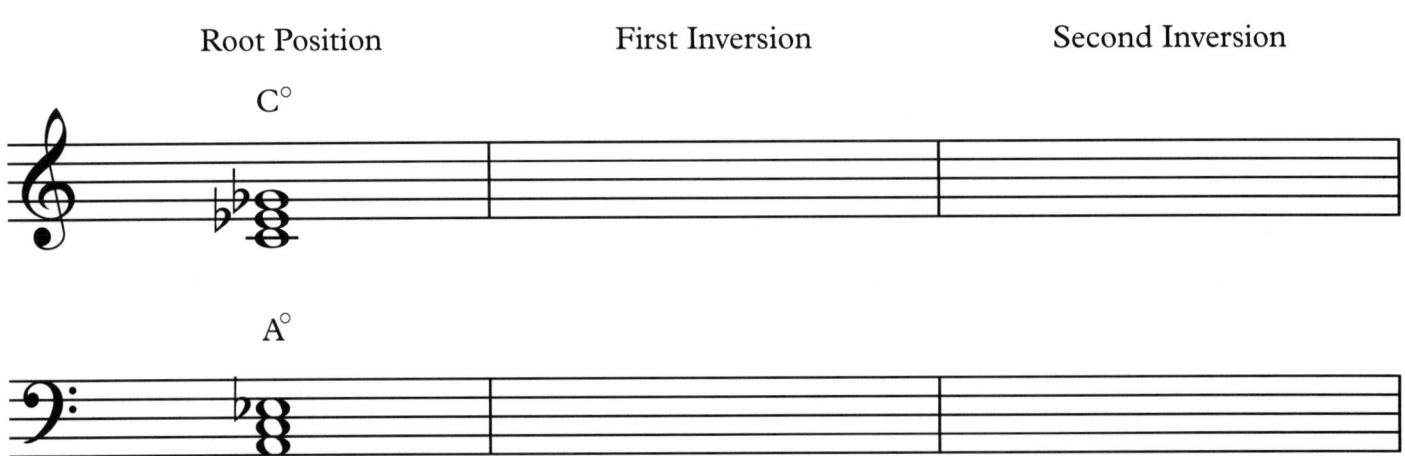

GP692

Time Signature 2/2; Dim. and Aug. Triads

Augmented triads are formed by raising the 5th of a Major triad a half step.
Augmented triads may be labeled with the abbreviation **Aug**, or a plus sign + .

Augmented triads in root position have the intervals of an Augmented 5th and a Major 3rd.

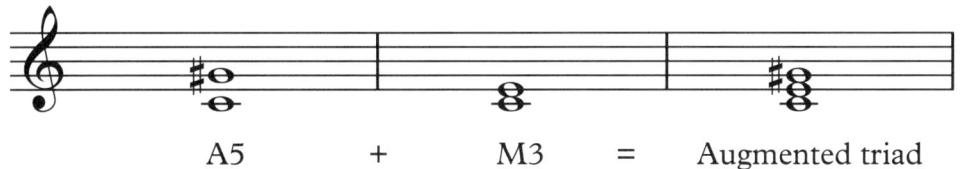

3. Draw an Augmented triad after each Major triad.

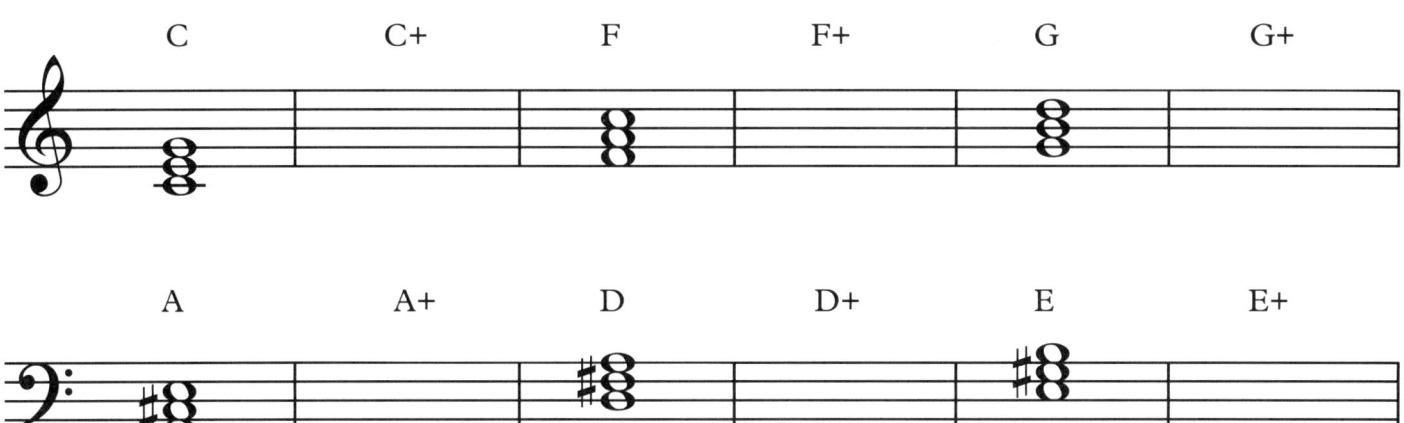

4. Draw the inversions for each root position Augmented triad.

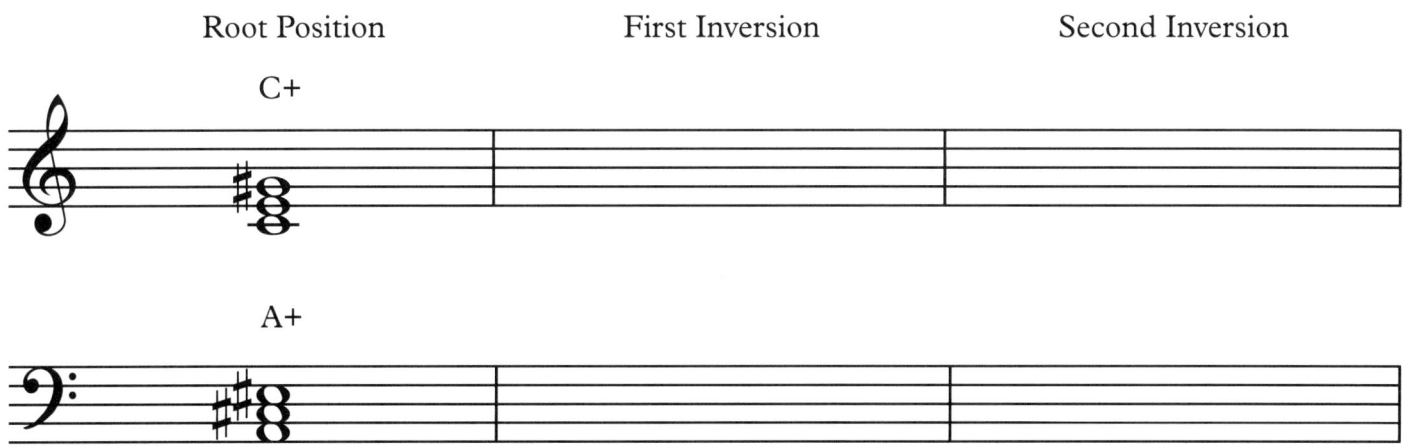

TECHNIC

1. Major, Augmented, minor and diminished triads.

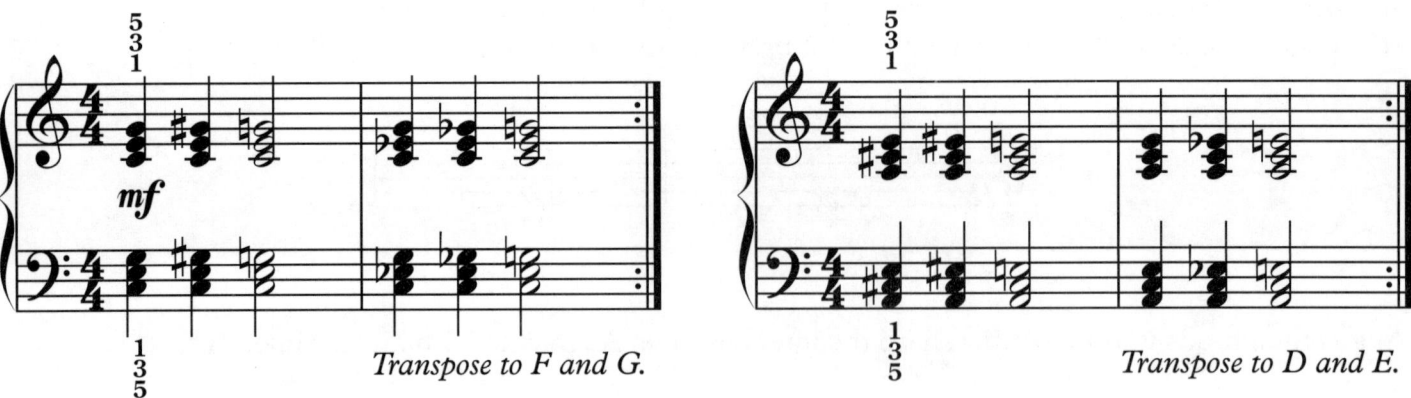

2. Major and Augmented arpeggios.
   Play hands separately first.

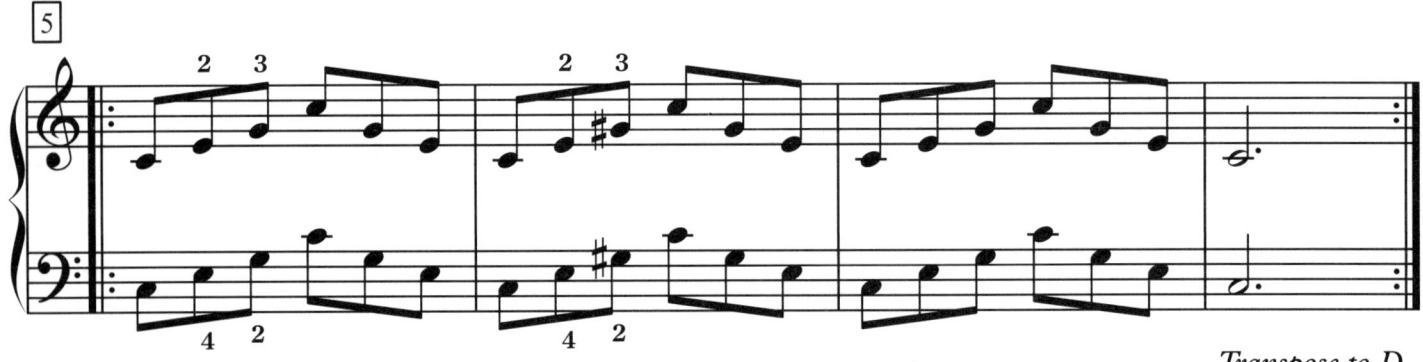

3. Minor and diminished arpeggios.
   Play hands separately first.

Time Signature 2/2; Dim. and Aug. Triads 83

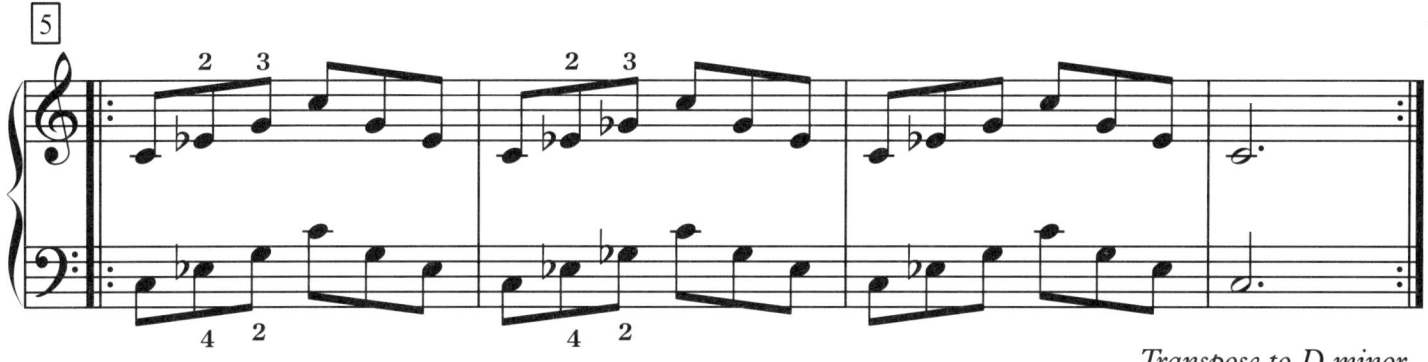

Transpose to D minor.

4. Etude for playing in cut time.

Benjamin Carr, an English pianist and composer, immigrated to the United States in 1793. He lived in Philadelphia, where he established one of the earliest music stores and publishing houses in the US.

The **gavotte** is a French dance, taking its name from "gavot," a name for an Alpine resident in the southeast of France, where the dance originated. It was a popular court dance throughout the 18th century and involved kissing — but this was eventually replaced by the presentation of flowers.

Gavotte

Moderato

Benjamin Carr
(1768-1831)

UNIT 8
SIXTEENTH NOTES; TIME SIGNATURE 3/8

Four to One

Four sixteenth notes equal one quarter note.

Transpose to E.

Two to One

Two sixteenth notes equal one eighth note.

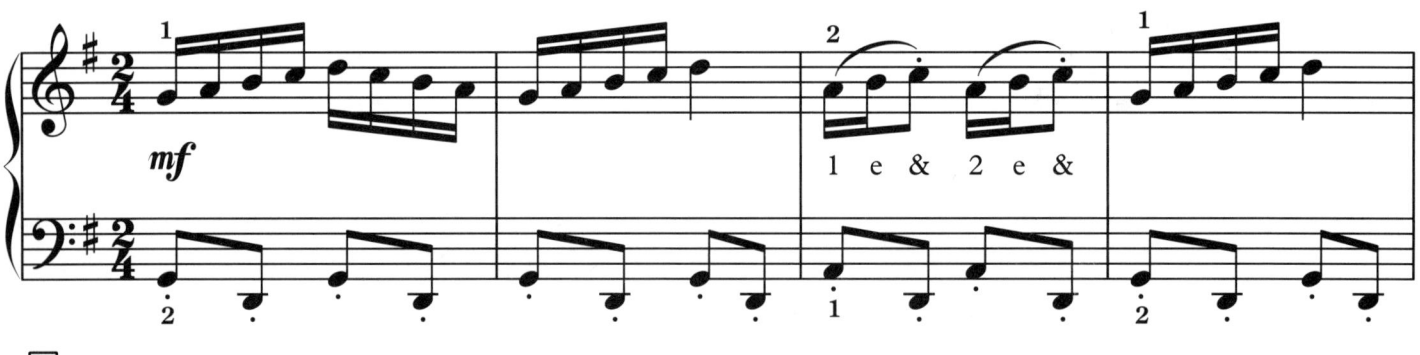

Transpose to F.

The **arabesque** is a form of artistic decoration consisting of a single design which can be seamlessly repeated as many times as desired. In music, an arabesque is meant to create the atmosphere of highly embelished Arabic music. However, it is derived from Western ideas about Arabic music. In actuality, arabesques and Arabic music have little in common.

Unit 8

This piece is from *The First Steps of the Young Pianist,* Op. 82. Gurlitt did not give titles to any of the pieces in his Op. 82, only numbers (this one is 52). Editors will often supply titles, as is the case here.

Sixteenth Rest
(See measure 7.)

Etude in A Minor
Op. 82, No. 52

Cornelius Gurlitt
(1820-1901)

GP692

Sixteenth Notes; Time Signature 3/8 ■ 87

Franz Joseph Haydn was an Austrian composer who spent more than thirty years in service to Hungarian nobleman Prince Esterhazy. Haydn was a major influence in the development of the symphony, sonata, and string quartet, and the "sonata allegro" form used in those genres.

Time Signature 3/8   Three counts in each measure, ♪ = 1 count   ♩ = 2 counts   ♩. = 3 counts

German Dance

Franz Joseph Haydn
(1732-1809)

GP692

Strolling

A **dotted eighth note** equals three sixteenth notes.

Transpose to D and G.

Singing

The length of an eighth note tied a sixteenth is the same as a dotted eight note.

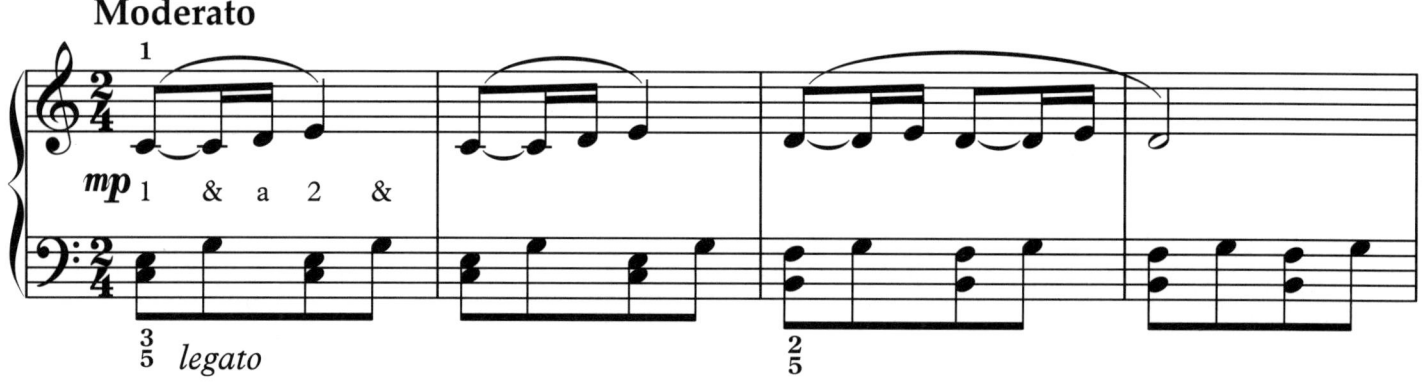

Transpose to F and E.

Sixteenth Notes; Time Signature 3/8 ■ 89

Ludwig van Beethoven, a German pianist and composer, was born in Bonn, Germany. At the age of 21, he moved to Vienna, where he lived until his death at age 56. He was one of the most recognized and influential musicians during his life, and is still considered one of the greatest composers of all time. Despite the deterioration of his hearing starting in 1801, which worsened to almost complete deafness by 1811, Beethoven composed nine symphonies, five piano concertos, one violin concerto, thirty-two piano sonatas, ten violin sonatas, five 'cello sonatas, sixteen string quartets, and many other important works. An estimated 20,000 people attended his funeral.

Russian Folk Song
Op. 107, No. 3

Ludwig van Beethoven
(1770-1827)

GP692

THEORY

Scale Degrees

Each degree of a scale has a name.

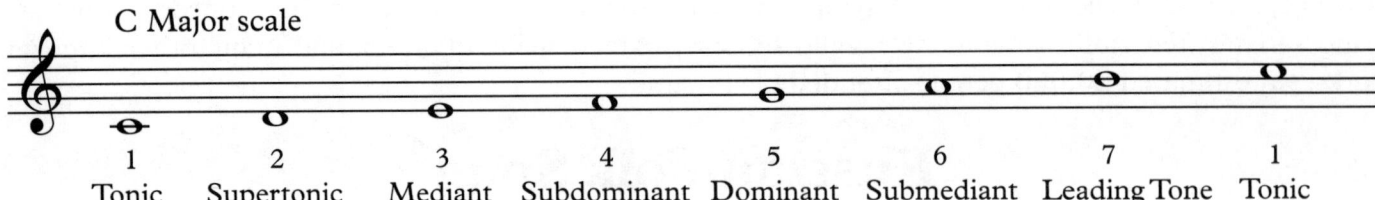

Each scale degree name refers to its position up or down from the tonic.

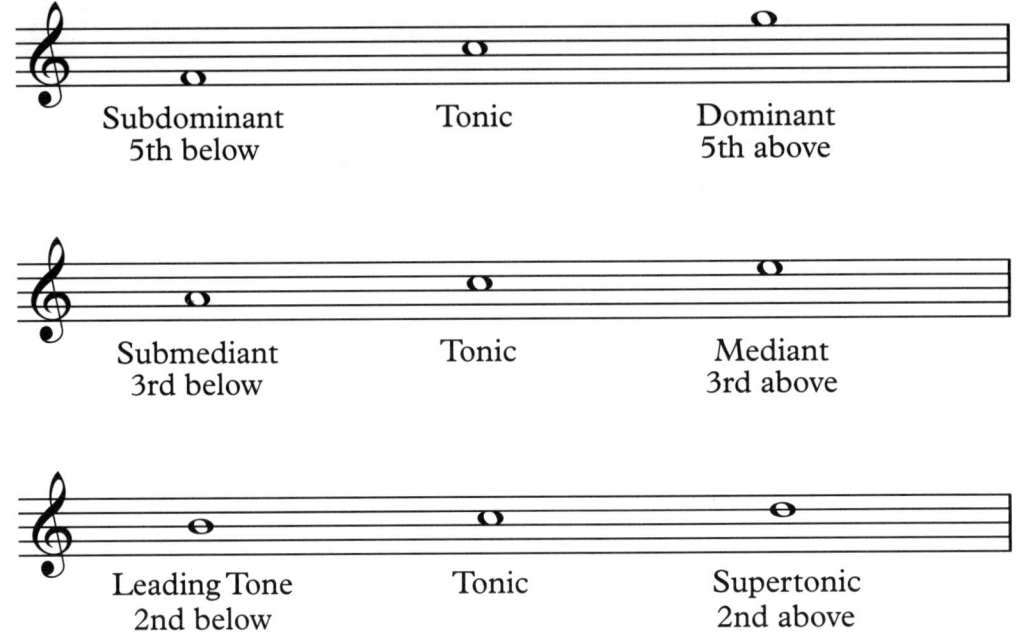

1. Write the scale degree name for each note of the F Major scale.

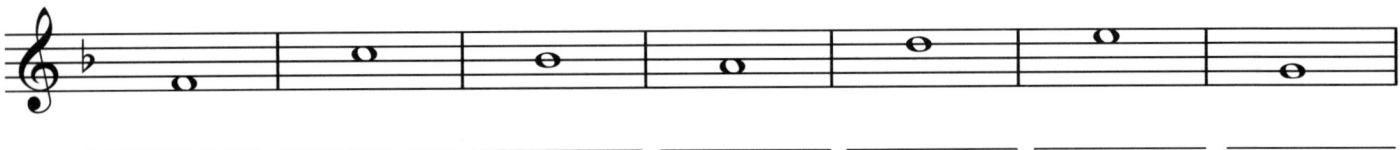

2. Draw the note for each scale degree name of the G Major scale. Use whole notes.

Triads of Major Scales

A triad may be built on each degree of the Major scale. Each triad is labeled with a Roman numeral and named for the scale degree of its root. Upper or lower case Roman numerals indicate triad quality.

    Major: upper case (I, IV, V)
    minor: lower case (ii, iii, vi)
    diminished: lower case and ° (vii°)

These triad qualities are the same for all Major scales.

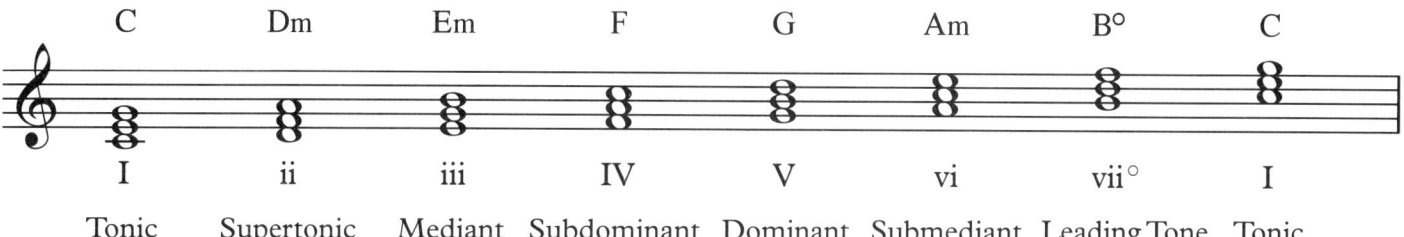

3. Write the Roman numeral below each triad of the D Major scale. Write the chord names above.

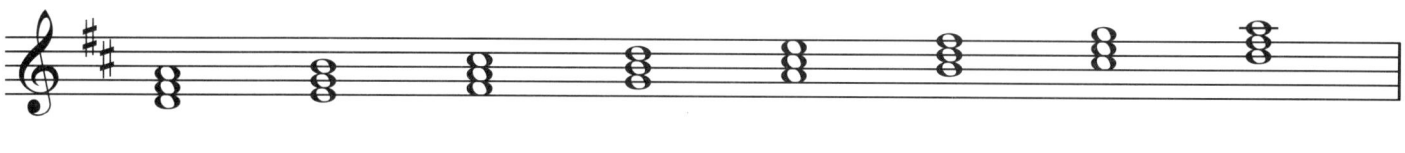

4. Write the Roman numeral below each triad of the B♭ Major scale. Write the chord names above.

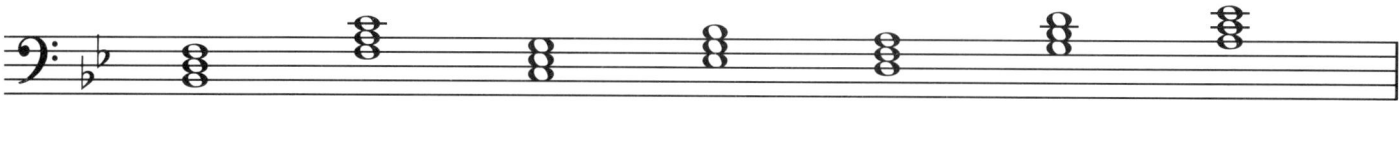

5. Draw each triad of the G Major scale according to the degree name.
   Write Roman numerals and chord names. Use whole notes.

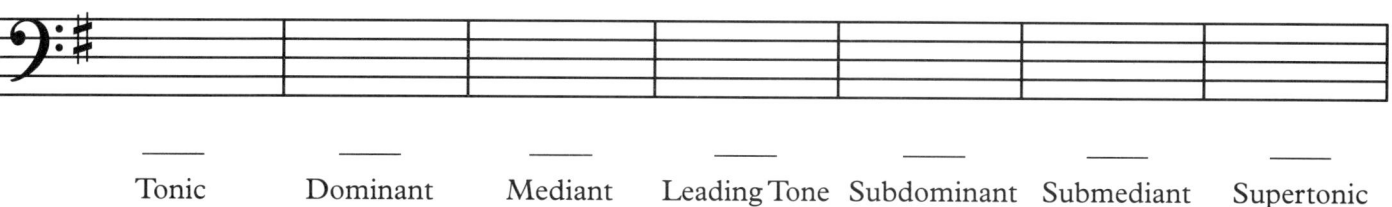

TECHNIC

1. Triads of the C Major scale, root position.

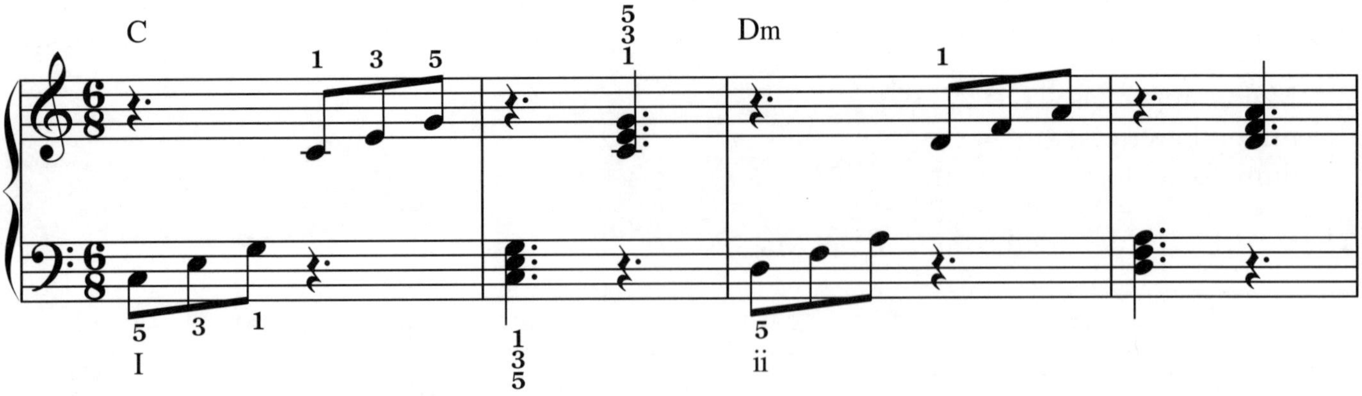

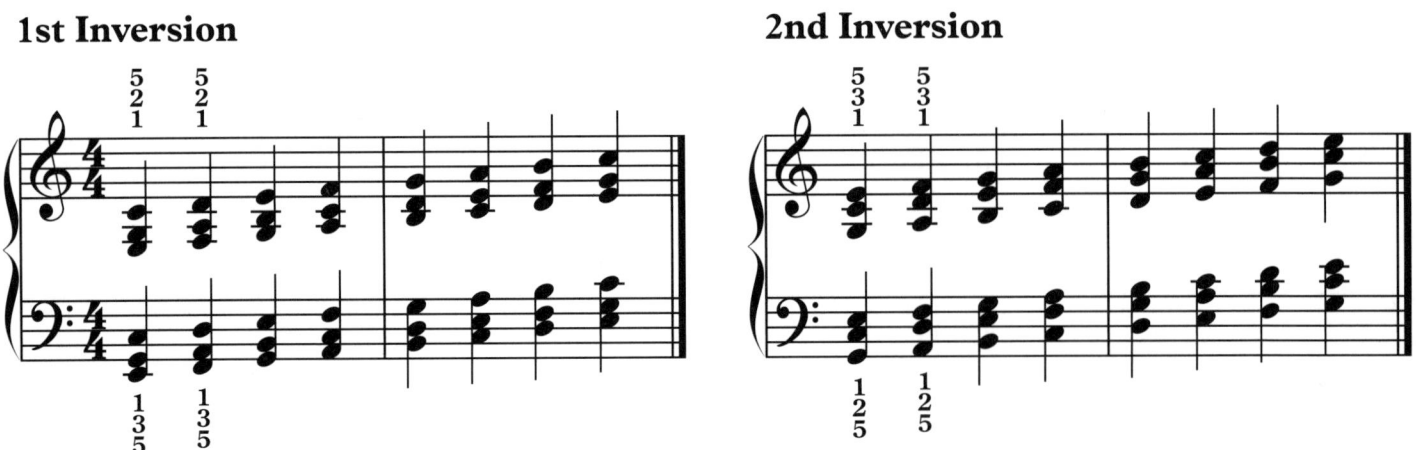

2. Triads of the C Major scale, 1st and 2nd inversions.
   These triads may also be played broken and blocked, in the same rhythm as above.

1st Inversion

2nd Inversion

Transpose exercises 1 and 2: G, D, A, E, F, and B♭ Major.

Carl Czerny was an Austrian pianist, composer, and piano teacher. His teachers included Clementi, Salieri, and Beethoven. He maintained a friendship with Beethoven throughout his life, becoming piano teacher to Beethoven's nephew Carl, and proof reading many of Beethoven's works prior to publication. Czerny was dedicated to teaching, often seeing as many as twelve students a day. His most famous student was Franz Liszt. Czerny wrote literally thousands of piano pieces, and was the first to use the word "etude" as a title. He is regarded as the "father of modern piano playing," as so many of his students became teachers, handing down his legacy through generations of teachers and students.

Etude
Op. 599, No. 33

Carl Czerny
(1791-1857)

UNIT 9
E♭ MAJOR, A♭ MAJOR, D♭ MAJOR

E♭ Major Scale and Key Signature

The key signature for E♭ Major has three flats: B♭, E♭, and A♭.

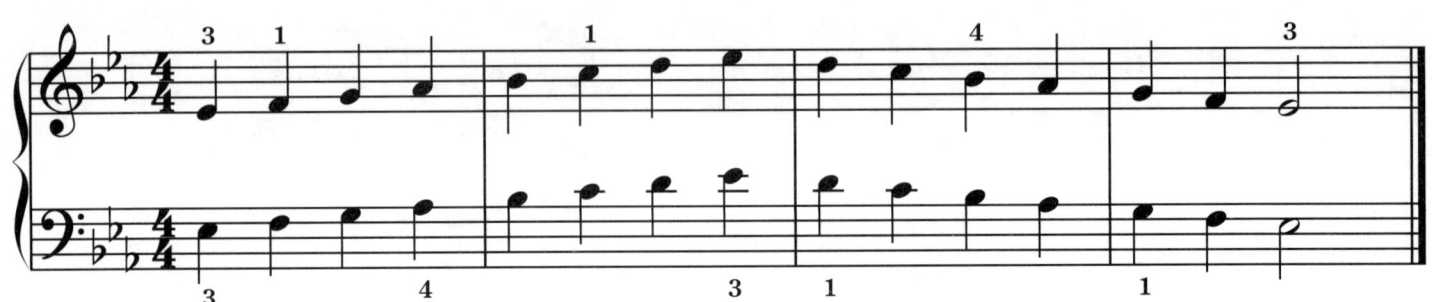

Primary Triads in E♭ Major

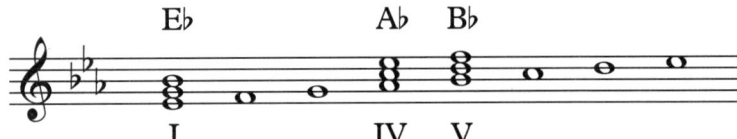

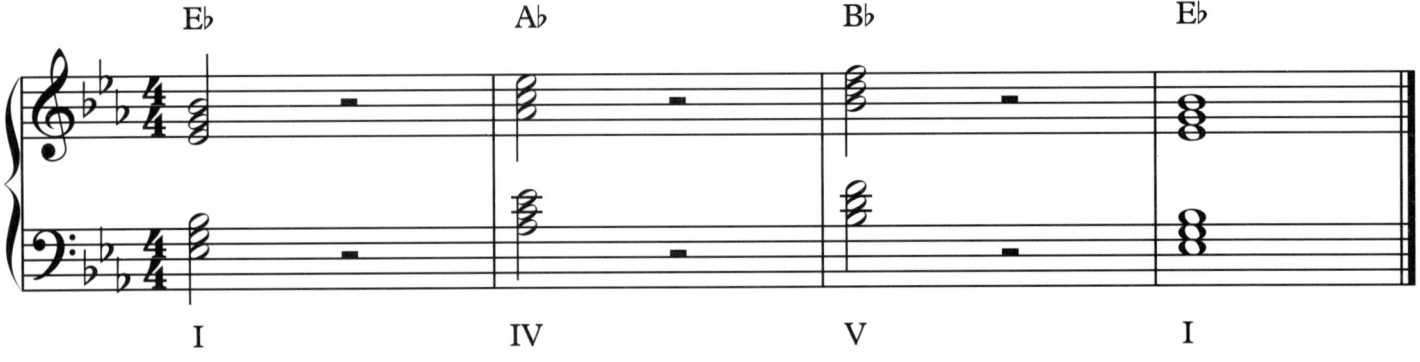

Primary Chord Progression

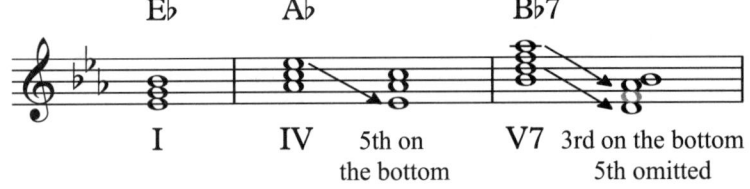

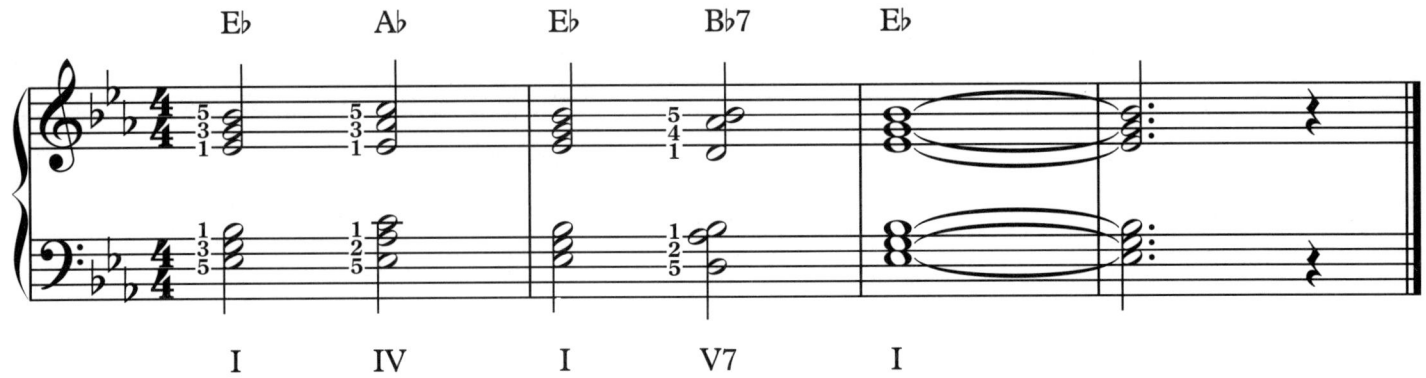

GP692

Eb Major, Ab Major, Db Major 95

Reading in Eb Major

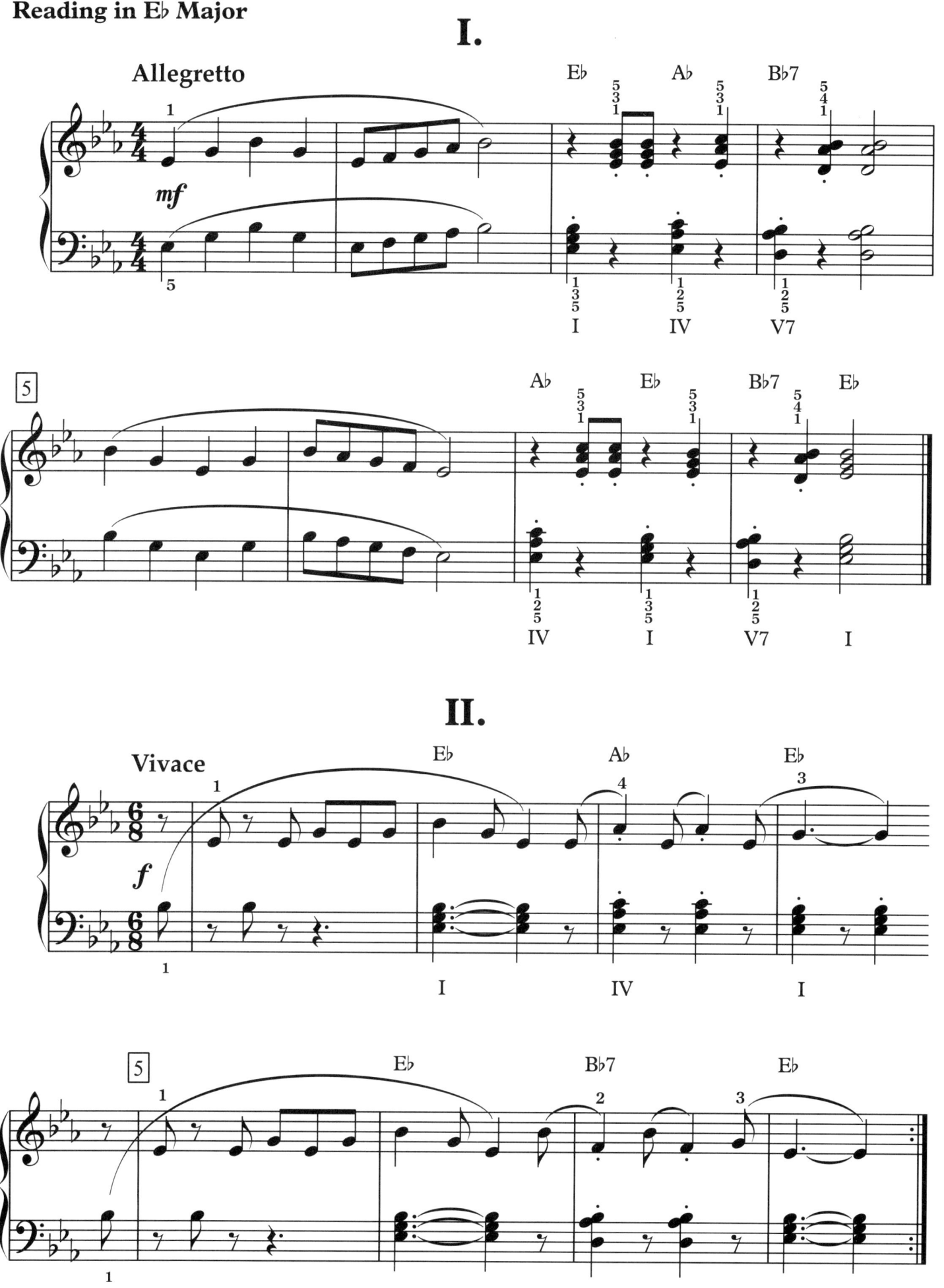

GP692

Largo
Theme from *New World Symphony*

Antonín Dvořák
(1841-1901)
Arranged

Écossaise, although French in origin, is in the style of a Scottish country dance that was popular in France and Great Britain in the late 18th and early 19th centuries. The écossaise, usually in 2/4 time, was danced in two lines, with men facing the women. The music for écossaises was mostly composed for piano, making it easily accessible for small gatherings. Two great composers who wrote many of them were Ludwig van Beethoven and Franz Schubert.

Écossaise
WoO 86*

Ludwig van Beethoven
(1770-1827)

Werke ohne Opuszahl (Works without Opus Number) is a catalogue of music by Beethoven published without opus number.

A♭ Major Scale and Key Signature

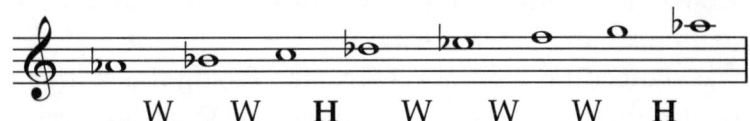

The key signature for A♭ Major has four flats: B♭, E♭, A♭, and D♭.

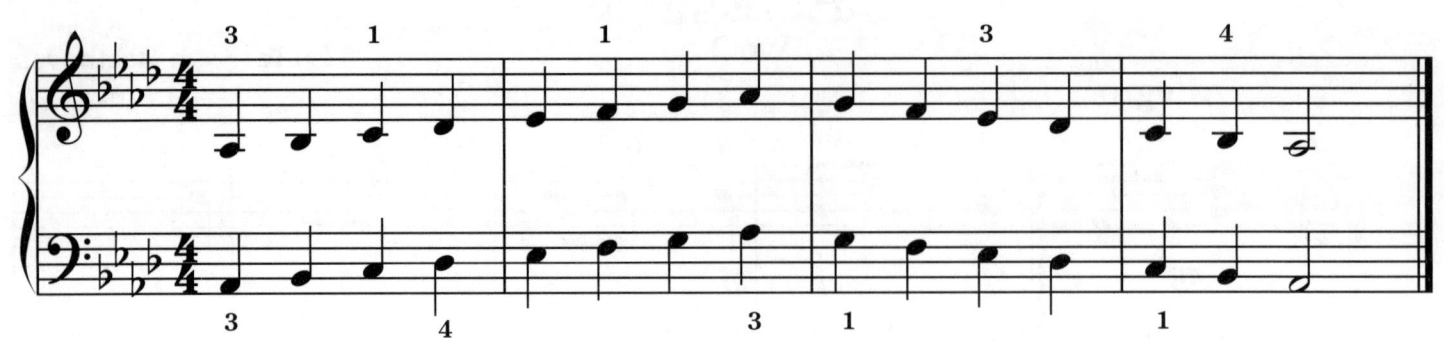

Primary Triads in A♭ Major

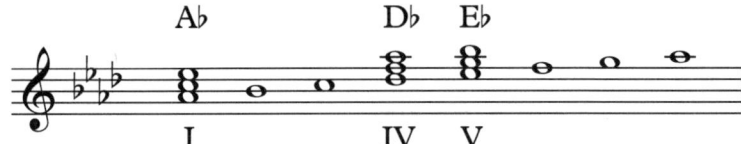

Primary Chord Progression

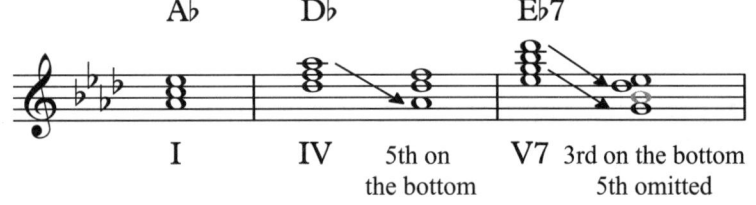

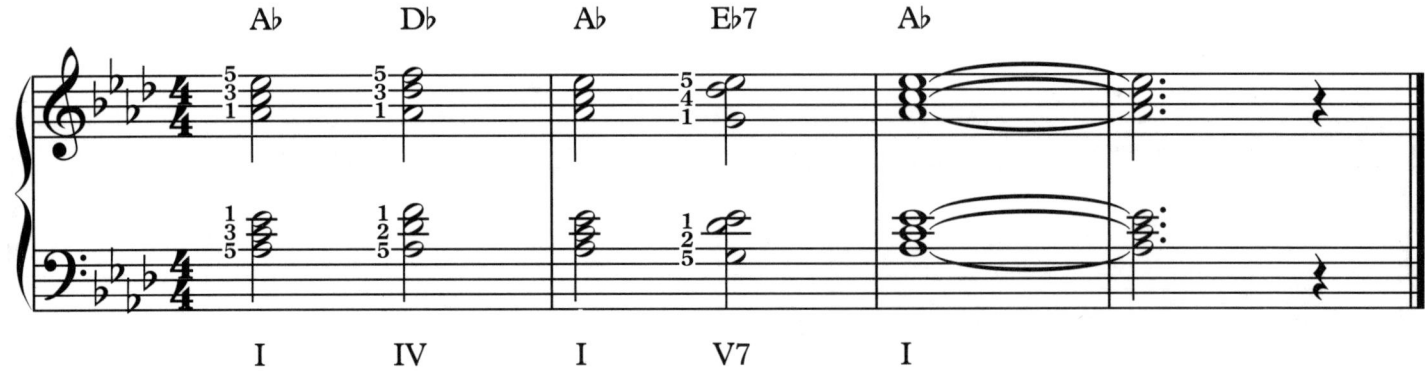

Reading in A♭ Major

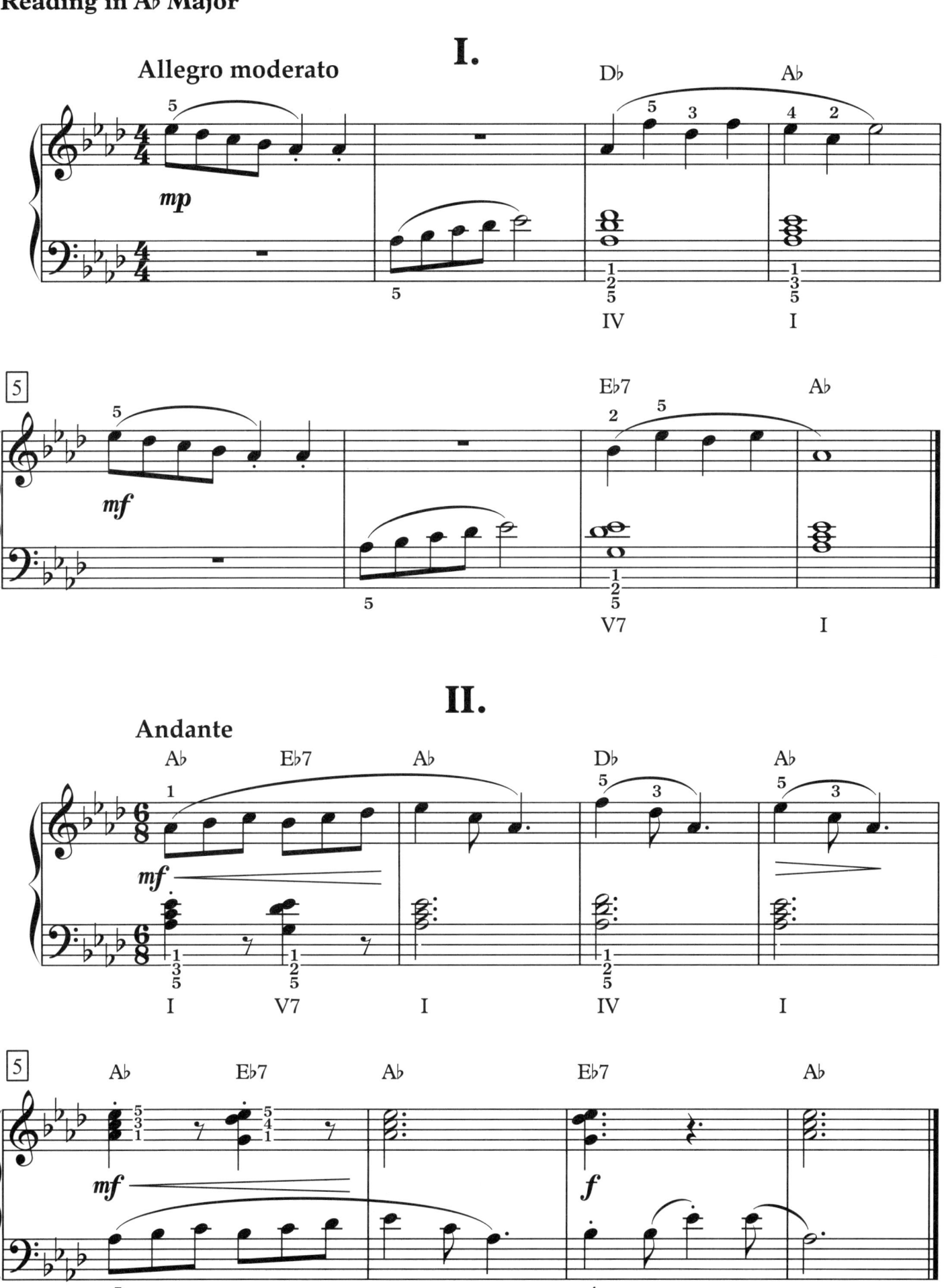

Sonata Theme
from *Piano Sonata No. 11, K. 331*

Wolfgang Amadeus Mozart
(1756-1791)
Arranged

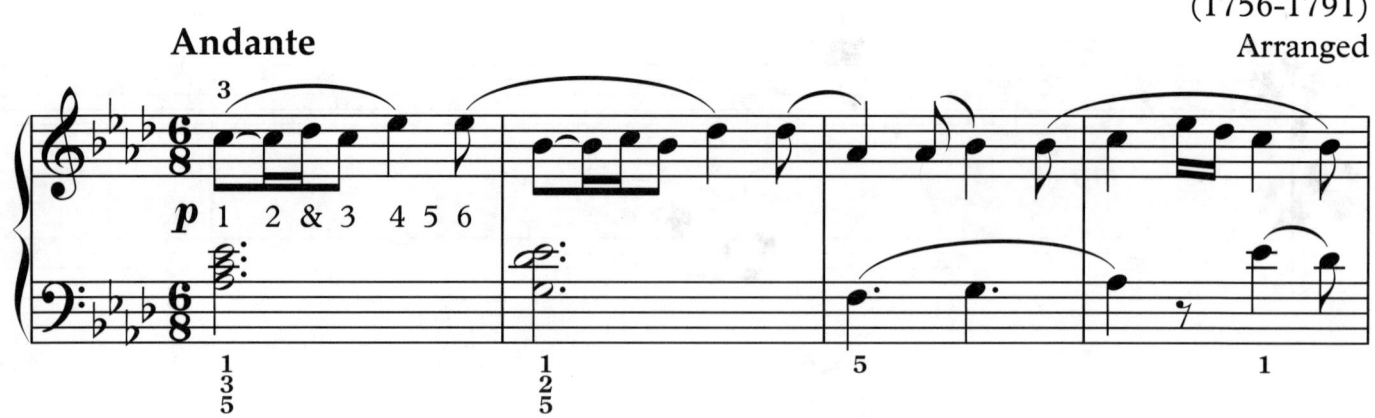

Transpose to A.

E♭ Major, A♭ Major, D♭ Major 101

Waltz
Op. 39, No. 15

Johannes Brahms
(1833-1897)
Arranged

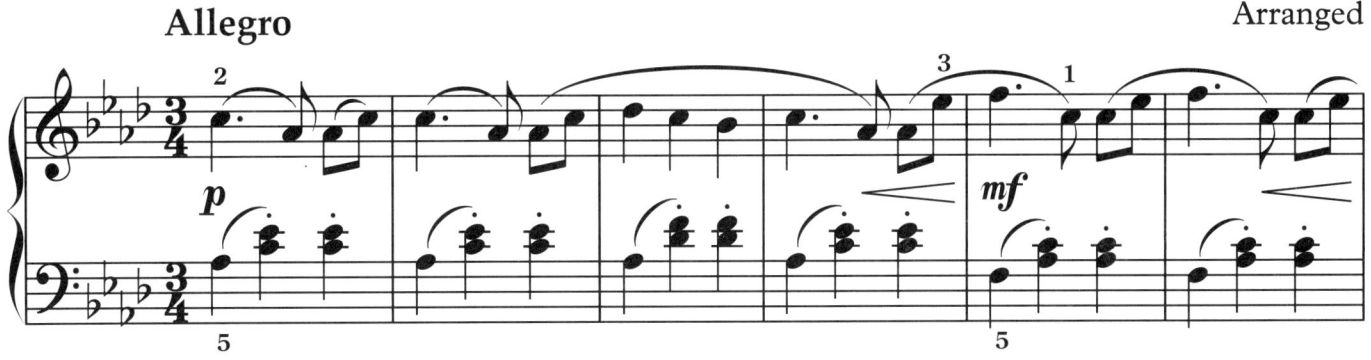
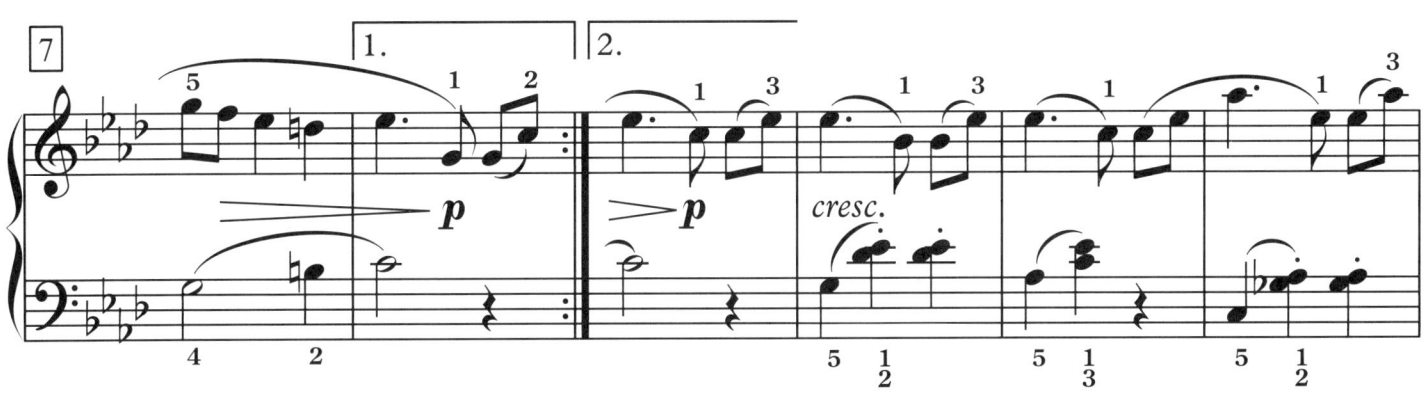
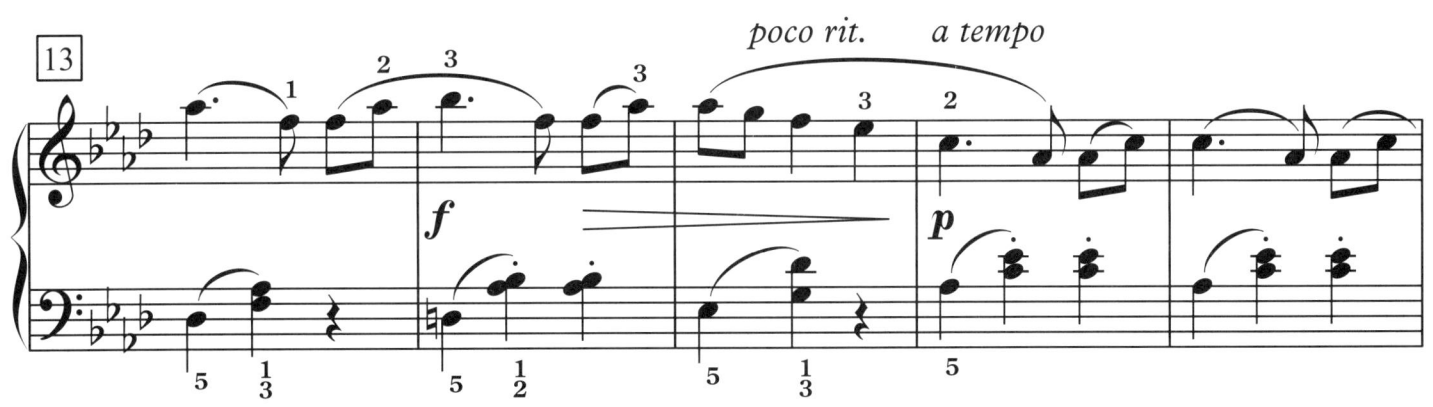
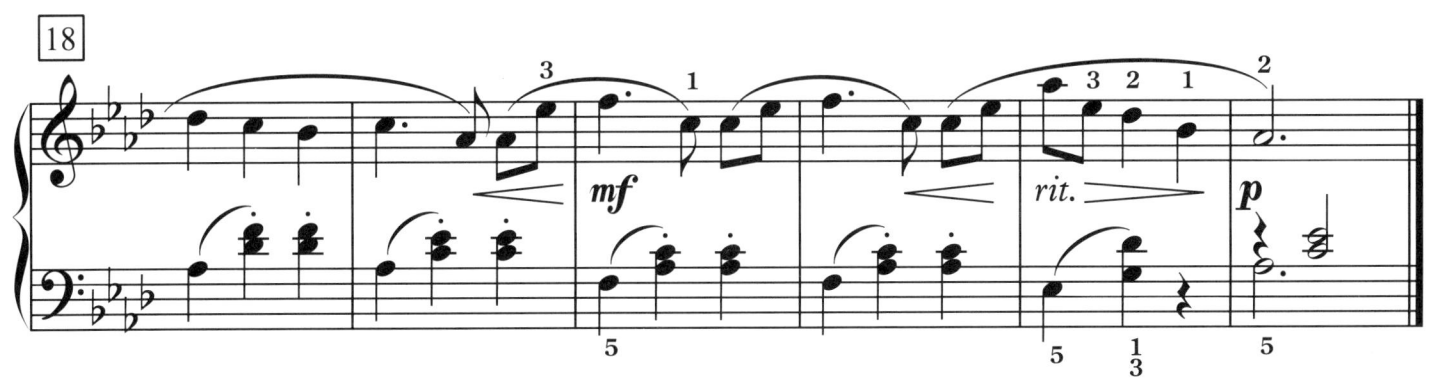

GP692

D♭ Major Scale and Key Signature

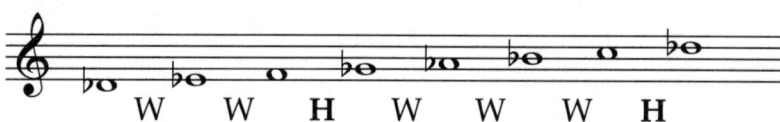

The key signature for D♭ Major has five flats: B♭, E♭, A♭, D♭, and G♭.

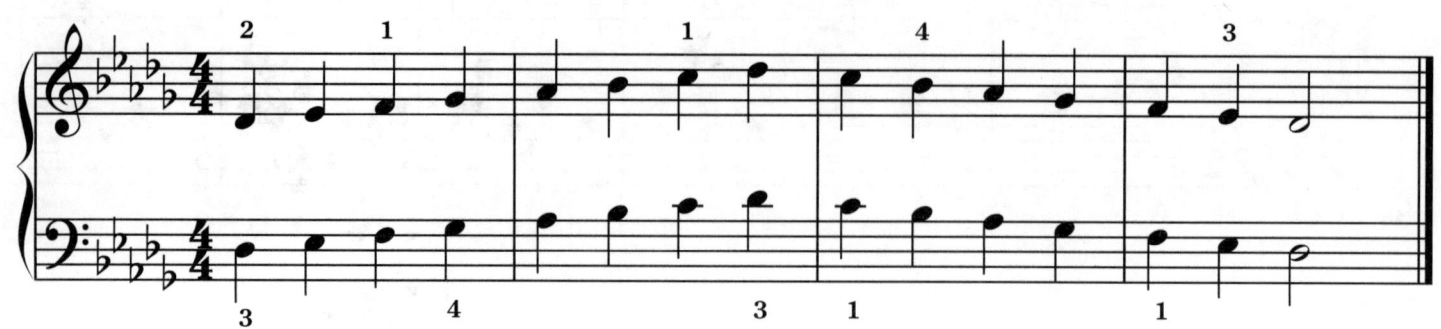

Primary Triads in D♭ Major

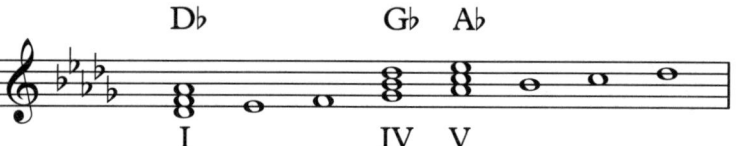

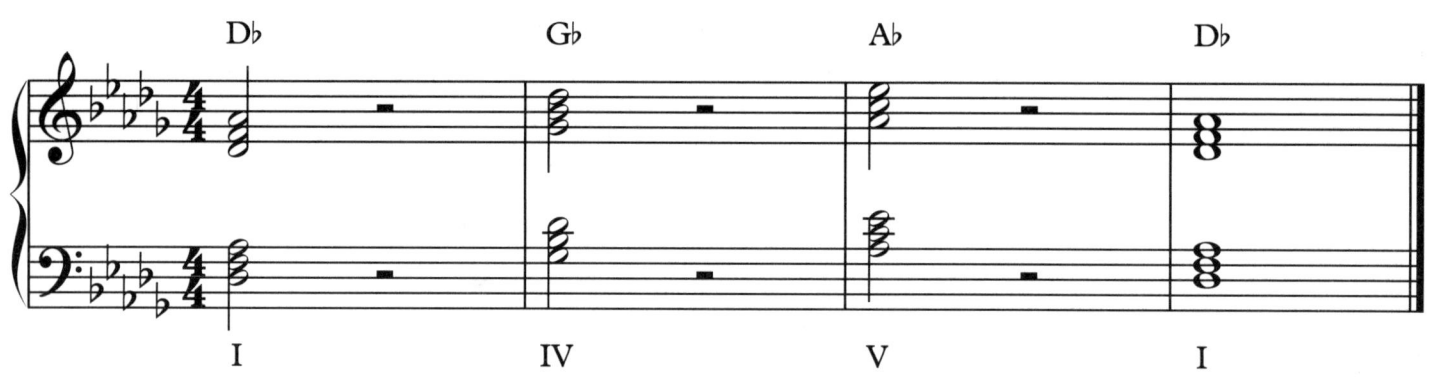

Primary Chord Progression

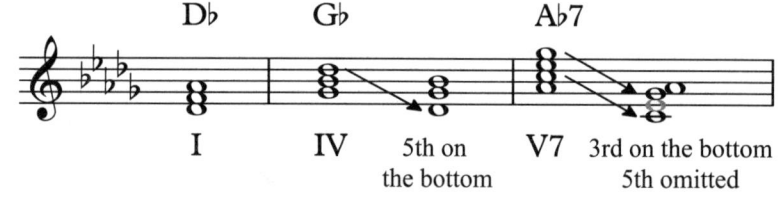

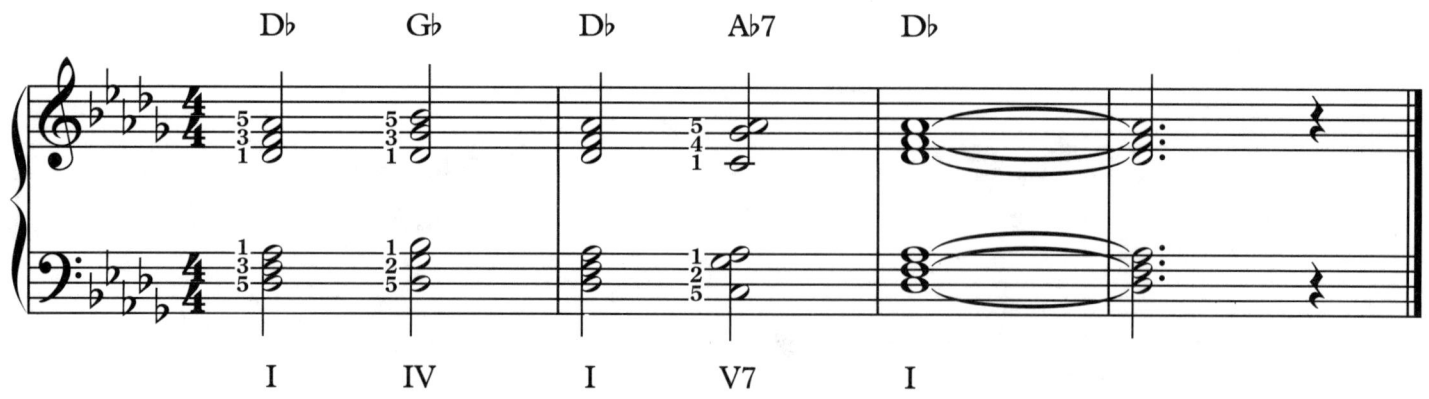

Reading in D♭ Major

I.

Moderato

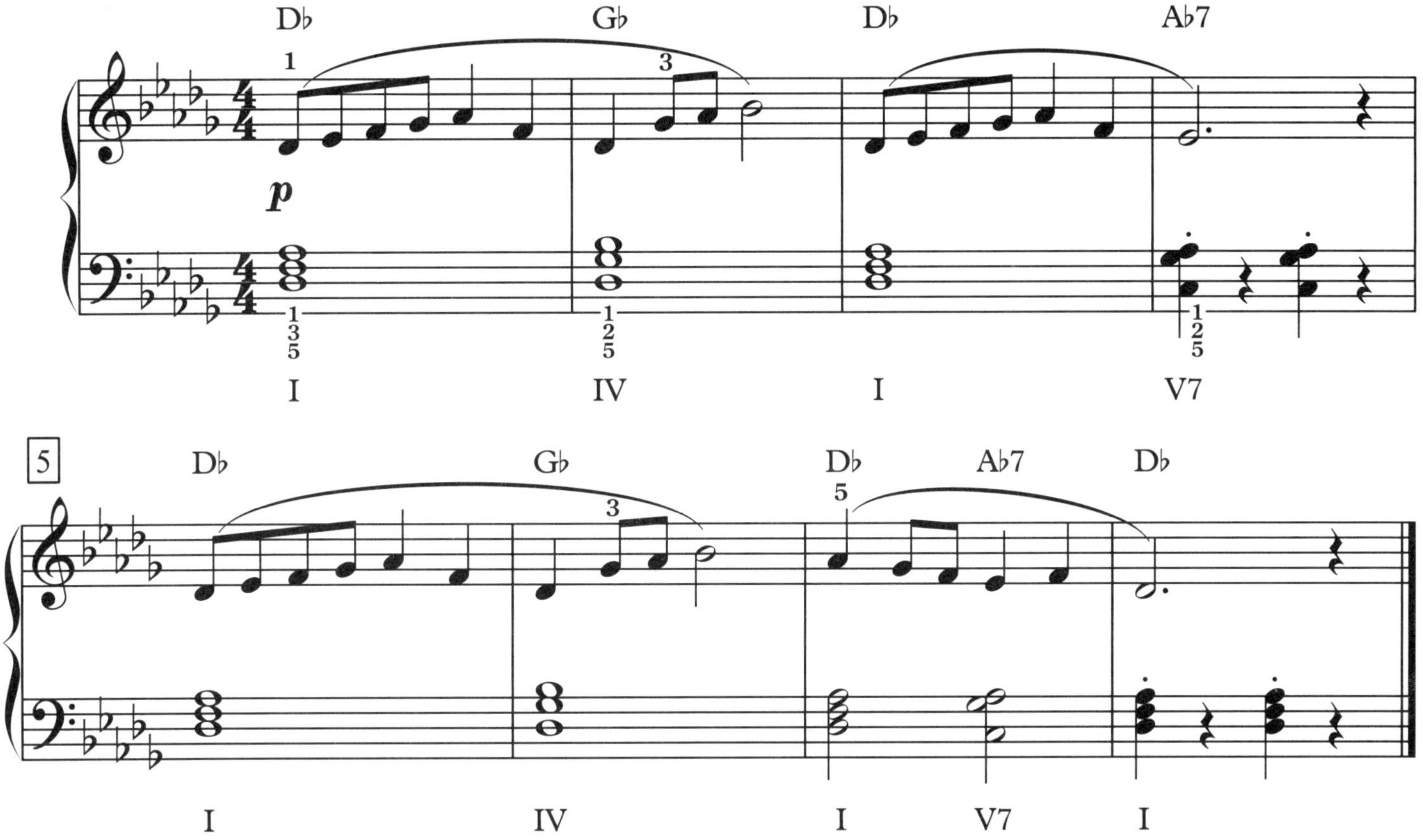

II.

Allegretto

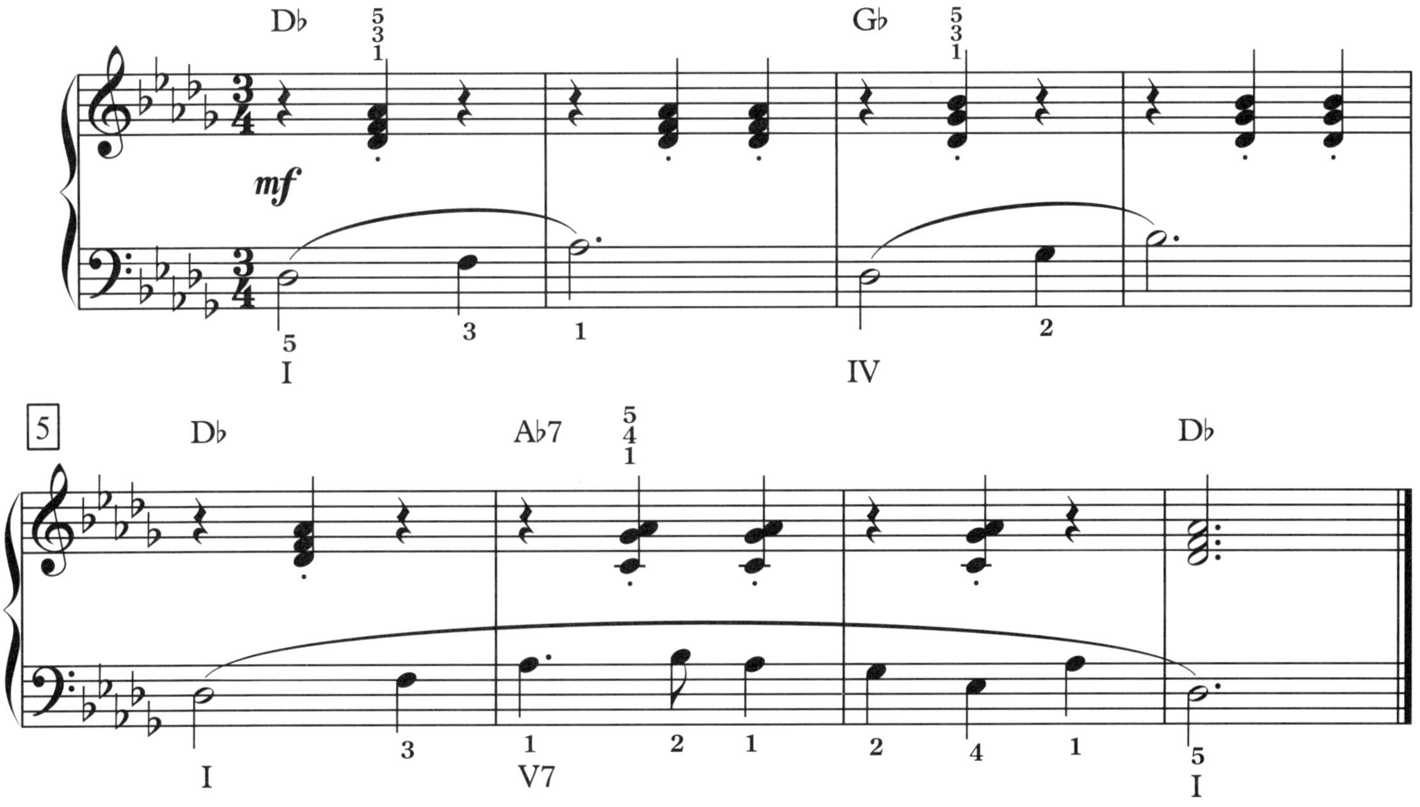

Barcarolle*

E♭ Major, A♭ Major, D♭ Major — 105

*A **barcarolle** is a Venetian gondoliers' song, or a piece of music composed in that style.

**Return to the beginning and play to the sign ⊕, then skip to the Coda to finish the piece.

THEORY

Major Flat Key Signatures

The Order of Flats

B E A D G C F

The flats in key signatures are always in the same order. Memorize the order of flats.

1. Trace the order of flats in the first measure, then draw the order of flats two more times.

There are seven **Major keys** that have flats in the key signature: F, B♭, E♭, A♭, D♭, G♭, and C♭ Major.

To recognize and name any Major flat key signature,* name the next-to-last flat in the key signature.

The name of the next to last flat is the name of the Major Key.

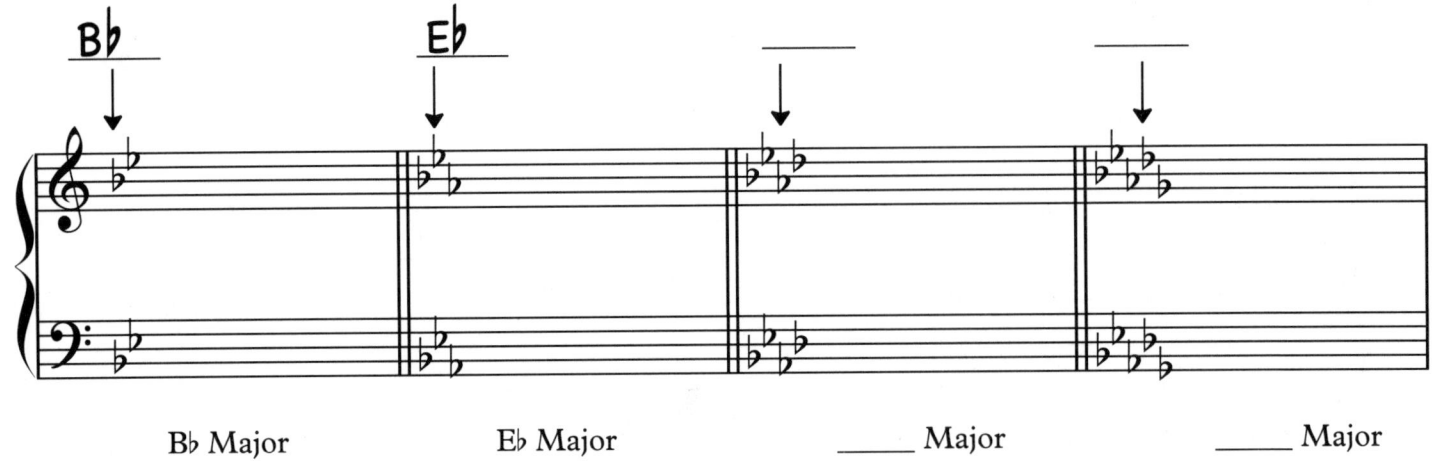

B♭ Major   E♭ Major   _____ Major   _____ Major

*Exception: the key of F Major has one flat, B♭.

2. Name each Major key signature.

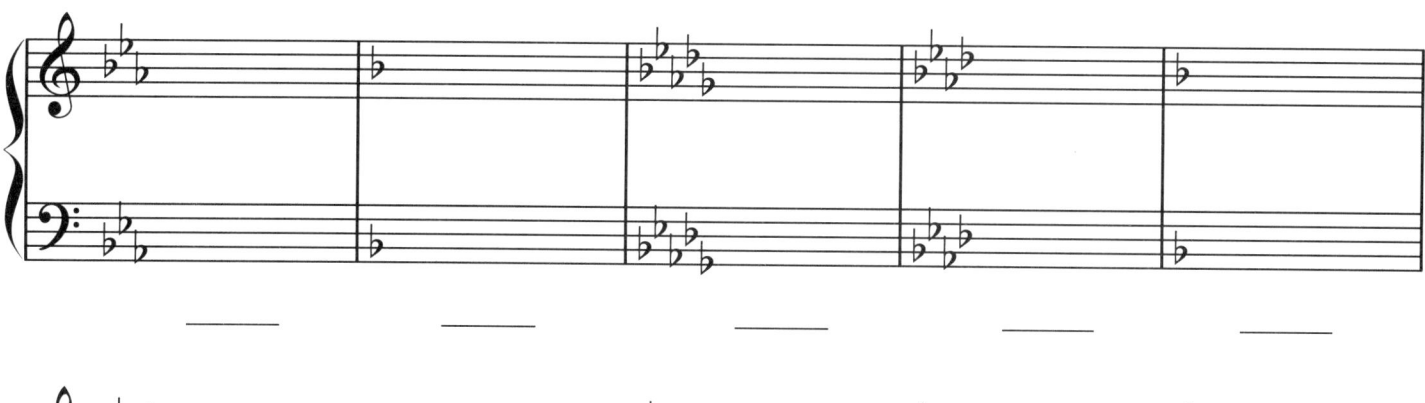

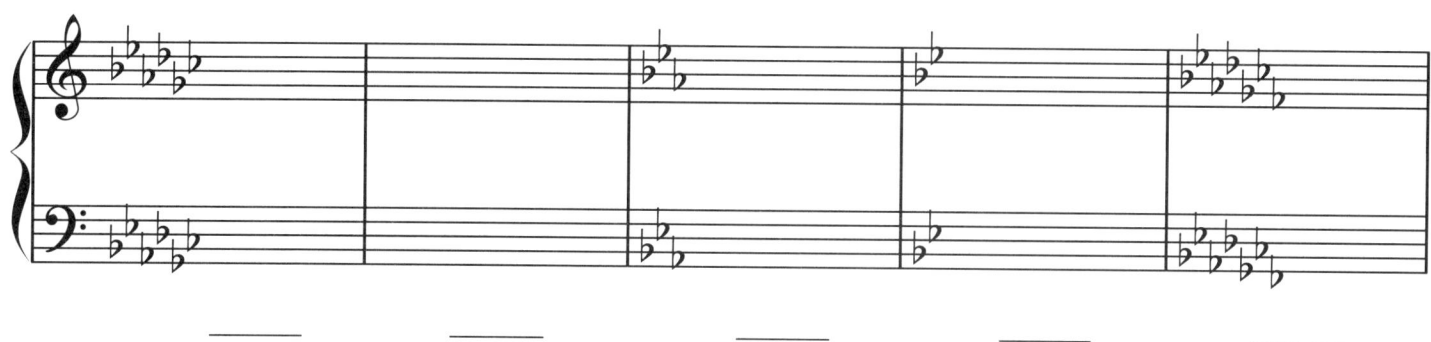

To write the key signature for any Major flat key, write the order of flats up to and including the flat after the key note.

Example: Key of A♭ Major:

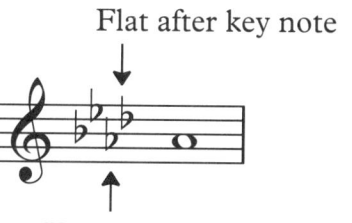

Flat after key note
Key note (A♭)

3. Write each Major key signature.

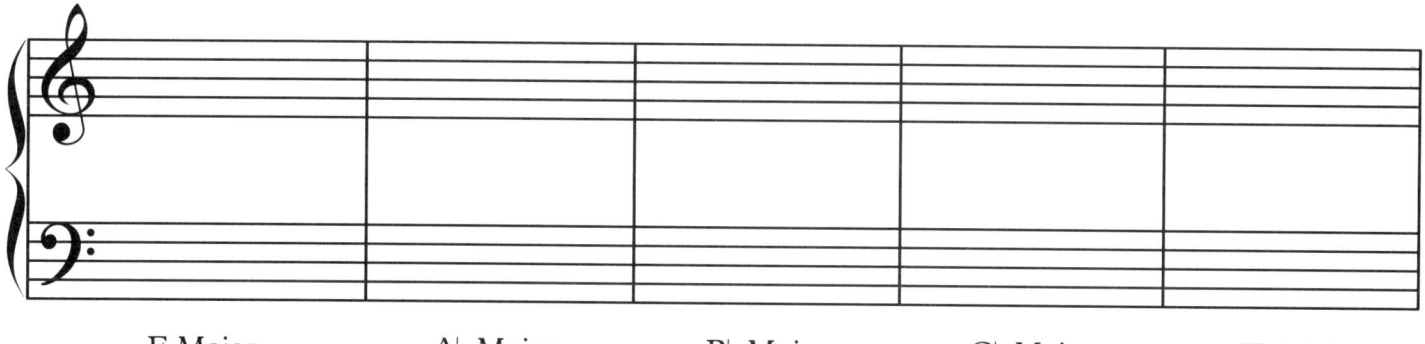

F Major   A♭ Major   B♭ Major   G♭ Major   E♭ Major

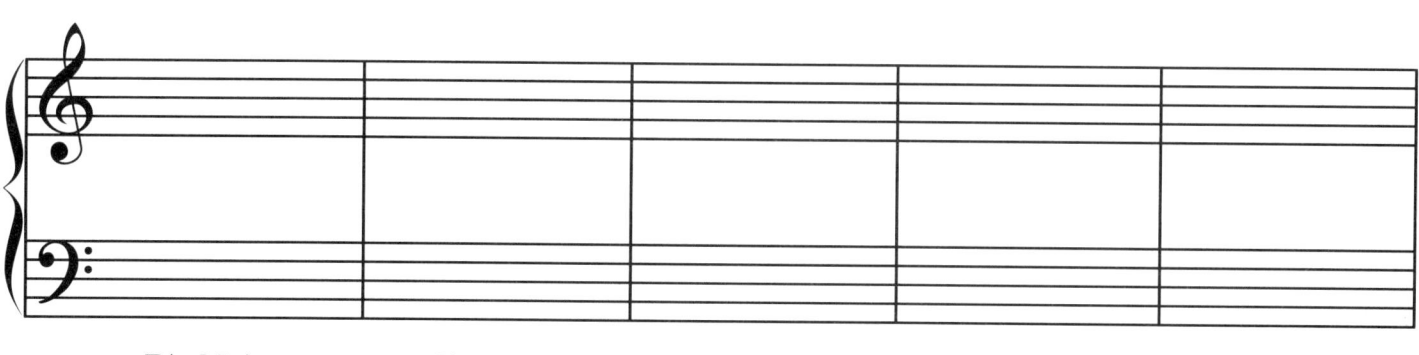

D♭ Major   C♭ Major   E♭ Major   A♭ Major   B♭ Major

E♭ Major Key Signature

The key signature for E♭ Major has three flats: B♭, E♭, and A♭.

4. Trace the first key signature, then draw two more.

Primary Chords in E♭ Major

Primary Chord Progression

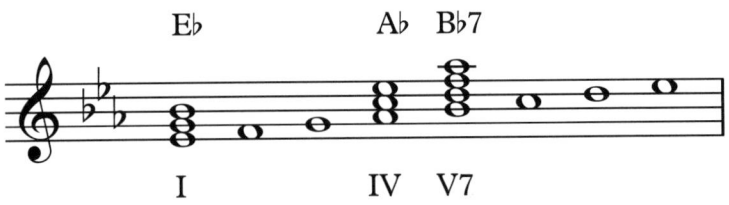 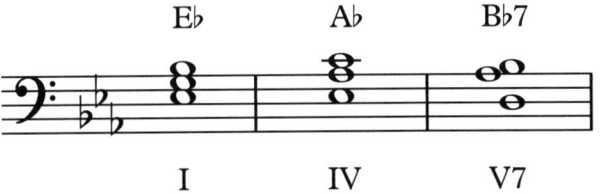

5. Draw this primary chord progression. Use whole notes.

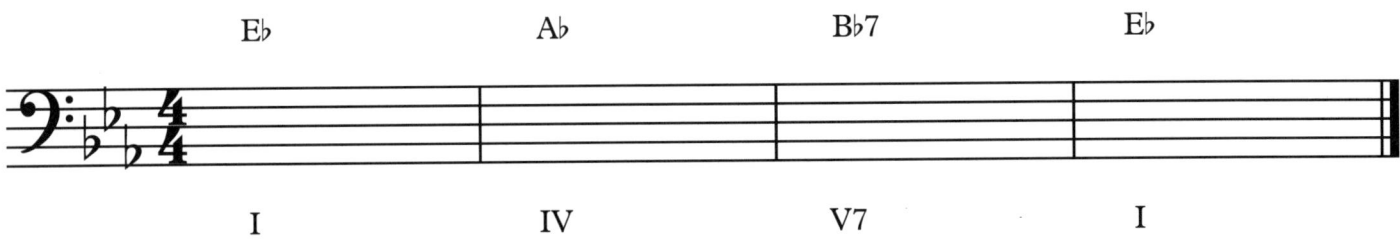

6. Harmonize each measure of this melody with I, IV, or V7. Use dotted quarter notes.
Write Roman numerals below the staff, and chord names above the staff.
Play what you have written.

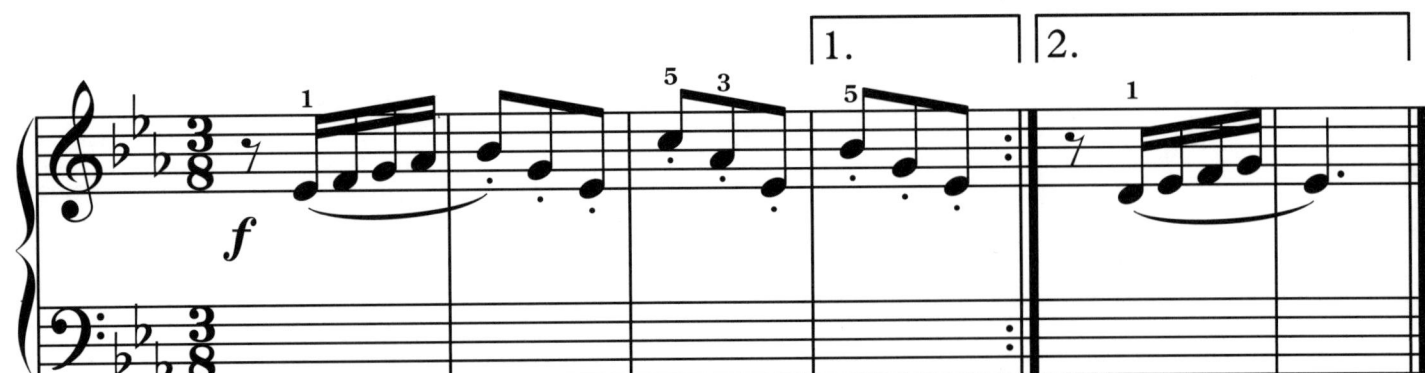

GP692

A♭ Major Key Signature

The key signature for A♭ Major has four flats: B♭, E♭, A♭, and D♭.

7. Trace the first key signature, then draw two more.

Primary Chords in A♭ Major   ### Primary Chord Progression

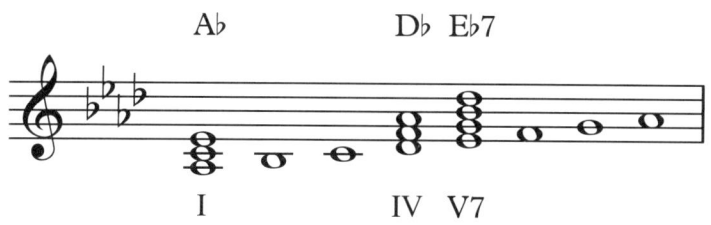 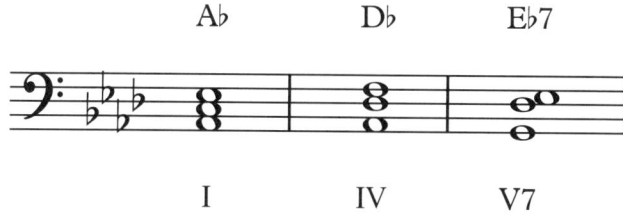

8. Draw this primary chord progression. Use whole notes.

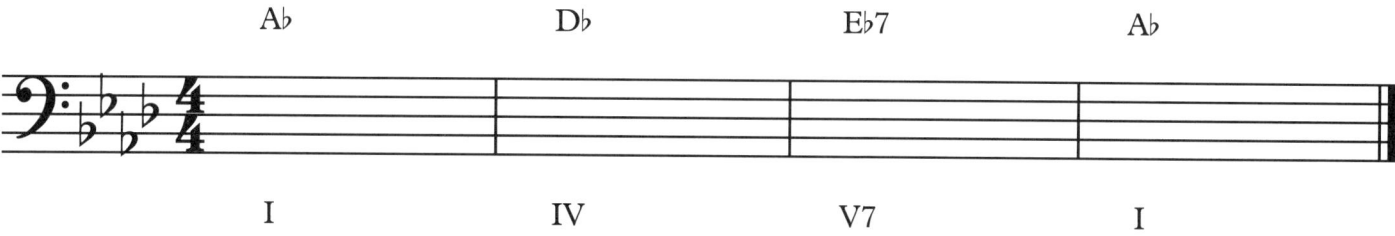

9. Harmonize each measure of this melody with I, IV, or V7. Use half notes.
   Write Roman numerals below the staff, and chord names above the staff.
   Play what you have written.

D♭ Major Key Signature

The key signature for D♭ Major has five flats: B♭, E♭, A♭, D♭, and G♭.

10. Trace the first key signature, then draw two more.

Primary Chords in D♭ Major

Primary Chord Progression

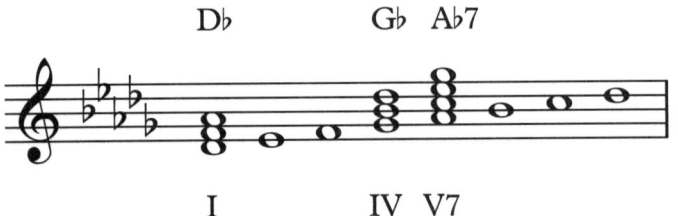 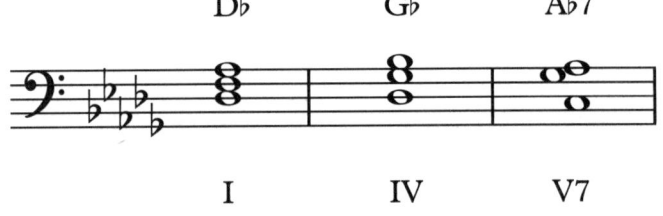

11. Draw this primary chord progression. Use whole notes.

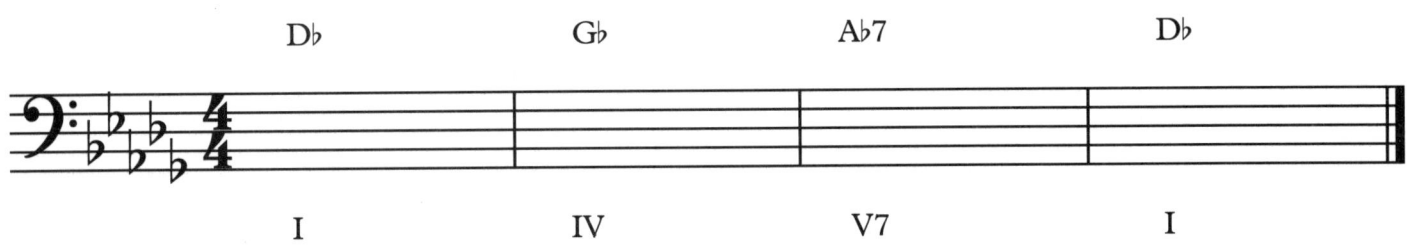

12. Harmonize each measure of this melody with I, IV, or V7. Use whole notes.
    Write Roman numerals below the staff, and chord names above the staff.
    Play what you have written.

GP692

Major Sharp Key Signature Review

The sharps in key signatures are always in the same order.

Memorize the order of sharps.

The Order of Sharps

F C G D A E B

10. Draw the order of sharps three times.

To write the key signature for any Major sharp key:

- Name the note a half step below the key note.

- Write the order of sharps up to and including the sharp that is a half step below the key note.

D Major

Key note

Sharp half step below key note

11. Write each Major key signature.

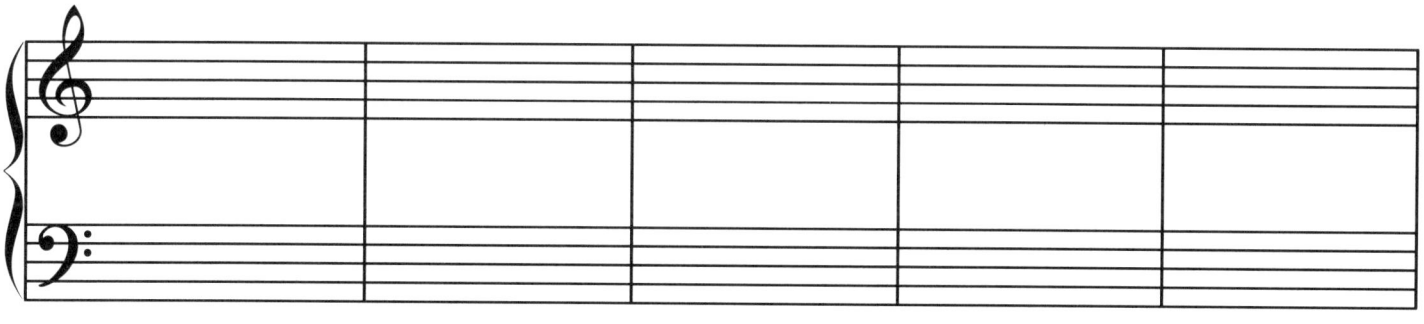

D Major   E Major   G Major   F♯ Major   A Major

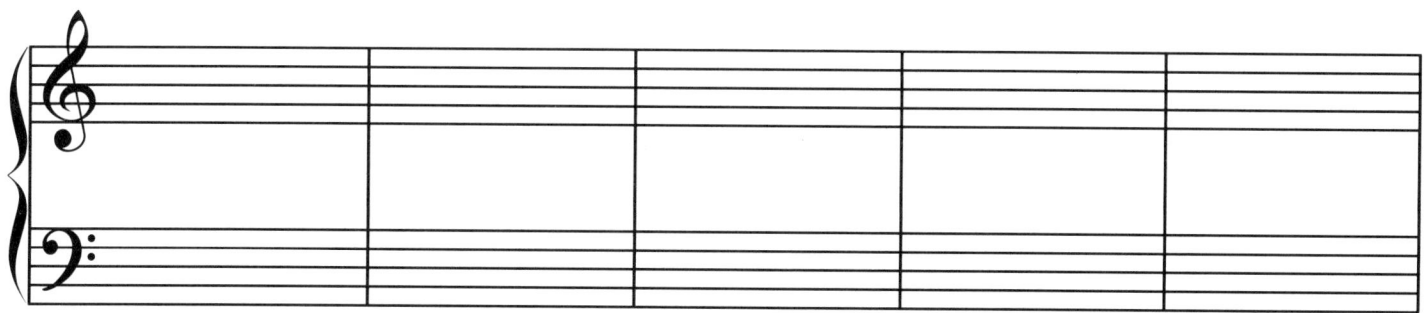

C Major   C♯ Major   B Major   D Major   E Major

TECHNIC

1. Major sharp scales and chord progressions review.

E♭ Major, A♭ Major, D♭ Major 113

2. Major flat scales and chord progressions review.

F Major

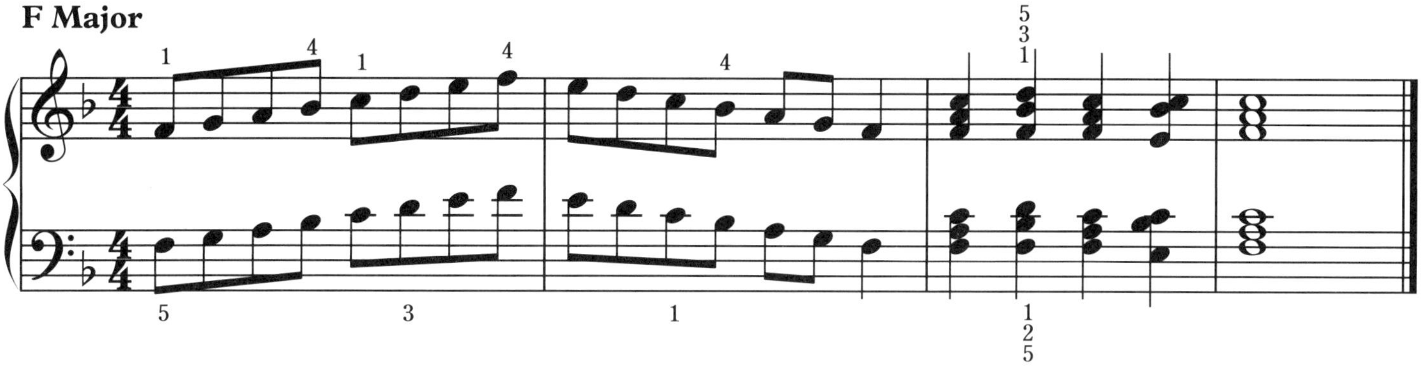

B♭ Major

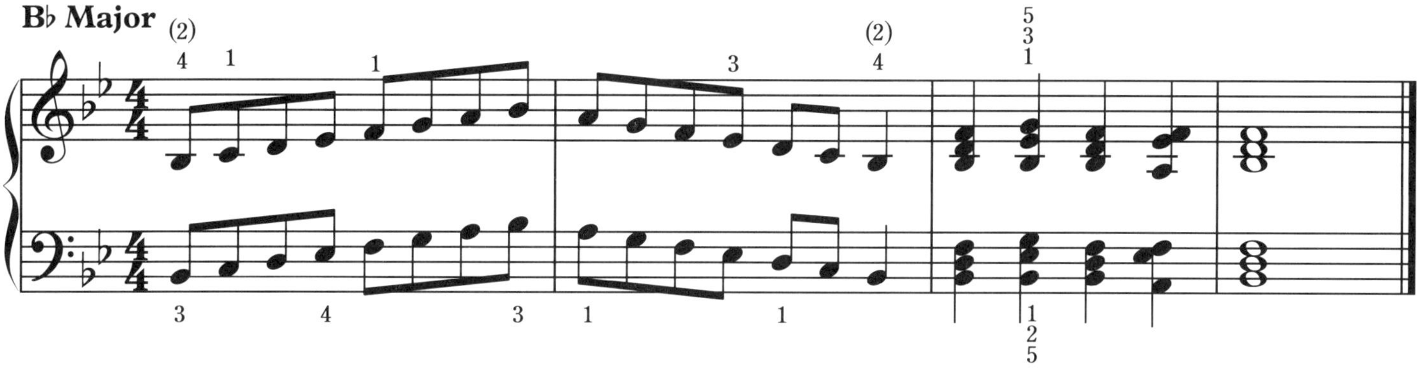

E♭ Major

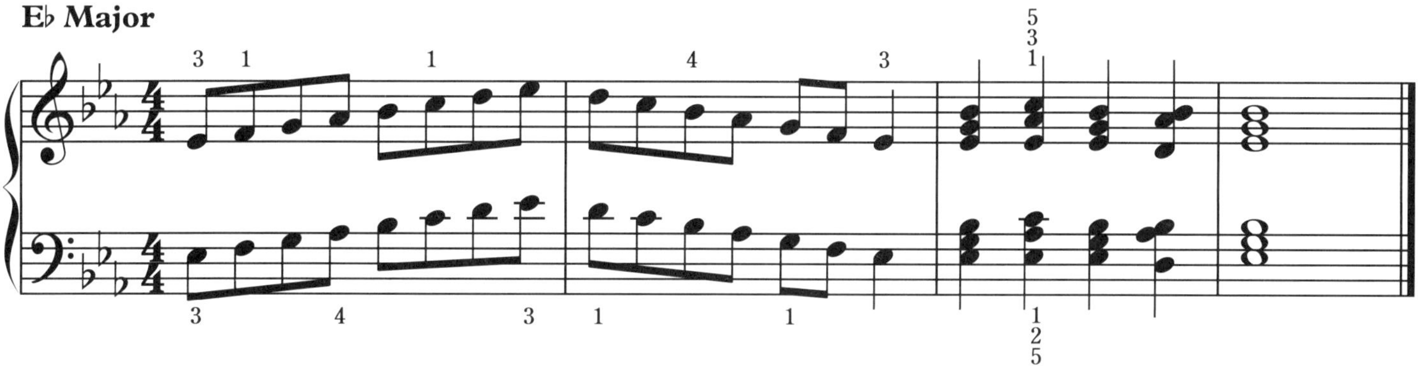

A♭ Major

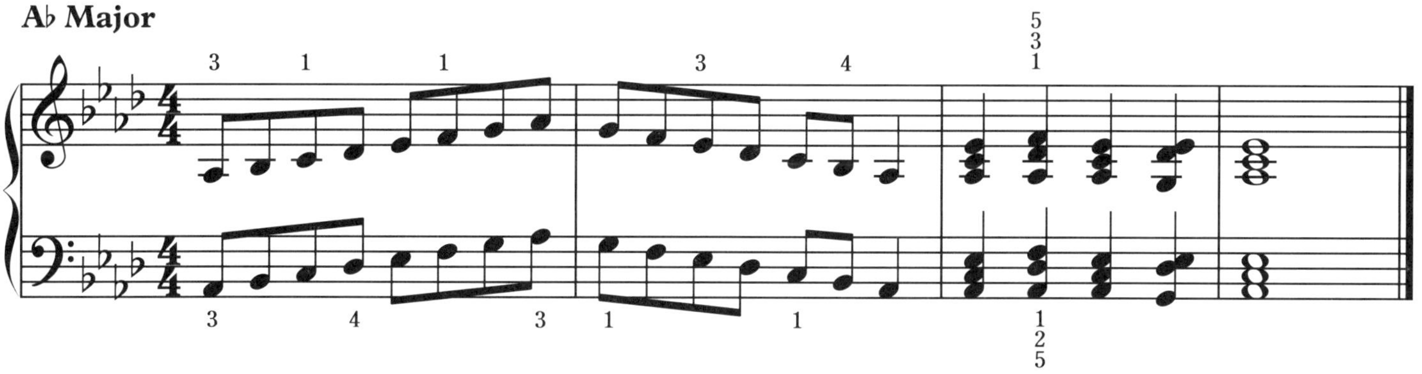

D♭ Major

GP692

UNIT 10
G♭ MAJOR, B MAJOR

G♭ Major Scale and Key Signature

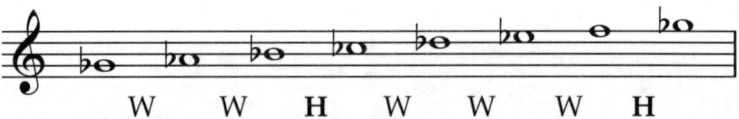

The key signature for G♭ Major has six flats: B♭, E♭, A♭, D♭, G♭, and C♭.

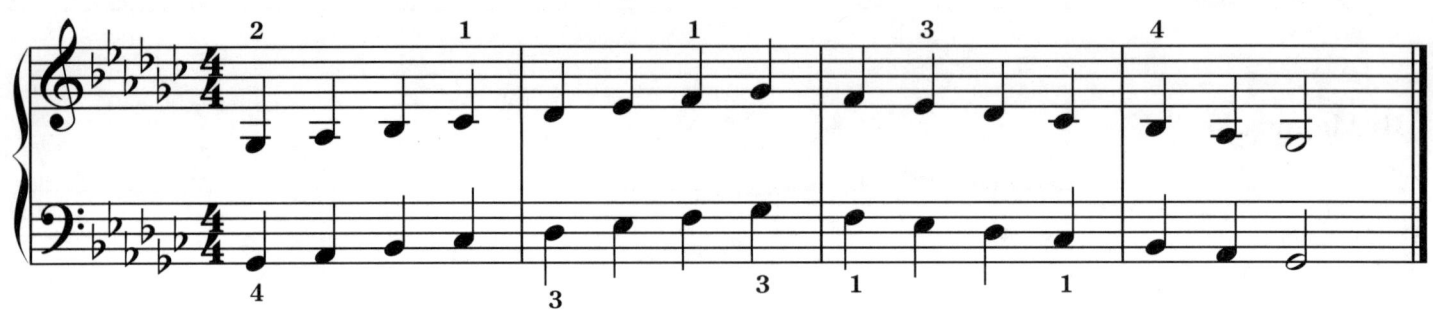

Primary Triads in G♭ Major

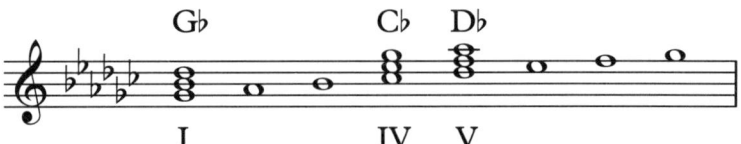

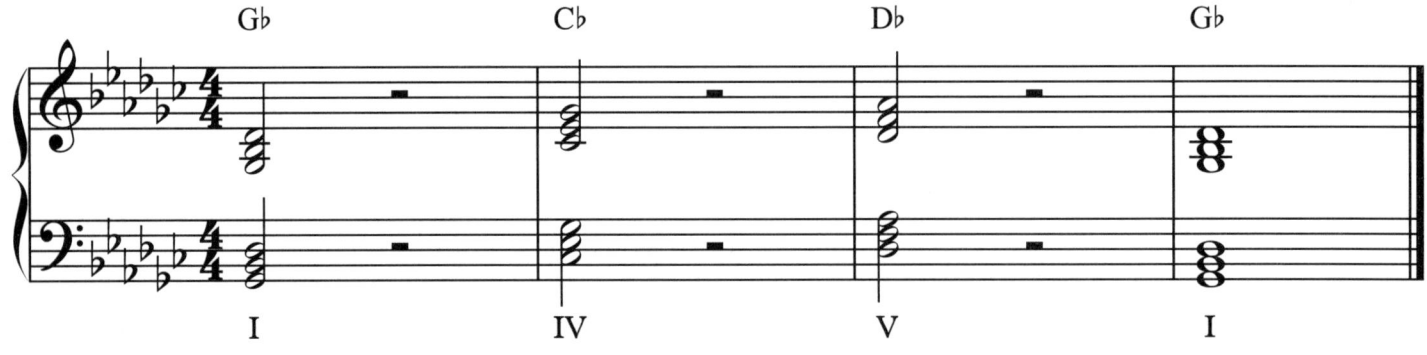

Primary Chord Progression

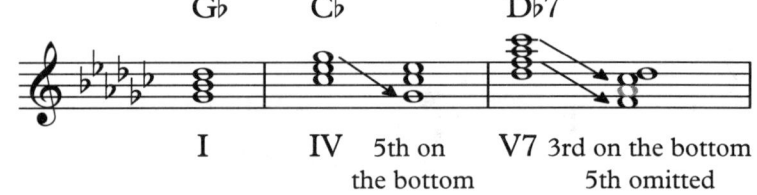

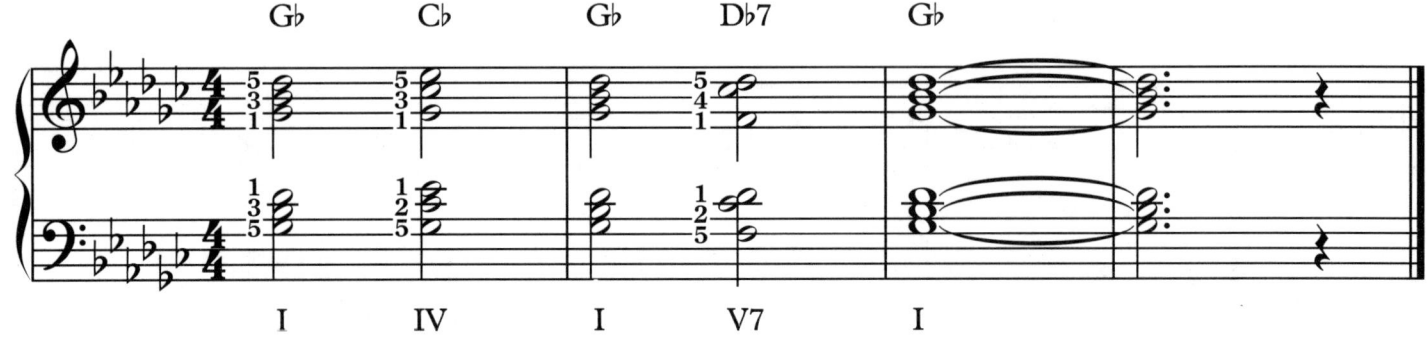

Gb Major, B Major — 115

Reading in Gb Major

I.

Allegretto

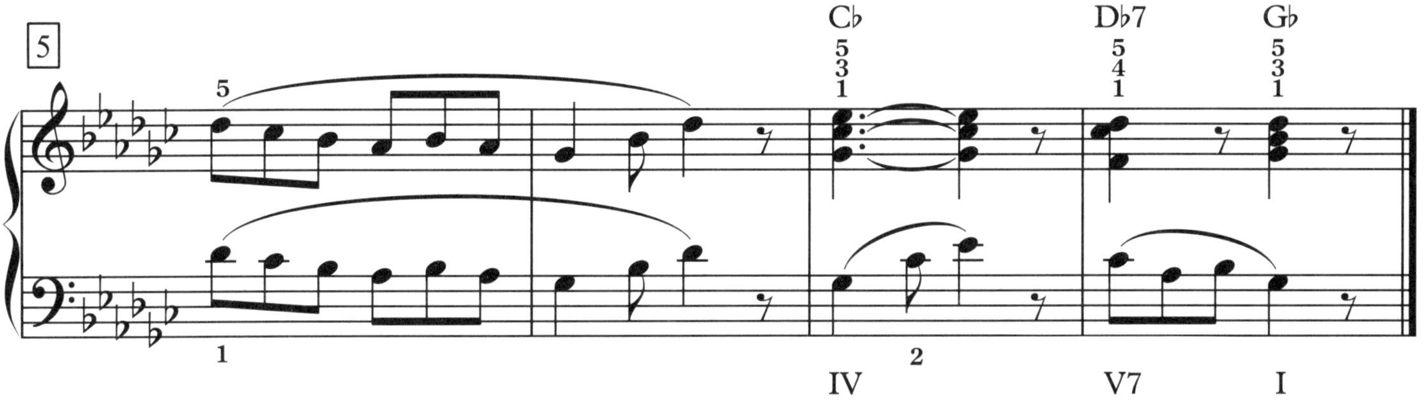

II.

Vivace

Carl Czerny
(1791-1857)

GP692

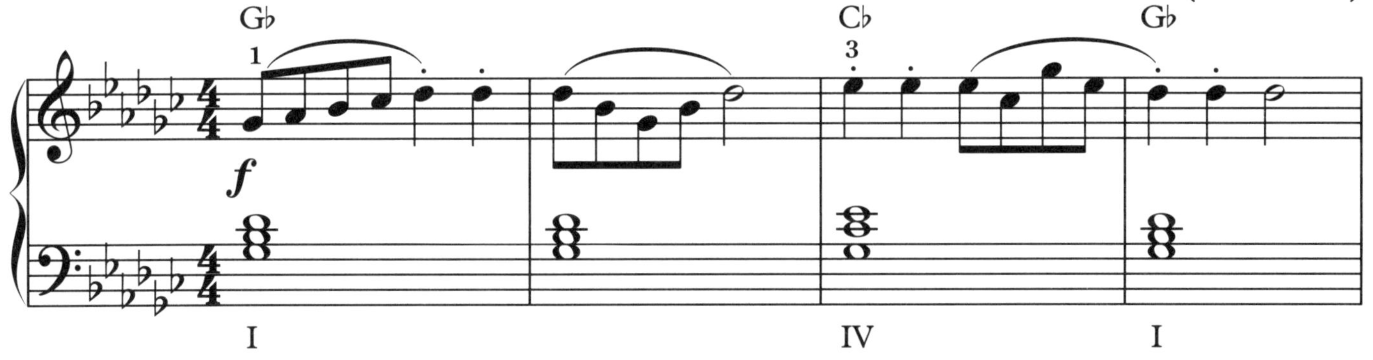

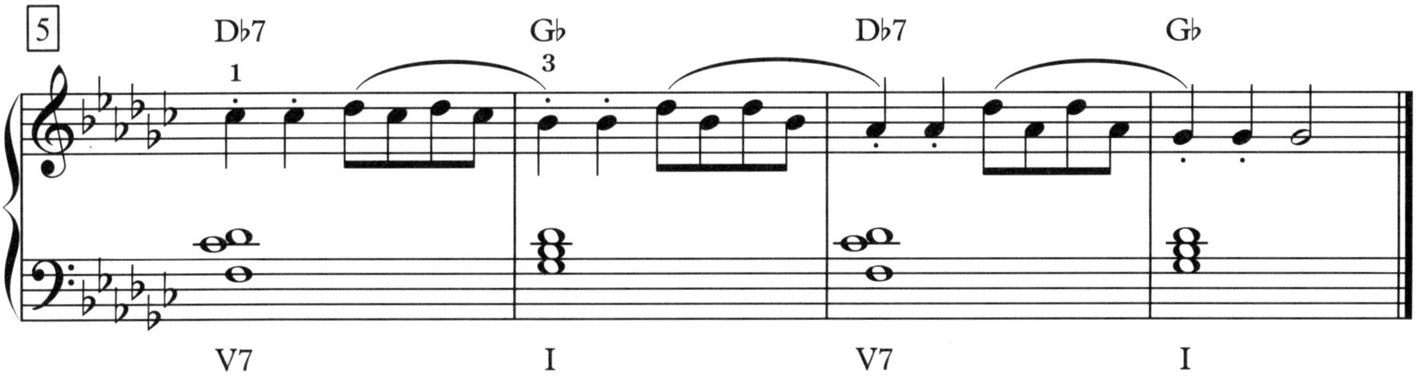

America
My Country 'Tis of Thee

Samuel Francis Smith

Melody of the British National Anthem

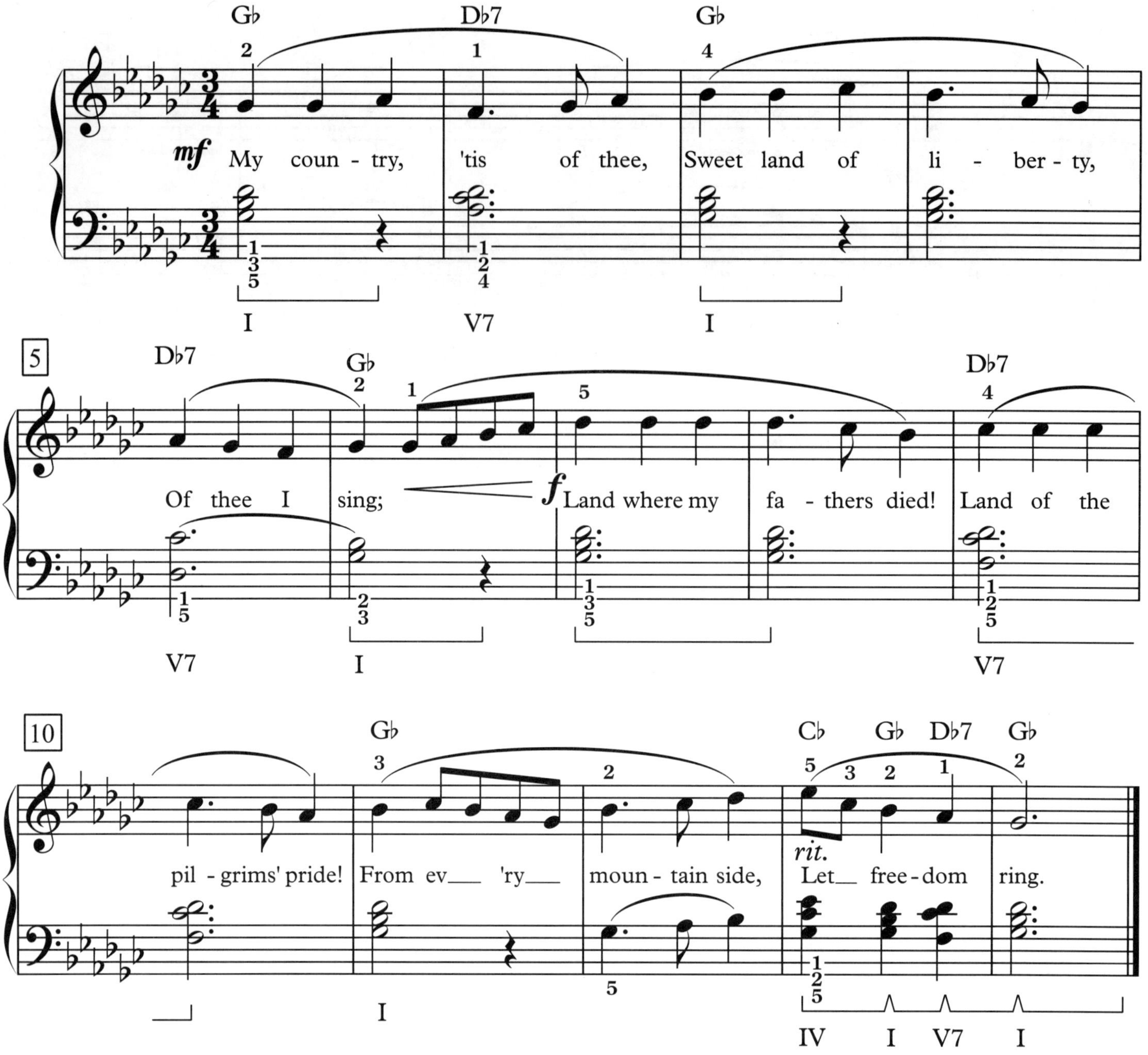

Monument Valley

B Major Scale and Key Signature

The key signature for B Major has five sharps: F#, C#, G#, D#, and A#.

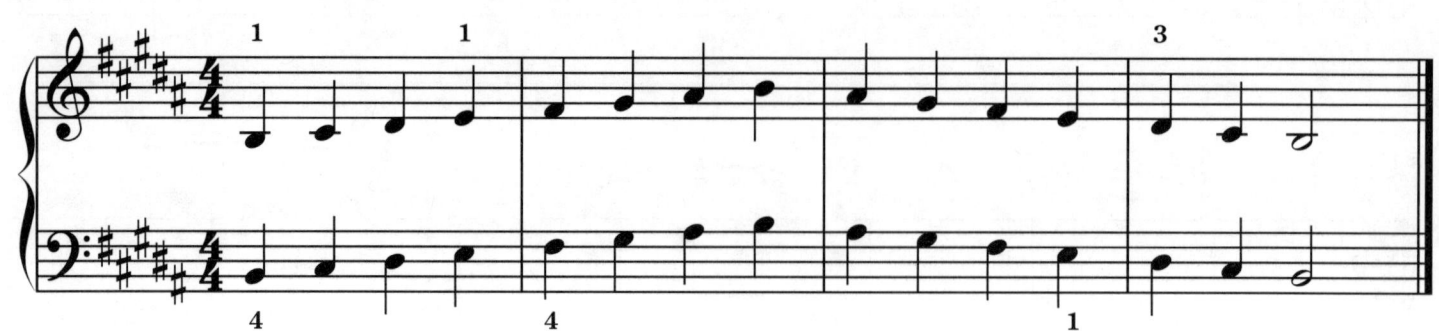

Primary Triads in B Major

Primary Chord Progression

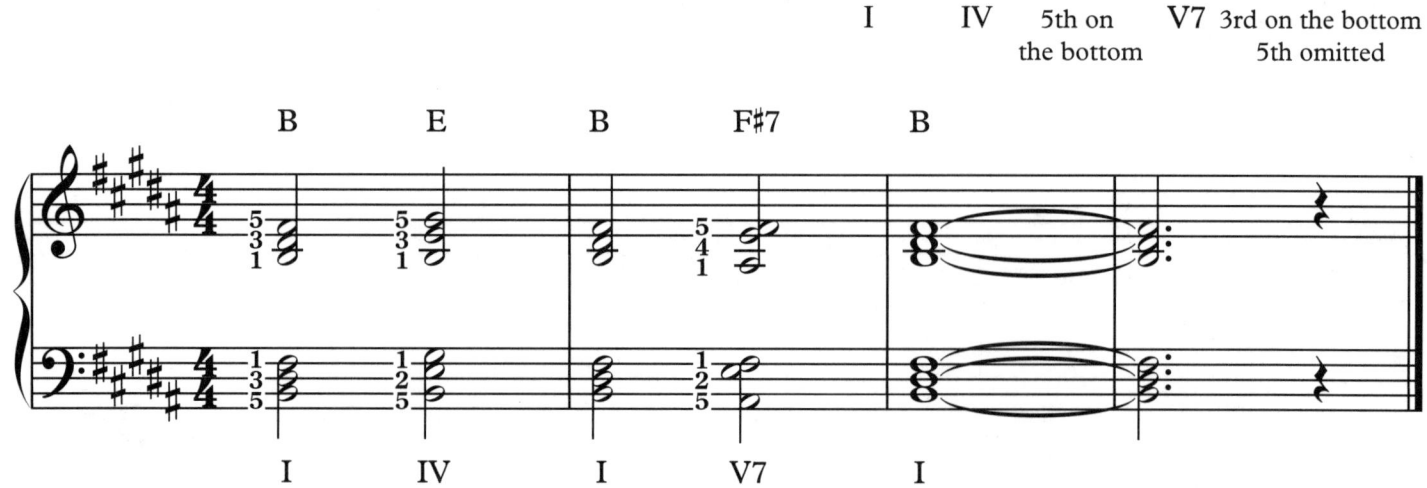

Reading in B Major

Unit 10

Double Sharp ×
Raises a note two half steps. (See measure 11.)

La donna e mobile
From the opera *Rigoletto*

Giuseppe Verdi
(1813-1901)

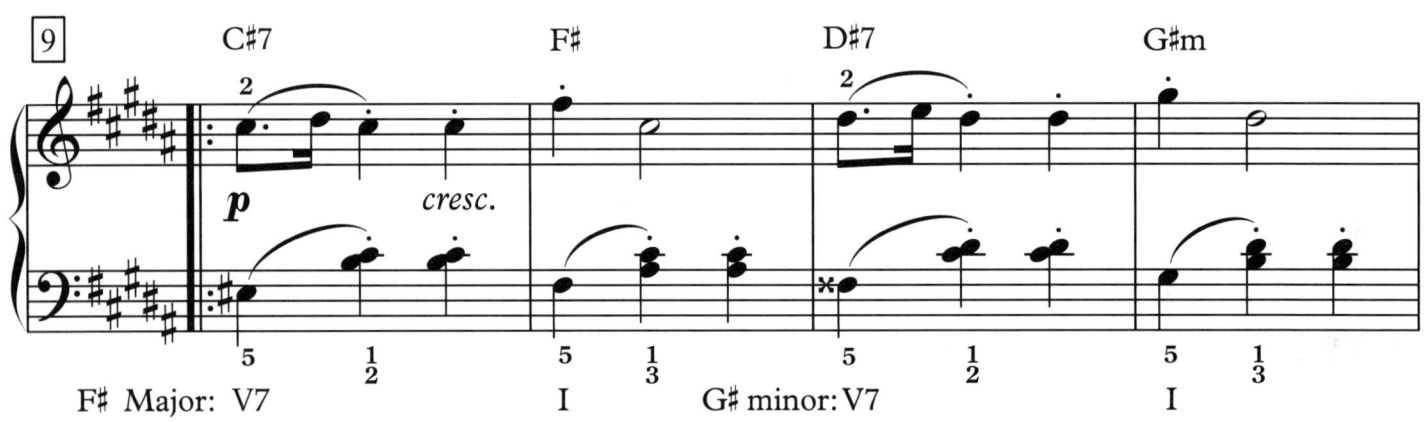

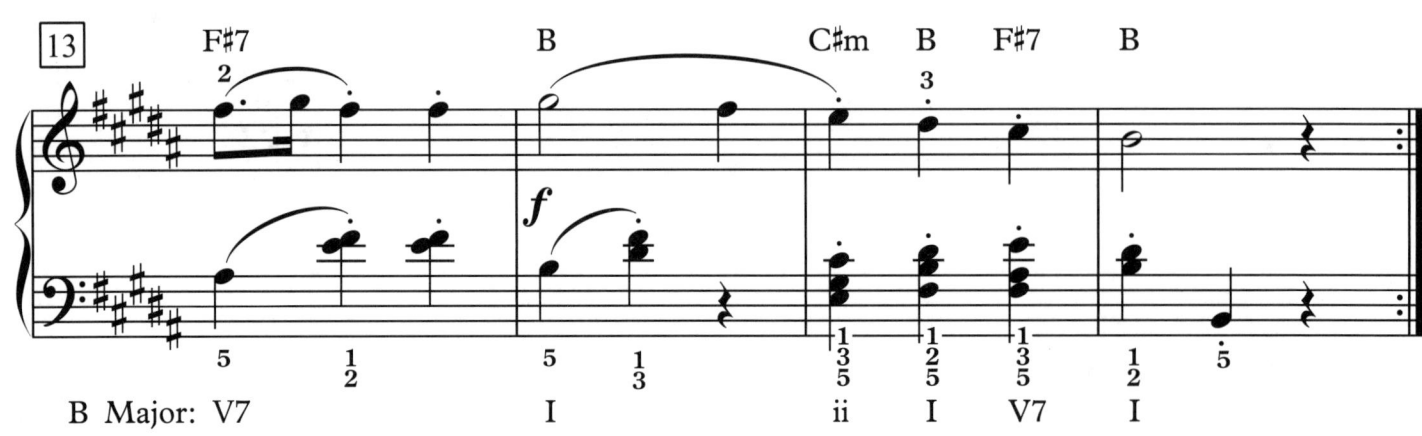

GP692

The **habanera** is a Cuban dance in slow duple time (two beats per measure).
It became popular in 19th century Europe when it was brought back to Spain by sailors.

Habanera
Dance of Havana

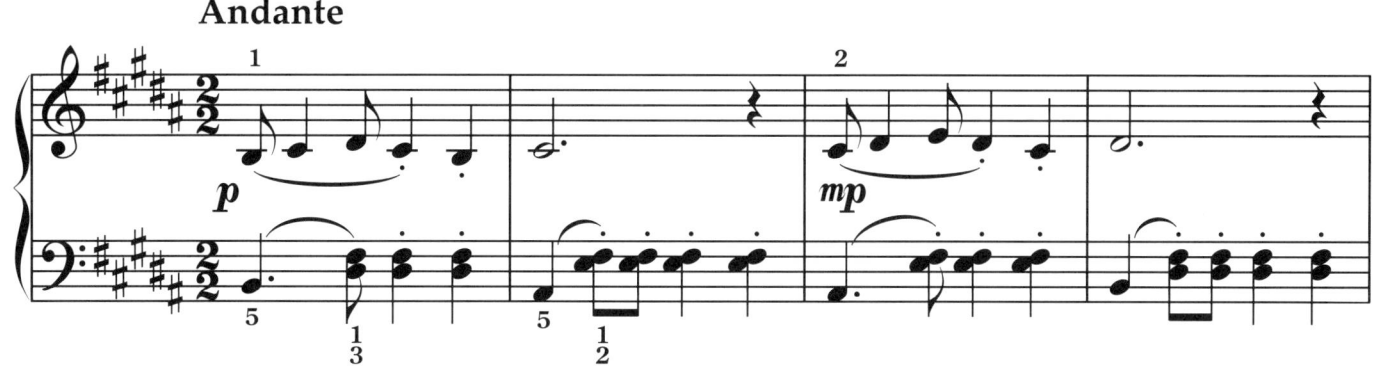

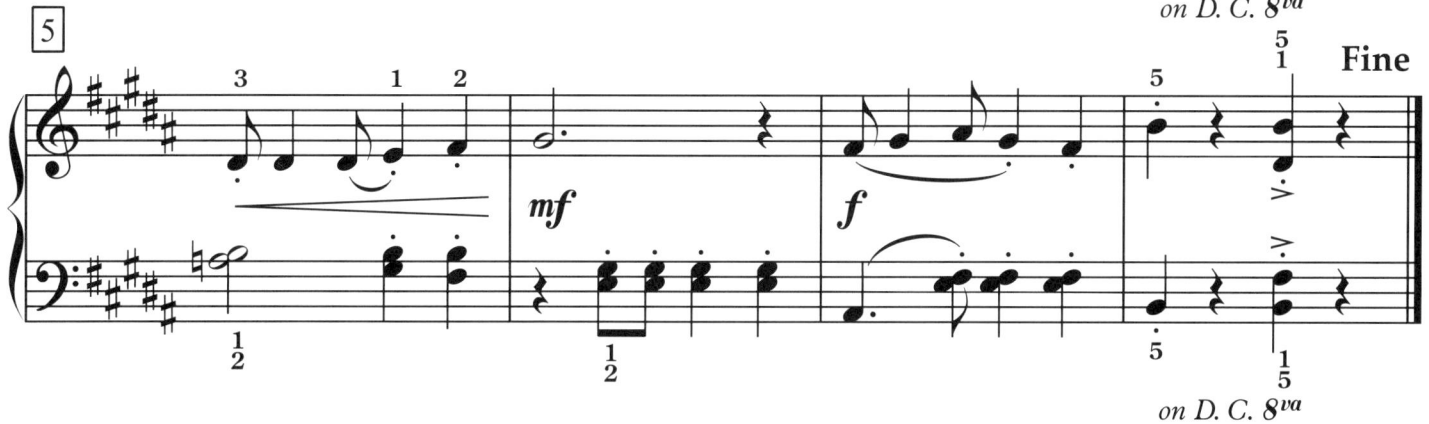

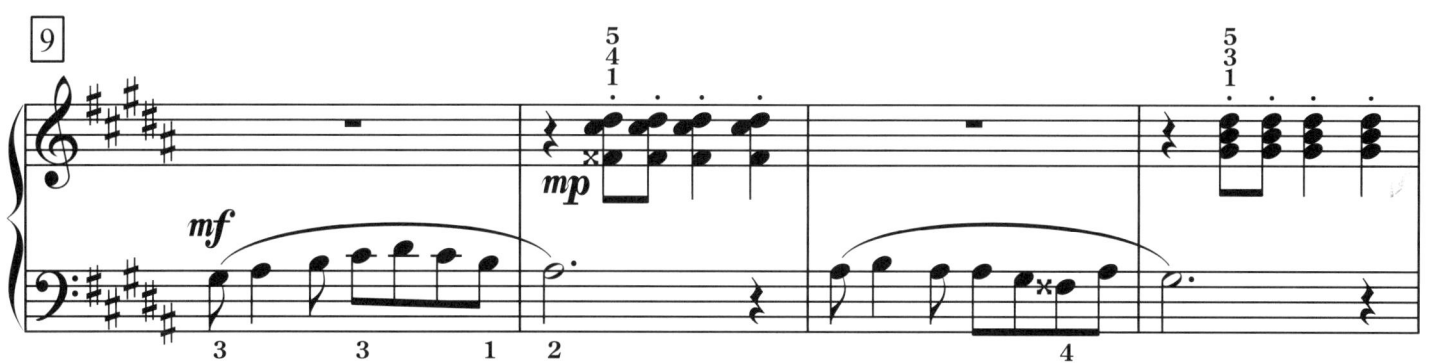

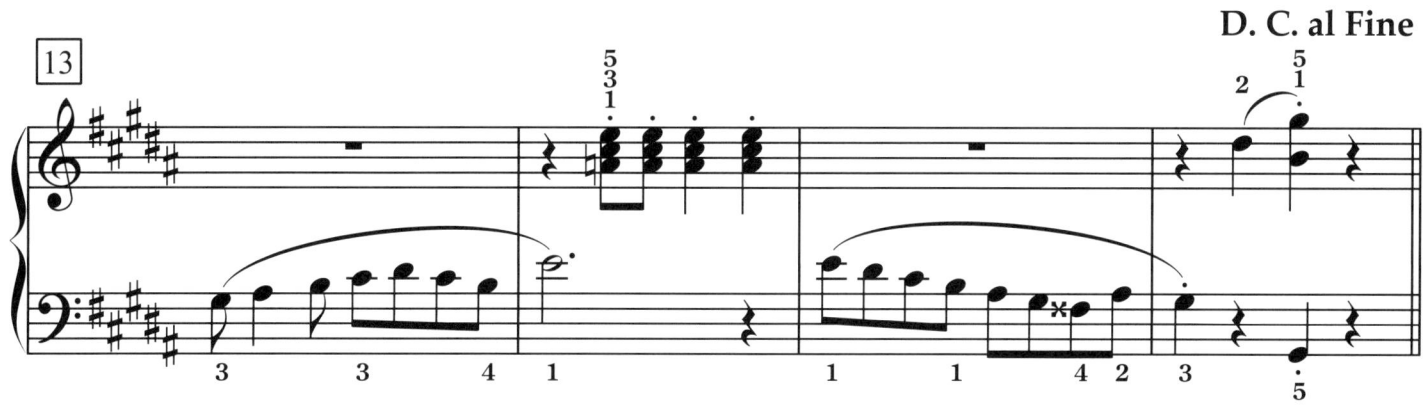

THEORY

G♭ Major Key Signature

The key signature for G♭ Major has six flats: B♭, E♭, A♭, D♭, G♭, and C♭.

1. Trace the first key signature, then draw two more.

Primary Chords in G♭ Major

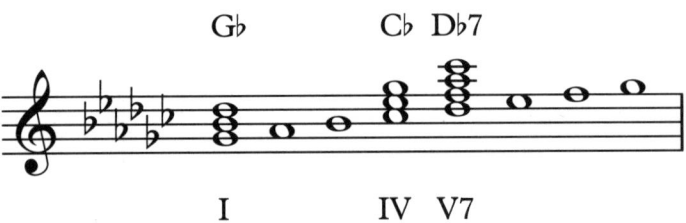

Primary Chord Progression

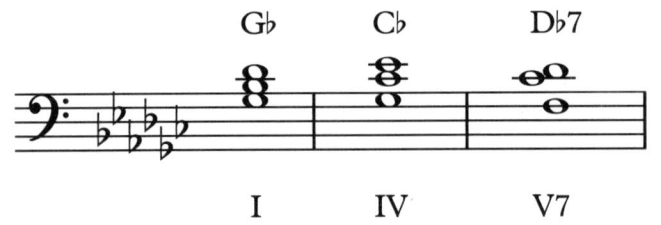

2. Draw this primary chord progression. Use whole notes.

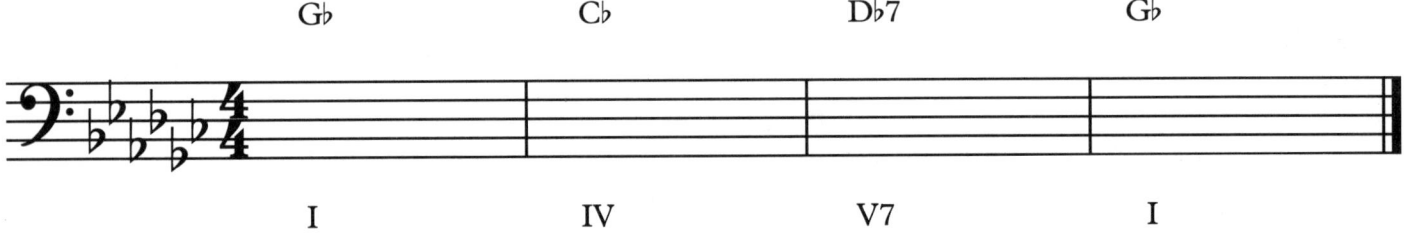

3. Harmonize each measure of this melody with I, IV, or V7. Use dotted quarter notes.
   Write Roman numerals below the staff, and chord names above the staff.
   Play what you have written.

B Major Key Signature

The key signature for B Major has five sharps: F♯, C♯, G♯, D♯, and A♯.

4. Trace the first key signature, then draw two more.

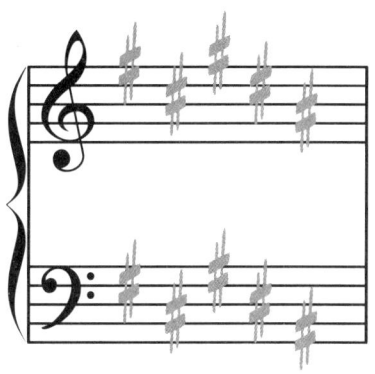  

Primary Chords in B Major

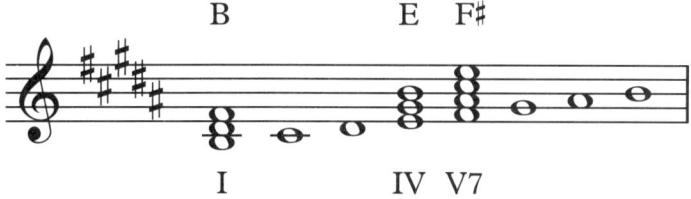

Primary Chord Progression

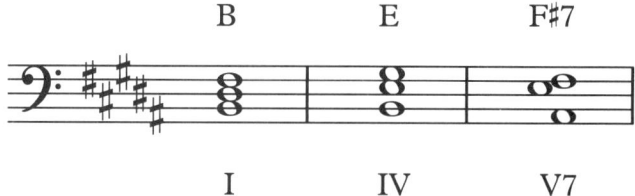

5. Draw this primary chord progression. Use whole notes.

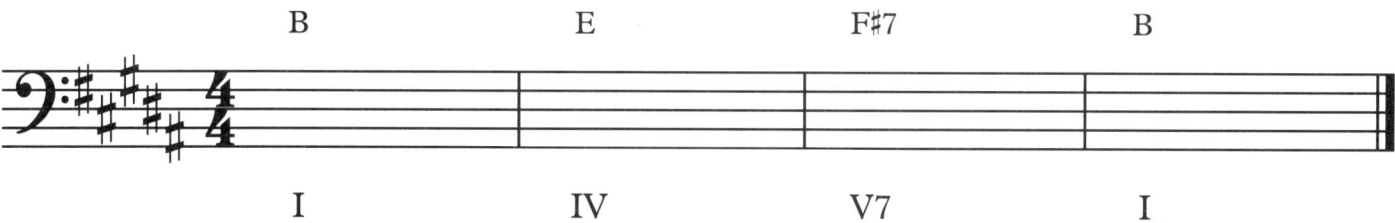

6. Harmonize each measure of this melody with I, IV, or V7. Use half notes.
   Write Roman numerals below the staff, and chord names above the staff.
   Play what you have written.

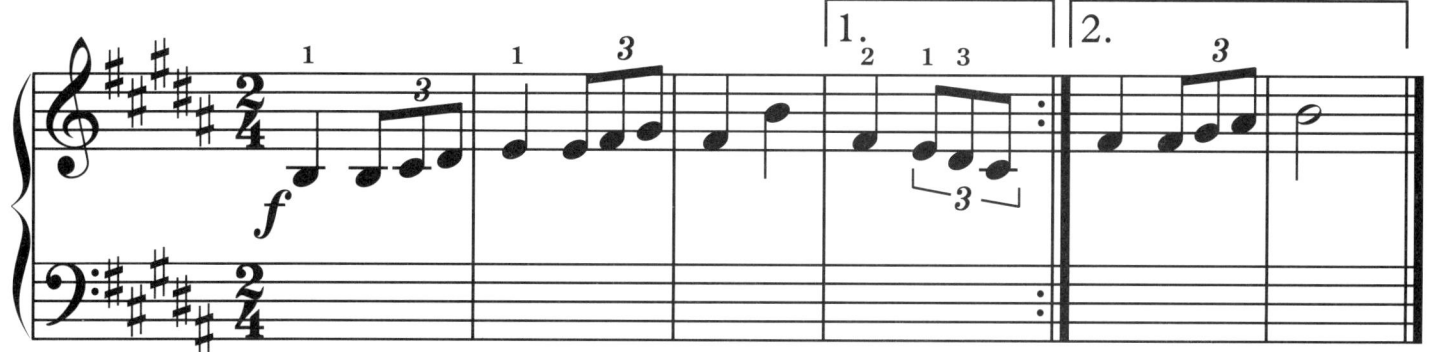

Minor Key Signature Review

Every key signature has a Major and minor name.

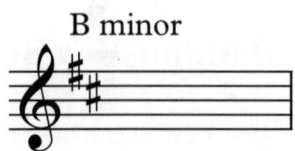

The minor key is found three half steps below the Major key.

7. Write the Major and minor name for each key signature.

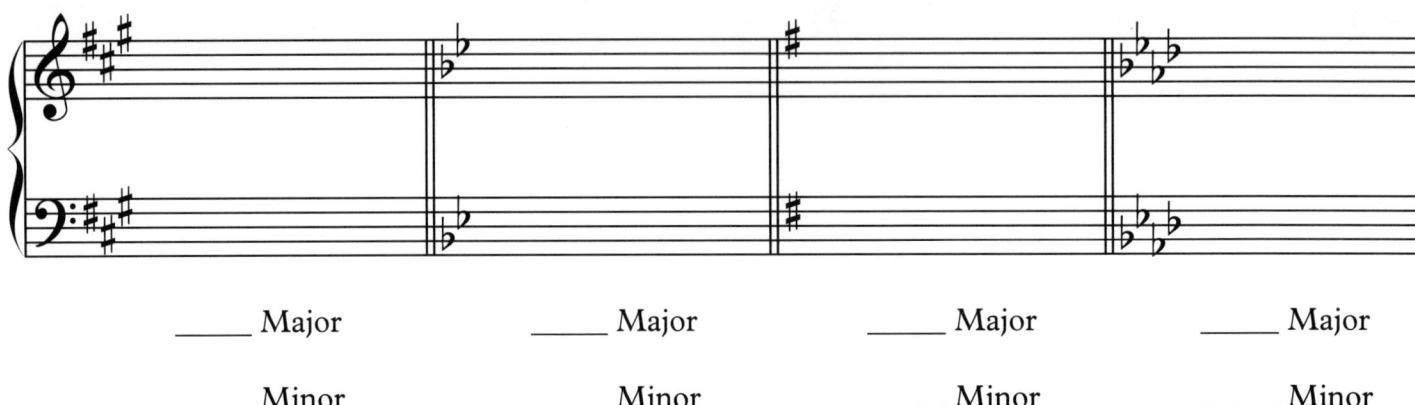

____ Major   ____ Major   ____ Major   ____ Major

____ Minor   ____ Minor   ____ Minor   ____ Minor

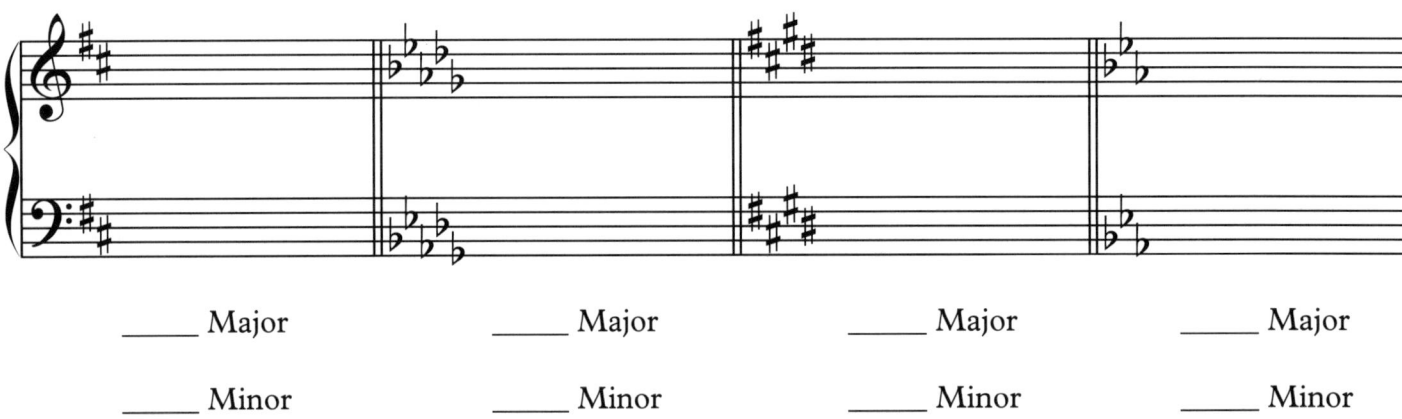

____ Major   ____ Major   ____ Major   ____ Major

____ Minor   ____ Minor   ____ Minor   ____ Minor

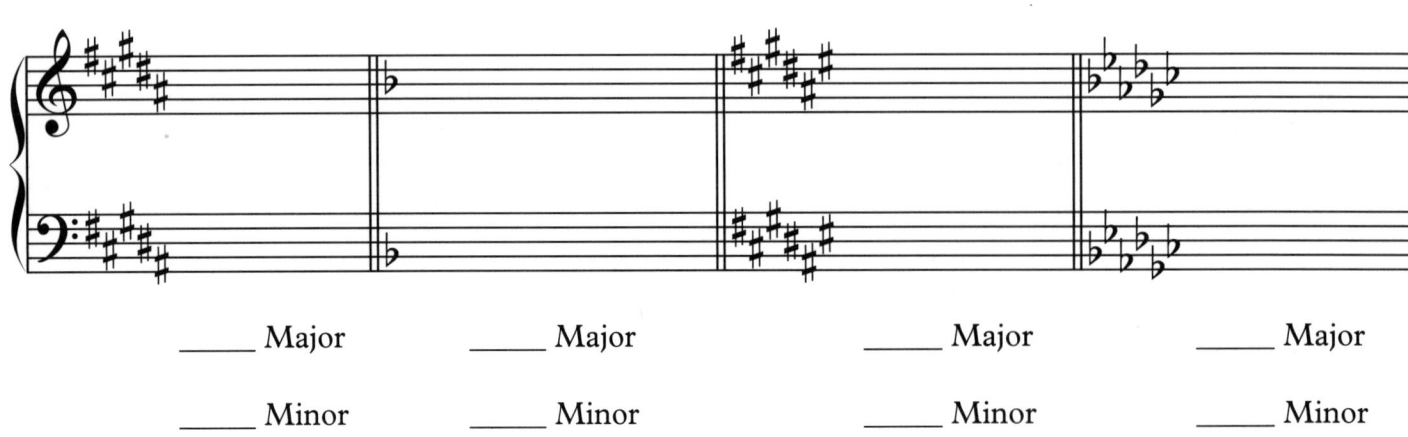

____ Major   ____ Major   ____ Major   ____ Major

____ Minor   ____ Minor   ____ Minor   ____ Minor

The Circle of Keys

The **circle of keys** is a diagram of all Major and minor key signatures. The sharp keys are arranged from the top, moving clockwise. The flats are arranged from the top, moving counterclockwise.

There are fifteen Major keys: seven sharp keys, seven flat keys, and one key with no sharps or flats. Likewise, there are fifteen relative minor keys.

The keys at the bottom of the circle are called **enharmonic** keys because their tones sound the same, but are named and written differently.

The circle of keys is sometimes called the **circle of fifths** because the keys are an interval of a fifth part. Notice that as you move around the circle of keys clockwise from the top, one new sharp is added to each key. As you move counterclockwise from the top, one new flat is added to each key.

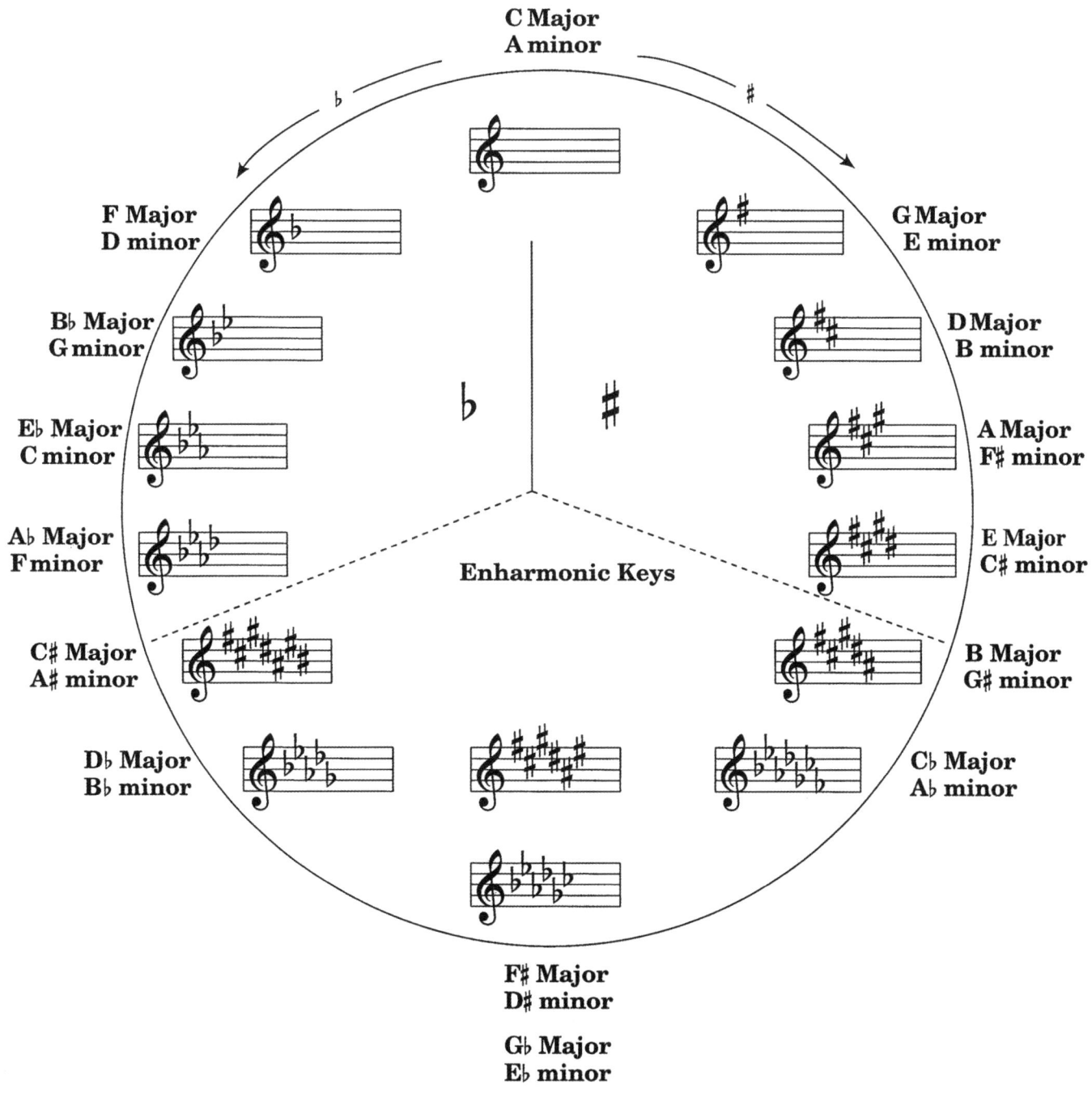

TECHNIC

1. Harmonic minor scales and chord progressions review.

Gb Major, B Major 127

2. Etude for legato 3rds.

Etude
Op. 101, Nos. 70 & 71

Ferdinand Beyer
(1803-1863)

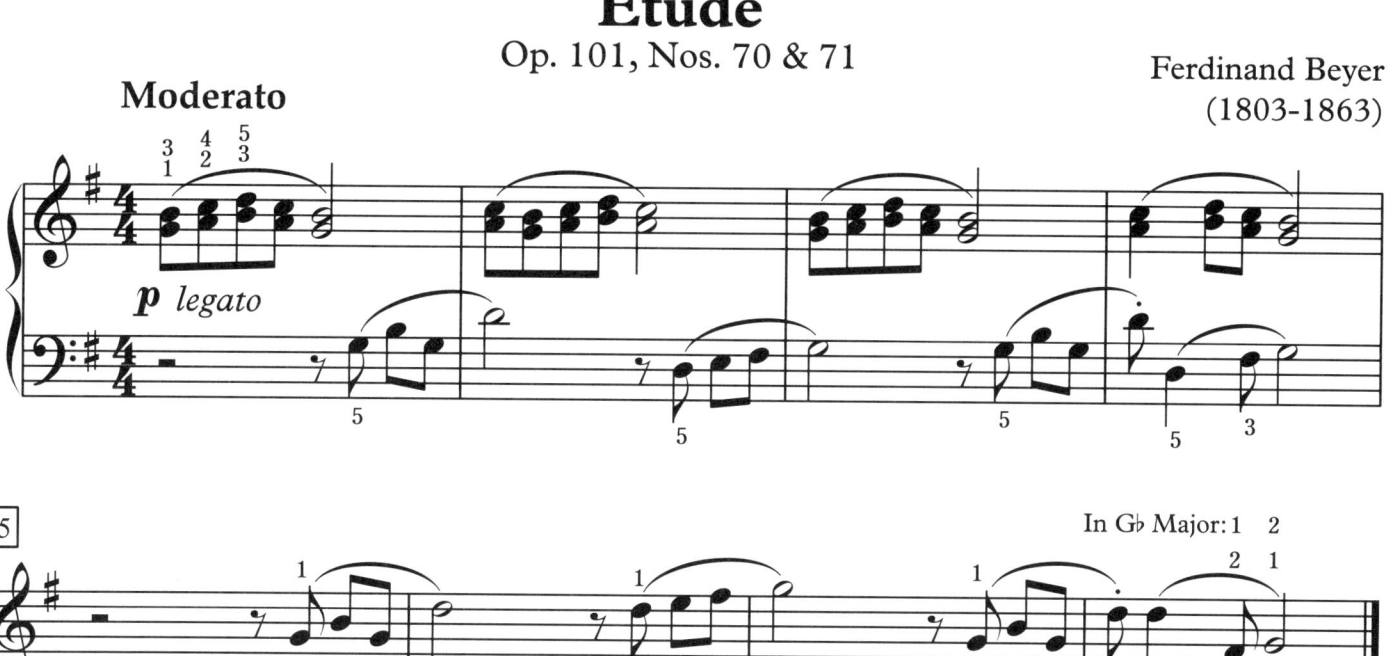

Transpose to Gb Major and D Major.

3. Etude for left hand scales.

Etude
Op. 821, No. 2

Carl Czerny
(1791-1857)

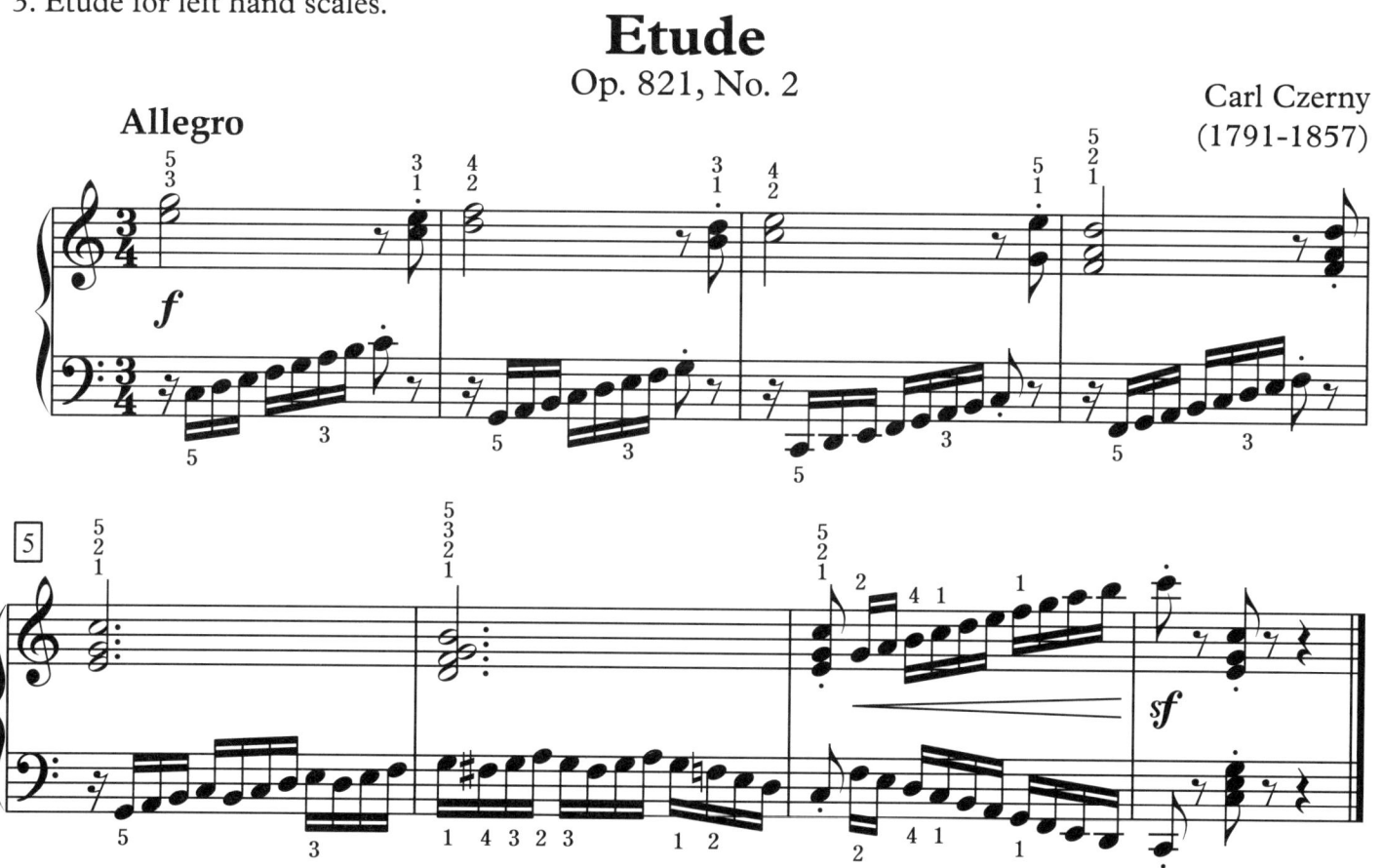

GP692

MUSIC DICTIONARY

Term	Sign	Meaning
A tempo		Return to the original tempo.
Accent	>	Play the note or notes louder.
Accidental		Any sharp, flat, or natural that appears in the music.
Allegretto		Somewhat fast.
Allegro		Fast.
Andante		Slow, walking tempo.
Arpeggio		See Broken chord.
Augmented triad		Formed by raising the 5th of Major triad one half step.
Binary form		A piece with two sections, section A and section B.
Blocked chord		The notes of a chord play together.
Broken chord		The notes of a chord played one at a time.
Chord		Three or more notes sounded for harmony.
Chord inversion		A chord is in an inversion if the 3rd, 5th, or 7th is the lowest note.
Crescendo (*cresc.*)	⟨	Gradually louder.
Chromatic scale		A scale formed entirely of half steps. It can begin on any note.
Con moto		With motion.
Cut time	¢	Another term for time signature 2/2.
Da capo al fine (D. C. al Fine)		Go back to the beginning and play to the fine.
Del segno al fine (D. S. al Fine)	𝄋	Play from the sign to the end (Fine).
Diminished triad		Formed by lowering the 5th of a minor triad one half step.
Diminuendo (*dim.*)	⟩	Gradually softer.
Espressivo		With expression, expressively.
Flat	♭	Play the note a half step lower than written.
Fermata	𝄐	Hold the note longer than its time value.
First inversion		When the 3rd of a chord is the lowest note.
Forte	*f*	Loud
Half step		The distance from one key to the next with no key between.
Harmonic interval		Two notes played together.
Harmonic minor		The 7th degree of the natural minor scale is raised one half step.
Implied harmony		A melody written in a way that in the absence of chords, the harmony is strongly suggested.
Inversion		See Chord inversion
Interval		The distance between two notes.
Key signature		Sharps or flats at the beginning of the staff that indicate the key of the music.
Key note		See Tonic.